R.A.Whitehead

GARRETT
TRACTION
&
PLOUGHING
ENGINES

R.A.Whitehead & Partners
Tonbridge,
Kent

1997

Fig.1. The gentle art of deception. An early 6NHP single, probably No.20800 (May, 1897) posed in a delightful scene at Knodishall Hall as the basis of a publicity brochure. Once the blockmaker had touched out the tuck in the belt doubtless many threshing men asked themselves how the gang came to be threshing with such a short belt.

Published by R.A.Whitehead & Partners
42 Hadlow Road
Tonbridge, Kent TN9 1NZ

© **Copyright 1997 by R.A.Whitehead**

All rights reserved. No part of this publication may be reproduced, stored in a retrieval system, or transmitted in any form or by any means - electronic, mechanical photocopying, recording, or otherwise - unless the permission of the publisher has been given beforehand.

Photographs: Unless otherwise acknowledged all illustrations are from the collections of the now defunct firm of Richard Garrett Engineering Ltd., or of the author. Illustrations from other sources are acknowledged individually.

Cover: In the generous stackyards of East Anglia and the South Midlands there was usually room for a big engine. Here 8NHP Garrett single No.25858, owned by William Townsend of Exning, Suffolk, close to Newmarket, is seen at work, the bagged corn being loaded onto the traction wagon visible behind the engine's smokebox.

Typeset in Times New Roman 10 by J.E.Whitehead.

Printed and bound by Biddles Ltd., Woodbridge Park, Guildford, GU1 1DA

ISBN 0-9508298-8-9

Contents

Foreword by Michael R. Lane, Esq.		Page 5
Preface		Page 6
Acknowledgements and thanks		Page 6
Chapter 1	Adventures with Boydells	Page 9
Chapter 2	Engines prior to 1890	Page 17
Chapter 3	Traction Engines Recommenced	Page 29
Chapter 4	Strawburners	Page 49
Chapter 5	Ploughing Engines and New Zealand Tractions	Page 57
Chapter 6	Road Locomotives and Showmen's Engines	Page 78
Chapter 7	Continental Traction Engines	Page 90
Chapter 8	Final Days	Page 98
Chapter 9	Agents and Buyers	Page 108
Chapter 10	An Evaluation	Page 117
Specification & Estimate for Garrett General Purpose Traction Engine		Page 129
Appendix 1	Table of Dimensions of Traction Engines & Tractors c.1909	Page 134
Appendix 2	The Garrett & Schmach Patent Differential Locking Arrangement	Page 136
Appendix 3	Key to Prefixes Applied to Drawing & Pattern Numbers	Page 136
Appendix 4	List of Garrett Tractions, Road Locomotives & Ploughing Engines	Page 137

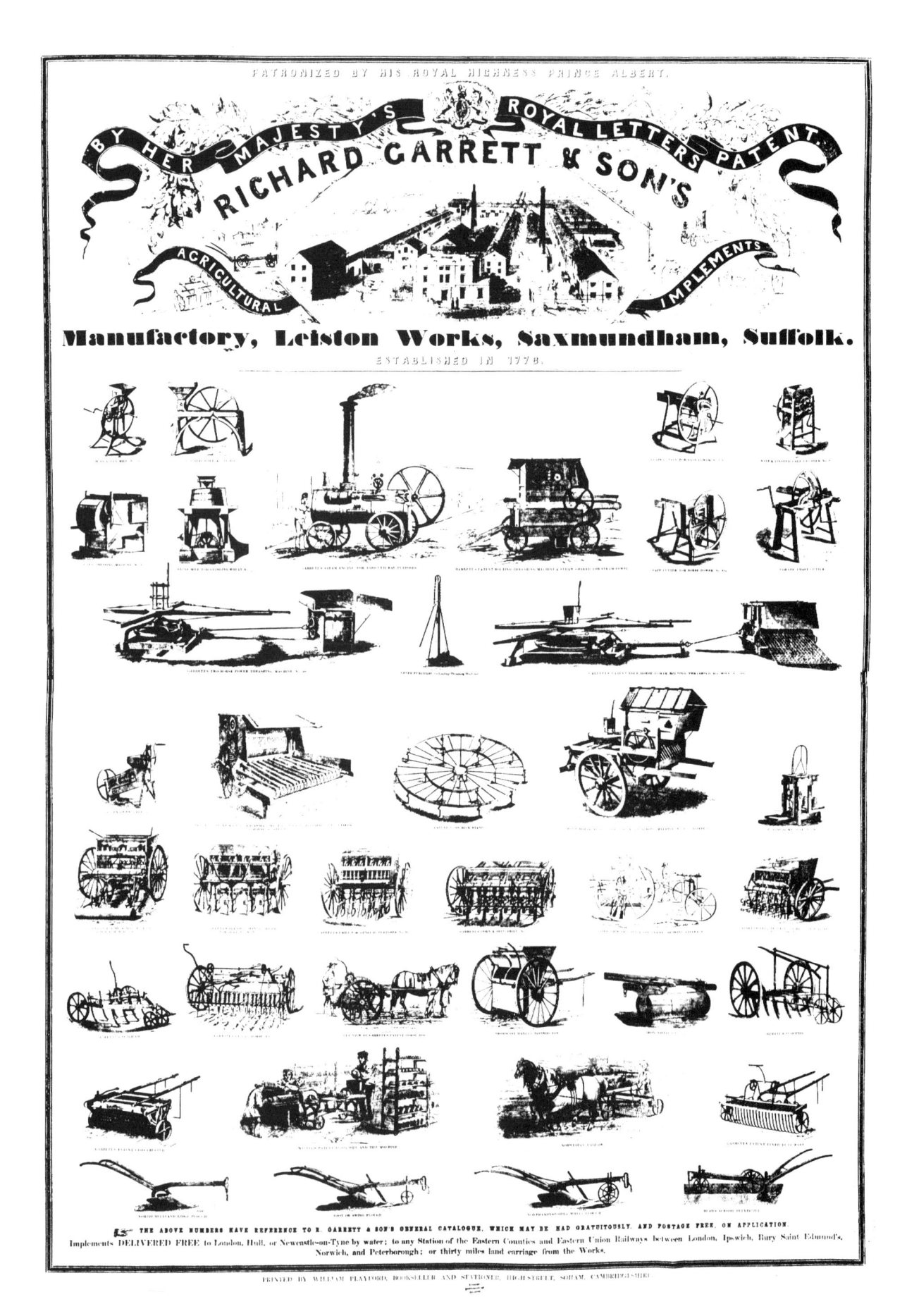

Fig.2. The history of Garretts prior to 1856 epitomised in the famous poster which forms part of the collection of the Rural History Centre at Reading University. Perhaps the only important element not shown is that of sickles and edge tools.

Fig.3. No.35461, the last Garrett traction engine to be built, delivered on June 12, 1931.

Foreword

By Michael R. Lane Esq.

I feel greatly honoured to be asked to write a foreword for this scholarly addition to Bob Whitehead's well-known series of books dealing with various facets of Richard Garrett & Sons Ltd. of Leiston in the County of Suffolk. His comprehensive history of the firm, first published in 1964, is now a treasured collector's item. This gave an overall perspective of the firm's many and varied engineering activities which were mainly associated with the needs of the agriculturalist and road transport. Having developed from modest beginnings in 1789 as bladesmiths and edge-tool manufacturers, Garretts had, by the middle of the last century, earned a world-wide reputation for their threshing machines and portable steam engines. They trained and built up a highly skilled workforce. Geographically they were well placed to meet the needs of East Anglian farmers in the boom years of *High Farming*, and were close to the east coast ports for the shipment of their products to the rapidly growing markets in the cereal producing areas of Eastern Europe.

The present volume is devoted to Garrett's range of self-moving steam traction engines and describes them and their derivations in fascinating detail. Their first self-moving engine was fitted with James Boydell's Patent Endless Railway wheels. Completed in 1856 it was exhibited at the Royal Show held in Chelmsford, participated in the Lord Mayor's Show in London, and was purchased in London by a wealthy Australian landowner. We learn that between 1856 and 1890 Garretts built about sixty traction engines. This was followed by a five year pause, after which the production of new designs was resumed in 1895. Road locomotives and similar specially adapted engines to meet the needs of travelling showmen appeared in 1903, and the first of the many one-man operation steam tractors were produced in 1905/6. By the time production finally ceased at Leiston, due to the collapse of the ill-fated Agricultural & General Engineers conglomerate who had acquired the company in 1919, a total of over 500 traction engines had been completed.

Although traction engines probably accounted for only about 2½% of the total number of steam engines built at Leiston, the number is significant when compared with the quantity built by many other UK traction engine builders. Undoubtedly, Richard Garrett & Sons Ltd. have earned a lasting place in the history of the traction engine, and will for ever form an important part in our steam heritage.

We are extremely fortunate that Bob Whitehead has been prepared to embark upon years of dedicated research to produce such comprehensive and competent records of this famous old Suffolk company. He is to be congratulated on compiling not only a most interesting book, but one that will be of great value to engineering historians in the years ahead. I wish it every success.

Preface

Though Garretts were not regarded as one of the pre-eminent firms of traction engine builders they were among the earliest of the famous firms to place a self-moving engine on the market. Moreover, because the preponderant part of their trade was provided by overseas clients, many of whom required a less sophisticated engine than did buyers in the home market, a fairly high proportion of their traction engine output was made up of engines that did not conform to the convention of the home trade.

When Richard Garrett & Sons Ltd. became part of the Agricultural & General Engineers combine in 1919 they surrendered the building of traction engines to fellow member Charles Burrell & Sons Ltd. Thereafter such building as they did was occasioned by special circumstances, sometimes customer preference, but at other times because a particular type - such as the engines built in the 1920s for Ed. Zehder of Riga - did not fit easily into the Burrell production system

The story of traction engine building at Leiston Works began well before the furthest extent of living memory even in the days (now nearly forty years ago) when I started systematic research into the history of the Works and its products. It was at its zenith in the first fifteen years or so of this century during most of which period Victor Garrett, my invaluable source of information from within the family circle, had no part in managerial decision making. Indeed for some years of that time he was absent in South Africa. Nevertheless, because the family kept fairly close contact, he knew a good deal of what went on. The origins of traction engine building lay, however, in an earlier period when even his father was a lad, and when the crucial decisions were taken by his grandfather and Uncle Richard.

For all these reasons, and others besides, the story related in this book relies rather more heavily upon the surviving written evidence than upon personal narratives. Though, as to facts, one has always to place the greatest reliance upon written evidence, for interpretation of the thinking that prompted decisions oral testimony is invaluable and it is really only for the latter part of the story that this was available.

It should perhaps be added that throughout the period of manufacture of traction engines the predominant source of income to the firm was the making of portable engines and of the machines they powered, mostly threshers. It would probably be overstating the case to describe other types of manufactures as side-lines, since the firm regarded themselves as general engineers, but to remember how important the portables and machines were to the economics of the Works gives appropriate perspective to the firm's endeavours in other directions.

Tonbridge, Kent. Robert Whitehead
March, 1997.

Acknowledgements and Thanks

Assembling the information for this book began nearly forty years ago. Because of this a considerable number of those I wish to thank are now dead. Foremost of these was Victor R. Garrett, the last surviving family member of the board of directors of Richard Garrett & Sons Ltd. Some of the events narrated happened in his lifetime but of earlier happenings he was able to relay the recollections of his father and elder brothers and sisters. He always regretted that both his grandfather and Uncle Richard (IV) had died before he was born and that he had to rely upon what others remembered of them. I am also greatly indebted to those who successively had charge of the Works during the period of my researches: the late Alfred R. King, Reginald J. Hadfield, and Michael Hilton. Other directors who gave valuable help were Frank Andrews, Ernest Cuthbert, and Reginald Clarke, all now dead, the latter of whom became a valued personal friend.

The drawing office staff were also very helpful, especially Leslie W. Farrow, chief designer for many years, and his deputy, Arthur Woodhead. The late Frank Waddell, latterly editor of the *Leiston Observer*, had been a draughtsman in the thresher department which had little directly to do with traction engines but the situation, taken with his gregarious and extrovert nature, made him acquainted with the remaining men in the drawing office who *were* concerned with them. We used often to stay with him and his wife,

Madge, in Victory Road, and had many good times with them. The late Herbert R. (Jack) Simpson joined the firm in 1907 and later was involved in testing the 5NHP piston valved traction engine in the twenties; George Hambling worked, as a young man, on traction engine boilers, whilst Walter Hall, Dick and Jack Feller, Arthur Pipe and Jimmy Drane worked as fitters or erectors on the latter examples. None did more to help, however, than the late Ted Dunn, a friend for many years.

Others who have been very helpful are the staffs of the National Motor Museum, Beaulieu; the Rural History Centre, Reading; the Library of the Institution of Mechanical Engineers; the County Records Office of Suffolk County Council; the Long Shop Museum, Leiston; and Stadtarchiv of Leipzig, particularly Herr Hillert.

Valuable help was given by the late Alan Duke, of the Road Locomotive Society, and by Robin Harding, his successor, by John Butler , by Alan Martin who loaned photographs, and by my son-in-law, Michael J. Walters who did much research, read, commented upon and contributed to the manuscript, and took a major role in preparing the list of engines in the Appendix. My wife, Jean, contributed a share beyond measure and without complaint to the twenty years or so of research we put in at Leiston Works and about eighteen years elsewhere, besides editing the manuscript and setting it into type. Over the years Barry Finch gave much help in copying old photographs.

To all those named above I extend my heartfelt and most sincere thanks as well as to all those who have contributed but whom consideration of space precludes from individual mention.

I am particularly grateful also to Michael Lane for his kindness in reading the draft manuscript and contributing the foreword, and for allowing me to draw freely upon his researches into the Garrett Boydell engine which he conducted in collaboration with David Manson of Chatsworth (NSW) and Graham Clegg of Young (NSW). Chapter 1 is based very largely upon their work, supplemented by investigations into Chelmsford Royal Show 1856, by Pat Freeman, who also read and commented upon the draft, for all of which I am very grateful to him.

Bibliography

The information contained in this book was, so far as possible, extracted from documents that existed at Leiston Works. Other sources that were consulted included the periodicals:

Engineer *Implement & Machinery Review* *Bells Weekly Messenger*
Engineering *Mark Lane Express* *East Anglian Daily Times*
The catalogues of the Shows of the Royal Agricultural Society of England

Other books by R.A.Whitehead
¶ denotes still in print

The Story of the Colne Valley (jointly with F.D.Simpson)	Oakwood Press [Reprint]
Garretts of Leiston	Percival Marshall
A Century of Service	Eddison Plant
The Age of the Traction Engine	Ian Allan
A Century of Steam Rolling	Ian Allan
Steam in the Village	David & Charles
Garrett 200	Transport Bookman
Kaleidoscope of Steam Wagons	Marshall Harris & Baldwin
Kaleidoscope of Traction Engines	Marshall Harris & Baldwin
Wallis & Steevens - a History	R.L.S.
¶ *A Review of Steam Tractors*	R.L.S.
¶ *Austrian Steam Locomotives 1837-1981*	R.A.Whitehead & Partners
¶ *The Beloved Coast & the Suffolk Sandlings*	Terence Dalton
¶ *Jesse Ellis & the Maidstone Wagons*	R.A.Whitehead & Partners
Steam is the Essence	R.A.Whitehead & Partners
¶ *Garrett Diesel Tractors*	R.A.Whitehead & Partners
¶ *Made by Garretts*	R.A.Whitehead & Partners
¶ *Garrett Wagons Part 1 - Pioneers & Overtypes*	R.A.Whitehead & Partners
¶ *Garrett Wagons Part 2 - Undertypes*	R.A.Whitehead & Partners
¶ *Garrett Wagons Part 3 - Electrics & Motors*	R.A.Whitehead & Partners

Fig. 4. *A carefully posed picture of the frames and wheels of the Boydell Garrett being worked upon in the yard of Boydell & Glasier at Hawley Crescent, Camden Town.*

Fig. 5. *The drawing attached to Boydell's patent No.431 of 1854, depicting, at least in outline, the form of the wheels that supported the engine work supplied by Garretts.*

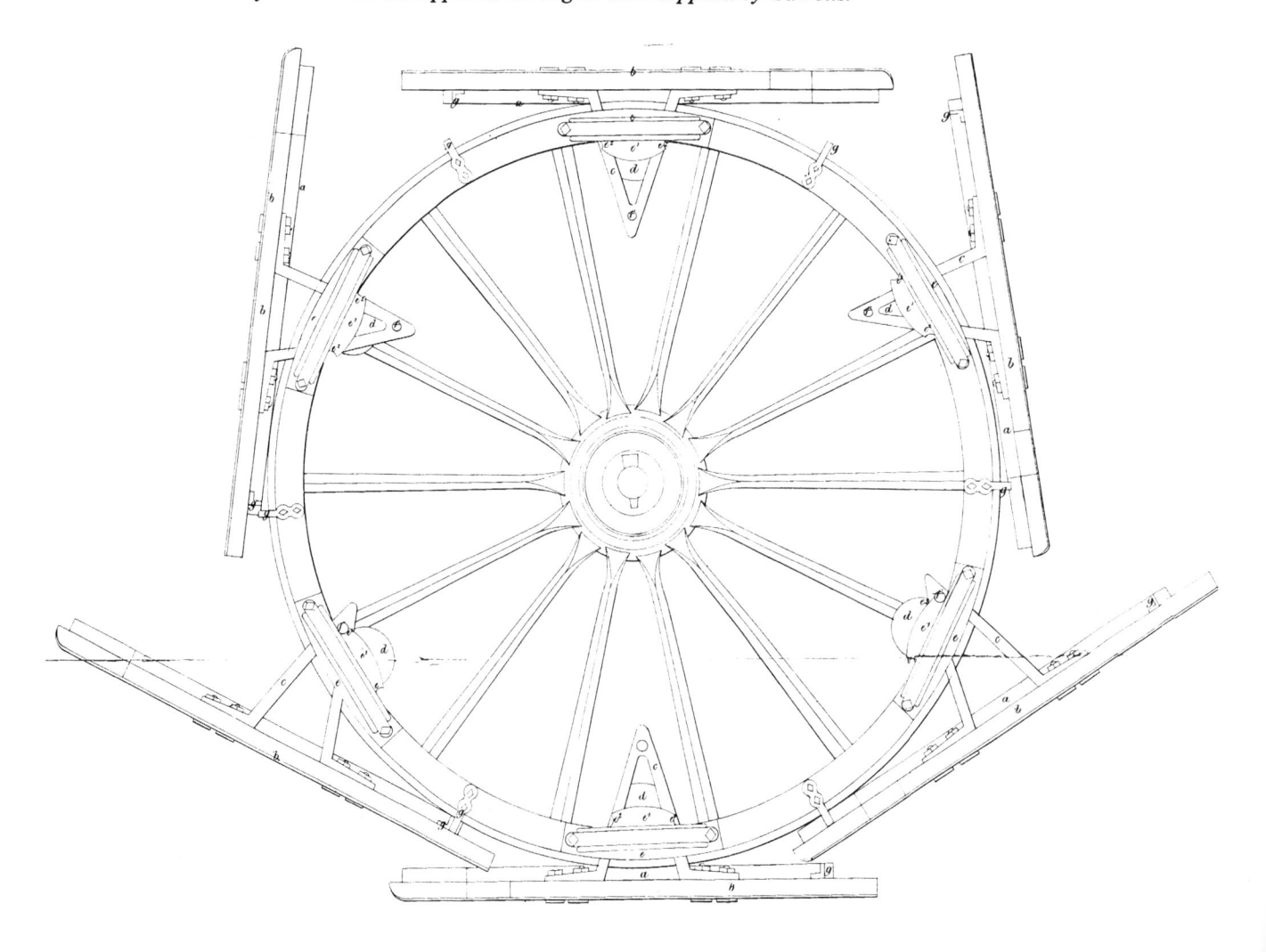

Chapter 1

Adventures with Boydells

It would seem that the involvement of the Garretts in the building of self-moving engines came about more or less by accident. As I have recounted elsewhere Richard Garrett III and his younger brother Newson, notwithstanding the fact that as well as their being brothers their respective wives were sisters, managed to spend the greater part of Richard's adult life in a state of rivalry, each endeavouring to match or excel every achievement of the other, though not perhaps in quite the ill-natured way that I have seen suggested. Nor did they disagree on every subject. Both felt strongly, for instance, on the subject of the shameful impositions made upon the public in the adulteration of food and drink. After Newson, in the course of advancing his career, had become the owner of the Bow Brewery in London's East End, an enterprise in which his son-in-law, James Smith, subsequently became a partner, (the firm thenceforward being known as Garrett, Smith & Co.), Richard, matching action for action, bought the Camden Brewery in Hawley Crescent, Camden Town, North London, later managed by his son-in-law, George Grimwood. It was through this brewery that Richard Garrett came to be acquainted with James Boydell, sometime senior managing partner in the Oak Farm Iron Company of Kingswinford near Dudley and inventor of the Boydell track-laying wheel patented, in its earliest form, in 1846.

Boydell left the Kingswinford firm in 1848, setting up practice as a land, mine and machinery valuer at 54 Threadneedle Street, in the City of London, and also forming a partnership with a Mr. Glasier to establish a factory in Hawley Crescent, Camden Town, both to make his patent wheels and to deal in the same type of goods as had been made at Kingswinford. Thus these two inventive spirits, Richard Garrett and James Boydell, found themselves with business premises only a few yards apart. Not only this but Boydell lived close-by at Regents Park Terrace, whilst Richard had a house in St. Johns Wood. Both had been exhibitors moreover at the Great Exhibition in 1851, Richard with the added prestige of a guarantor.

It would be deviating too widely from the subject of this book to reiterate a detailed description of Boydell's invention, the essence of which was to fit the periphery of the wheel with broad wooden shoes pivoted to it and carrying, on the side in contact with the wheel, short lengths of iron rail. As the shoes successively came into contact with the ground the wheel rim was presented with the iron rail upon which to run. Initially applied to carts the system was developed by its inventor to be employed upon self-moving steam engines also. The first such engine had been supplied by Richard Bach of Birmingham, whose firm subsequently became Belliss & Morcom. For reasons unknown to me the Boydell Bach cooperation did not proceed to a second example and one infers, with no direct documentary evidence, that the accidental juxtaposition of Boydell and Richard Garrett in North London led to an arrangement between the two men to build a second Boydell locomotive.

Richard Garrett had been producing portable engines for some years, having shown a 6NHP example, mounted on a return tube boiler, at the Royal Show at York in 1848. By the mid-1850's successive modifications in the Garrett designs had resulted in a range of larger portable engines that conformed in the salient points of layout with the arrangement that came to be considered the norm for portables in the second half of the nineteenth century i.e. the cylinders were mounted over the firebox of a locomotive type boiler and a forged crankshaft was carried in brackets on the leading end of the boiler barrel. Garrett engines of 10NHP and upwards were double cylindered. Therefore it is quite possible though, in the strict sense, unproven, that components of these portables formed the basis of the first Garrett self-mover.

The Boydell Bach engine was shown at the Royal Show of 1855, held at Carlisle in July. By the time of the next Royal Show at Chelmsford in 1856 Boydell had transferred his custom to the Garretts who, in the intervening year, had designed and built suitable engine parts. It seems likely that the project was initiated in the Autumn of 1855. Whilst resident in London Richard Garrett became a member of the Royal Society of Arts and a regular attender at its meetings. The subjects were varied and the speakers were usually men of substance respected for their knowledge and experience in their own fields. Sometimes he was merely a listener but at others the subject was one upon which he could speak with authority in the debate which followed the paper. Thus when, on January 30, 1856, John Fowler spoke on 'Cultivation by Steam - its past history and probable prospects', Richard spoke in the subsequent discussion. He confessed to having only recently become interested in the subject, but from observation and some personal experiments had concluded that the roundabout system, as then practised, entailed excessive loss of power. He ended by saying that Boydell's experiments in direct traction interested him more. This suggests that by that time some arrangement had been effected between him and Boydell.

Though portable engine components, or adaptations made from them, may have been used in the production of the engine, they were not arranged in portable engine form, the cylinders being mounted behind the chimney and the crankshaft being over the firebox. At that time Garretts had no boiler shop, buying in their boilers from either Wheatcroft or Horton & Co. (later Horton & Kendrick), both London boilermakers. Tradition says the latter provided the boiler for Boydell's engine. The drive to the road wheels was by a gear bolted to the spokes of the offside road wheel engaging with a pinion on the end of the crankshaft, capable of being clutched into or out of drive. In form if not in dimensions, this type of drive was carried forward into the first Boydell engine subsequently built by Charles Burrell which was the subject of a letter to the East India Company by Col. Sir Frederick Abbott in April, 1858, after observing at a trial of Burrell's engine at Woolwich in February 4, 1858. Col. Abbott put his finger on a great weakness when he wrote:
> Its power of draught is very great; but owing to its driving only one wheel it was unmanageable with a load as it could scarcely be turned to the right hand.

In published descriptions the Boydell Garrett engine is stated to have been of '12HP' and to have had cylinders 6½" in diameter by 10" stroke. This size of cylinder would not have resulted in a 10NHP engine, much less a 12NHP, under the RASE rating which calculated horse-power by taking the square of the piston diameter (doubled in the case of a double cylindered engine) and dividing the result by 10, in this case giving a result of 8½. The contemporary Garrett 10NHP portable had twin cylinders 6¾"diameter x 10" stroke, making it a dubious 10NHP at best, so there is an unexplained discrepancy hanging over the Boydell. Possibly the description meant brake horse-power, or perhaps it was no more than a sellers bombastic description. Published accounts of the engine say that the working pressure was 60 p.s.i. although then, or soon afterwards, the Garrett double cylinder portables used 70 p.s.i. Garretts contributed only the engine and boiler; the wheels came from Woolwich Arsenal; whilst the chassis and underworks were produced by Boydell and Glasier themselves or, if not built by them, then arranged directly by them. The finished machine had a belly tank and was arranged for front steerage by a vertical ship's type wheel. To help the steersman the steering mechanism was linked to a visual direction indicator. Among the features of the chassis was a screw levelling device intended to enable the horizontal centre line of the boiler to be kept level, or near it, when travelling down hill so as to protect the firebox crown. As finished the weight was 7 tons. Boydell claimed a travelling speed of 5 m.p.h. 'on good roads', a claim that appears doubtful to later eyes.

As noted, it made its first appearance at the Chelmsford Royal in 1856 after a private trial at Warren Farm, Writtle, two miles outside Chelmsford, on Saturday, July 5, where it was paired with the locally made Coleman & Morton plough with which it was to appear at the Royal. The *Chelmsford Chronicle* of July 11 reported that the engine had steamed from Camden Town to Chelmsford, (some twenty-seven miles incidentally) the day previous to the test, in about nine hours. After the experiment it steamed to Coleman's yard, almost certainly the first traction engine to be seen in Chelmsford. The *Chronicle* reporter commented '... we were certainly surprised to witness the regularity with which it was worked, the facility with which it was stopped, it being brought to a standstill or *backed* [my italics: R.A.W.] in an instant and the ease with which the steersman at its head guided it.' This ease of steering had apparently deserted it when it came to the time of the RASE practical trial a few days later. The *Chronicle* of July 18, reporting the engine's entry to the trial field, remarked 'This extraordinary invention ... is of a very cumbrous appearance. At the appointed time this stupendous affair left the Show Ground and came ambling along the road like a giant in loose wooden slippers.' The reporter described how at its first attempt to enter the narrow gateway of the field it struck a gate post. It then *backed* off and tried again, only to knock down the opposite gate post. Despite these set-backs he went on to say that the manoeuvring 'afforded practical proof of how much this unwieldy machine can be subjected to the easy control of the commonest engine driver.' I have twice italicised the word 'backed' in these references because it has usually been reported that the engine was non-reversible, whilst these two separate comments seem to suggest the contrary.

Coleman's plough carried ten plough breasts. These proved to be too much for the engine as it was able to plough only in short bursts before running out of steam. Removing two furrows improved matters somewhat but failed to solve the problem. This may have been a criticism of the plough as much as of the engine but, nevertheless, despite a good deal of favourable comment there remained a substantial body of sceptics. The *Journal of the RASE* commented drily: 'Mr. Boydell again exhibited his engine, drawing with ease the implements attached to it but it still remains to be proved if it will ever be found serviceable in agriculture.'

Upon the engine's return to Camden Town, supposedly under its own power, further demonstrations were given in the Works' yard, upon Mr. Francis Hamilton's farm at nearby Willesden, and on another farm at Hanworth, Hounslow owned by Mr. James Middleton, who subsequently became a director of the Traction Engine & Endless Railway Apparatus Co. Ltd. which took over from Boydell & Glasier early in 1857. A report of some of these trials appeared in the issue of *The Engineer* of October 3, 1856:

> On Tuesday week we visited the farm of Mr. Middleton, near Hounslow, where Mr. Boydell was trench-ploughing a small field with two of Cotgreave's trench ploughs, drawn by his traction engine by means of chains - Mr. Cotgreave himself superintending his ploughs. The work done was about twelve inches deep, and at the rate of five acres per day. It was executed in a superior manner, giving great satisfaction, especially to the market gardeners of the neighbourhood, who valued it at 30s. per acre, estimated as if done by horses. The total cost of the engine and attendance was 30s. per day, so that the expense per acre was only 6s., leaving a profit (according to the foregoing estimate), over similar work done by horses, of 24s. per acre, or £6 per day, a profit which would redeem the first cost of the engine in less than a season.
> Two large fields upon the same farm we also examined, a good deal of land the engine had ploughed, with four of Howard's ploughs, going nine inches deep, and at the rate of eight to ten acres per day. The quality of work gave universal satisfaction to all who examined it.
> On Friday we visited Mr. James Middleton's farm, Hanworth. This gentleman was ploughing in a large field with the above engine, and four of Howard's ploughs, going nine inches deep, and when timed, at the rate of fully an acre per hour, or ten acres per day of ten hours. The workmanship was better than any we examined on the previous day, and far superior to that done by horses in the same field. On the first farm named the soil was as dry as at Midsummer, stubbornly hard in the bottom, and difficult to plough; but on the latter farm, although equally dry, it was more sandy in the bottom and friable throughout, enabling the ploughmen to execute their work accordingly. The field was comparatively level, and nearly half a mile in length; at each end a single furrow was drawn across it, to mark off the breadth of the headland. As the ploughs respectively reached these they were regularly entered at the one and taken out at the other, the same as when ploughing with horses. On the headland, however, the steam-horse never offered to loiter, as is too commonly the case with his rivals, the former turning in less time than the latter.

Notwithstanding this enthusiasm on the part of *The Engineer's* reporter practically none of the predictions as to ploughing costs with Boydell engines were realised in sustained work, not even by the later and most developed examples made by Burrells.

Meanwhile comment upon the Boydell wheel from another source had furthered the inventor's efforts to gain public recognition for it. A message home from General Sir William Codrington, the Commander-in-Chief of the British troops before Sebastopol in the Crimean war, written in February, 1856, said:

> I saw the 'Mud Sling Cart' used during a deep, sticky, wet, Crimean mud. I understand that at that time the 95 cwt. gun could not have been moved at all by common means on such ground, and though an excessively clumsy-looking affair, I saw five horses move it at once on the level, stop at the rise, have two more horses put on, then move again. It crossed the railroad and the little ditches by the side of it without difficulty.

Although Sir William's command of grammar and syntax may leave something to be desired his approval of Boydell's wheels was plain. The Government of the day (Lord Palmerston's Whig ministry) responded by doing what so many governments have done, before and since, namely it appointed a committee, under Lord Panmure (later Lord Dalhousie), the Chairman of the Select Committee of the Board of Ordnance, to examine the matter. Besides military members from the Royal Engineers the Panmure committee included civilian scientists and engineers. With great common sense the committee set about determining the usefulness of the engine by arranging a practical trial on June 24, 1856, and reported upon it as follows:

> The experiments of the 24th instant were two in number, as follows:
> First. The engine, with a sufficiency of water for a good long working, weighing 9 tons fully laden, hauled a heavy siege gun (5 tons 12 cwt), a carriage and tender (2 tons 7 cwt) and sixteen men (say 1 ton 2cwt), making a total of 18 tons, from the Arsenal up Burrage Road to Plumstead Common, and down the steep incline to Waterman's Fields in return. The steepest party of the ascent is 1 in 10, and of the descent 1 in 8. Of the two, descending was considered by all present the master part of this experiment. No brake or drag was placed upon any of the wheels, those of the gun carriage and tender being without Endless Rails. In the very steepest part of the inclination our MEGATHERIUM war-horse had complete control over its ponderous load. Moreover, in going up Burrage Road, the wheels of the gun carriage sank from 1 to 3 inches in the shingle of which the road was made, a circumstance which greatly added to the draught; nevertheless the war-horse dauntlessly took the ascent with that dignity of bearing and self-confidence which characterises the genius of steam when master of its work, and would soon have enabled the men to place the huge gun at the top of Shooter's Hill, had not Colonel Tulloch, Superintendent, Royal Carriage Department, Woolwich, ordered the road train down the steep descent to try its mettle there.

> The second experiment was in hauling a gun of the same size over a marshy bog in the lower part of the Arsenal grounds, a bog too soft to bear the feet of horses when standing. The wheels of the gun carriage were, in this instance, fitted with Endless Railway rails, and the engine was yoked to the gun by means of a rope capable of sustaining a strain of 10 tons. This rope was broken by fair pulling several times owing to the abrupt inequalities in the ground, but these were overcome triumphantly over the quagmire. A result which all the artillery horses in Her Majesty's service could not have effected.

The conclusion of the committee was that the experiments had demonstrated the ability of the engine to haul 54 tons on a level ordinary road, reducing to 40 tons where the road was inclined at 1 in 30, and to 10 tons, on a grade of 1 in 10. The issue of *The Engineer* for July 4, 1856, reported these results, emphasising that on the downhill journey the unbraked train of vehicles was held solely by the engine, thereby confirming, albeit obliquely, that it must have had reversing gear.

Whether or not the Boydell engine tested at Woolwich was the same one that appeared at the Chelmsford Royal is at least questionable as is shown by two excerpts from *The Engineer*. The first appeared on November 6, 1857:

> NEW LOCOMOTIVE - At Moscow, lately, great curiosity was excited by an experiment being made with a new description of locomotive, running along the streets, and so constructed as to cause the wheels to lay down a sort of wooden rails as they advanced. The locomotive dragged after it a number of carts heavily laden. The experiment, though the first made, had perfectly succeeded. The author of the invention is a trader of Moscow, named Prokhoroff. (This is surely one of Boydell's?)

The following week a further comment appeared:

> THE NEW RUSSIAN LOCOMOTIVE - The locomotive noticed in our last number, and stated to be the invention of a M. Prockeroff [sic!] and which we fancied was identical with Boydell's endless railway engine, turns out to have been manufactured by Messrs. Garrett, of Saxmundham, for Mr. Boydell. It is the one, in fact, which was tried at Woolwich some time ago.

By that date, Boydell had entered into an arrangement with Burrell, and it may be that this Moscow engine had been supplied by Burrell. Journalists, like authors, are capable of error, but, on the face of it, the statement does indicate that it was by Garrett.

The trials of the first engine in Essex had brought it to the notice of Alderman John Mechi, at that time Sheriff of Middlesex. Mechi, a member of the London Italian community, had made a sizeable fortune from his invention of a patent razor strop. With commendable public spirit he used this fortune, at least in part, to establish a model farm at Tiptree, Essex, where, as a gentleman farmer, he was able to conduct experiments into agricultural improvements and farm mechanisation. As a result of his patronage the Boydell Garrett took part in the Lord Mayor's procession through the City of London on November 10, 1856.

Mechi may have been also responsible for bringing the engine to the notice of Mr. E.G. Clerk, a New South Wales pastoralist, who was on a visit to Britain with the object of buying plant and machinery for the further development of his property, known as Clerkness, near Bundarra in the northern part of the colony. Apart from ploughs and cultivating machinery he is known to have bought machinery for flour milling and brickmaking. After the Lord Mayor's Show he purchased the Boydell Garrett for £500. This and all of his other purchases left London on Christmas Day, 1856, aboard the *Lady Hodgkinson* to arrive in Sydney early in April, 1857. Clerk must have been a man of some importance in the colony as, according to the *Sydney Morning Herald* of Friday, April 10, to celebrate the arrival of the engine he arranged on board the ship a lavish luncheon attended by the Governor, Sir William Davison, and an entourage of notables, the engine itself being on display on deck for the occasion. After being unloaded the following week it was shown in the streets of Sydney, and gave ploughing demonstrations before embarking itself onto the coastal steamer *The Clarence* by means of a specially constructed gangway. The *Morning Herald* (May 23, 1857) related the event thus:

> This stately stepper crossed the wharf, taking as it does lengthy strides, placing its ponderous pattens very heavily wherever it treads. This unwieldy passenger, with steam up, succeeded in walking himself like a huge elephant on board *The Clarence* at the Australian Steam Navigation Company's Wharf.

The Clarence transported the engine to the town of Morpeth, 20 miles up the Hunter River from the coastal port of Newcastle. Supposedly it was unloaded there by a reversal of the way in which it had boarded the ship at Sydney for in the issue of the *Morning Herald* for July 10, 1857, its departure on the first stage of the journey to Bundarra is described:

> The Megaethon started from Morpeth at about ten o'clock yesterday, and overcoming the obstacles that lay in its way, passed on until near East Maitland, where it stopped awhile. It then proceeded onwards, crossing the Victoria Bridge in safety amidst the cheers of the bystanders. The next halt took place near the Cross Keys, in West Maitland. After a short delay the ponderous locomotive slowly moved on through the High Street at three

miles an hour, surrounded on all sides by a crowd and accompanied by several horsemen. The wood that had been used as fuel proved unsatisfactory and a supply of coal was obtained from a Mr. Sawyer, the benefits of which were soon apparent. The Megaethon then reached the Long Bridge and after traversing about two-thirds of the length, steam was shut off and the boiler screwed into the correct position preparatory to the ascent of Campbell's Hill. The ascent was accomplished with great steadiness, the boiler pressure remaining at 60 lbs. A short stoppage took place at Mr. Eckford's, and another, a quarter of an hour later, at Mr. Turner's tannery. The Megaethon then continued its way over the uneven ground that lies between the tannery and the road to Storey Creek, passing over several rather steep holes caused by the bullock teams and dray wheels in wet weather. Neither the holes, nor the roughness of the ground impeded the engine's progress. When it reached Captain Russell's Storey Creek the coal and water supplies were replenished. The time occupied in travelling from Cross Keys to Captain Russell's was two and a half hours, inclusive of stoppages caused chiefly by the necessity of oiling the machinery.

The Megaethon was enveloped in a cloud of dust nearly the whole way, the effects of which were evident. Whilst the engine had been at Morpeth the spur wheel attached to the driving wheel had been protected by a curved iron plate. The want of this protection had contributed greatly to the enforced stoppages when the engine was in use before. The shoes, loaded with mud as they revolved with the wheel, overhung the gearing, and mud frequently fell between the teeth of the gear wheels. This is now prevented. The steering apparatus appears to give the driver a perfect facility in guiding the engine on its way, and the Megaethon presented a formidable appearance as it moved along. The action of the shoes was admirable, each retaining its position on the ground, sustaining the weight resting upon it, until the succeeding shoe was ready to replace it.

The tender with the saw bench for providing fuel for the engine was not attached, but was carried on bullock drays which followed behind. It was Mr. Clerk's intention to proceed as far as Cowhill Paddock yesterday, and then push on through New England steadily. We wish him good speed on his journey.

At Singleton, some twenty-five miles from Morpeth, the convoy found itself unable to continue. The *Newcastle Telegraph* of November 13, 1857, reported its misfortunes in mocking words:

We learn from a reliable source that the lumbering, snorting monster, Megaethon, is laying this side of Singleton in a disabled condition. A long pole has been fitted to the engine, which will now have to continue its journey north through the agency of bullocks.

Megaethon made but a poor display in Sydney, where they have good roads, and therefore we never anticipated he would make a quick passage through New England. It is pretty certain our roads are too much for him, or any other known locomotive. He might be made useful to cut timber and saw wood, or drive a threshing machine, or pump water, but travelling with him is out of the question.

Notwithstanding this knocking and pessimism the engine eventually arrived at Clerkness on December 29, 1857, an event chronicled more sympathetically on January 6, 1858, by the *Maitland Mercury* - published in a town on its route:

It is with much pleasure that we are enabled by a correspondent to inform our readers of the safe arrival at Clerkness, Bundarra, of the Megaethon, about which the learned and inquisitive were so curious when it was in this neighbourhood some time since. Many were the prophecies that it would never make its destination, or that if it did it would be so maimed as to be useless. Unheard of were the number of bullocks suggested as the only chance of taking it over the rough ground of the Khyber Pass in the Moonbies. Nevertheless, and in spite of the avalanche of croaking hurled upon him, Mr. E.G. Clerk, thinking, with Napoleon, that nothing is impossible, started upon his perilous journey from Singleton, which he completed in twenty-six travelling days. The engine arrived at Clerkness on Tuesday, December 29, 1857. A team of twelve bullocks accomplished the impossible, requiring assistance only at Liverpool, the Moonbies and other steep pitches. No accidents of any importance occurred on the journey, and the leviathan now rests from its fatigues in perfect health and spirits.

It was the *Country News* of January 23, 1858, that told of the final misfortune:

The Megaethon which has safely arrived at Clerkness, has kept the inhabitants of this neighbourhood all alive for the last fortnight. Mr. E.G. Clerk certainly deserves the credit of all the district for his perseverance in having, in the face of undeserved ridicule and ill-omens of the would be wise, brought the Megaethon successfully up to Clerkness with the aid of twelve bullocks.

On Friday last, the Megaethon was put under steam for the first time here in the presence of leading gentlemen of the district. Though perhaps unsightly in appearance, the machine was quite as easily turned whilst under steam as a team of horses would be. It was proved to the satisfaction of all present that it was the fault of the roads and weather and not the impracticability of the machinery, that the Megaethon could not arrive here with the aid of her own natural powers. The Megaethon divested of her rather cumbersome wheels and railway is a perfect model of an effective engine, and from the manner in which she worked when attached to a saw table, it was evident that the time was drawing to a close when slabs only should be used in the building of our houses.

On Friday last Mr. Clerk entertained a large party of gentlemen from the Armidale district, when the Megaethon was again put in motion. So far as the sawing was concerned, she performed her duty admirably, but in consequence of some mismanagement the ploughing was not so successful. Mr. Clerk then attempted to steam across the river, but unfortunately the steering pole accidentally broke, which rendered the Megaethon incapable of any further performances in a moveable form.

Perhaps soon after this Mr. Clerk came to the conclusion that conditions in Clerkness were not yet ripe for steam traction. The locomotive was reported in 1879 as providing power for the Clerkness flour mill, having been stripped of its Boydell equipment. Later still it was recalled locally as the power unit of a pumping plant on the banks of the Gwydir river from which it was swept away and lost in a huge flood in 1926.

It is thus clearly established that there were at least two Boydell Garretts in existence in November, 1857, one making its way across New South Wales and the other giving a demonstration in Moscow. The interesting question arises as to whether or not a third was built since in an inventory of 1858 (Stock Book A dated May 24, page 39), at the time of writing lodged in the Long Shop Museum, the pages relating to the engine shop contain the entry 'A Boydell's Engine complete (out of repair) £250.0.0.' No subsequent reference has been found to this engine nor what became of it. It antedates by a few months the earliest surviving engine register which begins in 1858, so no help can be obtained from that quarter. Possibly it found a purchaser; alternatively, it may have been sold, minus its Boydell wheels, as a portable; or it may have been broken up. Whilst the possibility cannot entirely be dismissed that the engine in the inventory is the Moscow engine repatriated it certainly seems a strong inference that it was a third example.

Other entries in Stock Book A raise the possibility of whether it was intended to build a fourth, as the inventory goes on to list sundry components of a Boydell. Thus on page 46 the entry occurs: Wrought iron platform with wrought iron tool and coal boxes for Boydells; and again on page 48: Bracket saddle for Boydell engine. On the next page there is an entry: 2 boxes for Boydell's engine; followed on page 57 by Saddle for Boydell's engine; and on page 58 by Tank for Boydell's engine.

The only catalogue reference to Boydell engines occurs in that of December, 1857, in which there is a note which reads 'R.G. & S. have made arrangements for the manufacture of Boydell's Patent Locomotive Traction Engines, full particulars of which will be forwarded upon application'. This was not repeated in later catalogues. No photograph is known to exist of a complete Boydell Garrett, the nearest being a photograph (Fig.4) of the chassis and wheels taken in the Boydell & Glasier yard at Hawley Crescent, but there is an engraving of one on the cover of the prospectus issued in 1858 for the limited company. This is reproduced as Fig.6. Although not a technically correct drawing there are features in the illustration, such as the throttle lever and the circular plate behind it, which tie in with known Garrett practice on other engines and suggest that it does portray, albeit not completely or perfectly, what the Boydell Garrett looked like.

As will be seen in the next chapter Garretts later made intermittent use of an annular drive for self-moving engines for a period of some eight to ten years, distinguishing, by so doing, engines of the 'self-moving portable' category from full traction engines. Because of the propensity of the shoes for picking up and elevating mud and stones from their path Boydell engines fitted with annular drive were especially vulnerable to damage to the ring of cast iron gear teeth. The dropping of the drive to a ring of gear bolted to the spokes of the rear wheel in favour of geared drive to a live rear axle was one of the earlier major improvements to Boydell engines put into effect by Charles Burrell & Sons when they took over their manufacture. In the practical sense Boydell wheels quickly wore or broke the hardwood shoes and, moreover, demanded strength and wearing qualities in the metal components that were beyond the capabilities of contemporary metallurgy. Had manganese steels been available in 1856 more might have been achieved. As it was, however, the expense and inconvenience of breakdowns combined with high initial cost diminished the wheel's economic prospects which were blighted even more by Boydell's death in 1859, removing the force that might have fathered further improvements. Hindsight leads one to applaud Boydell's perception that tracklaying vehicles had great commercial possibilities but, on the other hand, the methods he used in an attempt to achieve that objective can be seen to have been inherently incapable of delivering satisfactory wearing qualities. Nevertheless the idea of making portables self-moving had been seeded into the thinking of the Garrett partners, and even as the 1858 inventory was being drafted some chain engines of their own design throughout were in the process of manufacture.

Fig.6. The Boydell Garrett as shown on the 1857 prospectus of the Traction Engine & Endless Railway Apparatus Co. Ltd. No reversing lever is shown though written references suggest it must have been reversible. Artist's licence or artist's ignorance may explain this.

Fig.7. The end of the Boydell connection more or less coincided with the launch of the first wholly Garrett self-mover. This is the 8NHP version though the picture also appeared against descriptions of the 12NHP.

Fig.8. A 10NHP traction engine, to Aveling's design, built at Leiston. It may have been No.3-82, the firm's exhibit at the Worcester Royal Show of 1863.

Figs. 9 and 10. *The second Aveling design (of 1862) later built under licence at Leiston, with details of the engine, driving sprocket and steering. The cylinder, with its steam jacket, and lagging was a workman-like job but a weak point was the placing of the intermediate pinion and sprocket upon a stub shaft with inadequate support from the carrying bracket.*

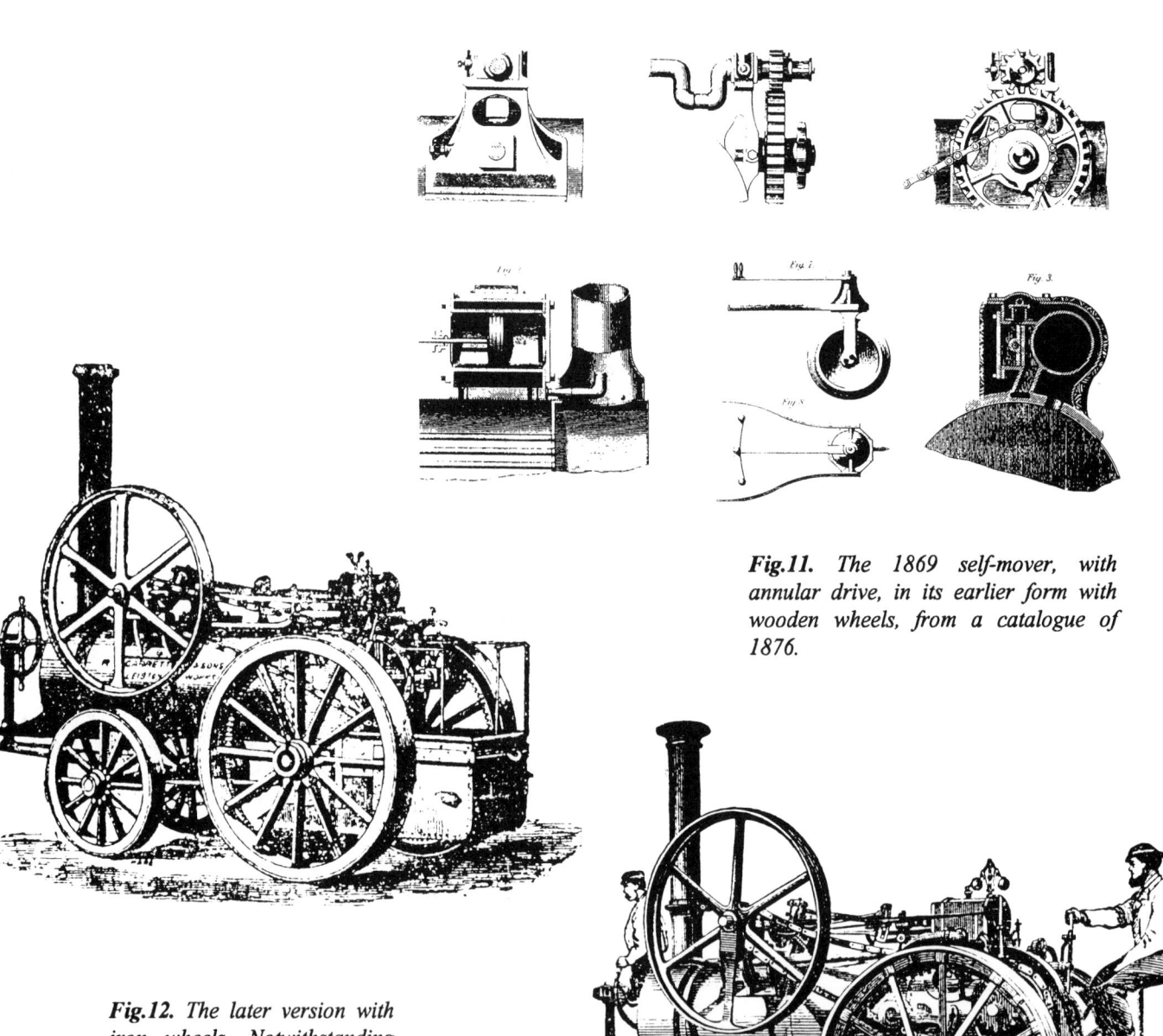

Fig. 11. *The 1869 self-mover, with annular drive, in its earlier form with wooden wheels, from a catalogue of 1876.*

Fig. 12. *The later version with iron wheels. Notwithstanding their unpromising appearance engines of this design had long lives. A new firebox for one of them was supplied in 1898 to Wm. O'Neill of Athy.*

16

Chapter 2

Engines Prior to 1890

Although the company stated in catalogues of the 1920's that their first steam traction engine had been built as early as 1854, lengthy research has produced nothing to suggest that any Garrett self-moving engine ante-dated the Boydell Garretts described in Chapter 1. Whether or not the Garretts were induced solely by the latter to build self-moving engines of their own design or whether the burgeoning interest generally in the idea prompted them to continue is now unlikely to be known. They must, in fact, have continued from the Boydells, virtually without an interval, into designing their own self-movers.

Their first venture was an 8NHP single cylinder engine (No.252) delivered locally to James Barber at Snape on March 1, 1858. Barber was a farmer and had a pottery at Iken where he produced flower pots and similar items for domestic use. He seems also to have been a threshing machine proprietor and his purchase of the 8NHP probably reflected a wish to be able to move his engine and machine without the aid of horses. Possibly he had the engine on a trial basis only or it may have proved disappointing to him for it was returned to the Works on August 18, 1858, and credited in full. As it found no other purchaser as a self-propeller it was stripped of its self-moving parts before being sold as a portable on March 14, 1859, to a Mr. Lipton, whose home village was variously stated in the books as Holton, Houghton, or Haughton. It is my belief that a photograph of this engine must have been in front of the engraver of the catalogue illustration (Fig.7) purporting to be of the 12NHP self-mover completed in summer, 1858, which will be described a little later on in this chapter.

What the illustration shows is a portable, still with horse-shafts for steering but made self-propelling by the provision of a chain sprocket upon the crankshaft behind the flywheel, from which power was taken by a pitch chain to a larger driven sprocket between the near side rear wheel and the firebox side. One assumes, though the presence of the chain sprocket prevents one from verifying the fact, that the dead axle was continuous and carried in brackets on the firebox throat plate. It also seems likely that the driven sprocket was bolted to the wooden spokes of the wheel, a better and stronger arrangement than taking the drive through the nave of the wooden wheel. Whether or not the driving sprocket could be clutched into and out of drive is neither shown nor described. If such a provision was not made the chain would necessarily have had to be taken off whenever the engine took up its main role as a stationary power source.

A manstand, probably with a small tank beneath, was provided on which a little coal might have been carried though the space available on the manstand for water and fuel was so limited as to make it virtually certain that the engine was intended to draw a tender. A draw strap ran round the manstand and was screwed to the firebox plates. No reversing lever is shown and there is no evidence of reversing gear. To compensate for the absence of braking action from the engine a cross brake shaft is shown above the firehole door, actuated by lever from a handwheel and fast thread and acting via wooden brake blocks onto the near wheel tyres. The cylinder is placed to the side of the firebox, driving onto an overhung crank.

In the inventory set out in Stock Book A (already referred to in Chapter 1) a number of parts for an 8NHP self-moving engine were listed whilst on page 48 under Finished Engines besides noting the complete Boydell engine it also included: One 8 horse with endless chain, single cylinder £200.0.0. As, by the date of the inventory (May 1858), No.252 had already been sent, on March 1, to James Barber, not to return until August this entry must have related to a second example, about which we know nothing further. The 12NHP self-mover was probably similar in many respects to the engine just described, but as it was of 12NHP, having duplex cylinders, it was necessarily provided with a crankshaft. This was 3½" in diameter, and the 54" flywheel weighed 6¾ cwt. A 36" diameter secondary pulley was fitted. There was a Watt-type governor set to give a speed of 125 r.p.m. The boiler pressure was not stated but was probably 70 p.s.i. Some details survive of the plate thicknesses in the wrought iron boiler in which the shell was $^3/_8$" thick, whilst the firebox and tubeplate were $^5/_{16}$" and ½" thick respectively. The material for the firebox and tubeplate were described as 'Lowmoor iron' but the barrel was said to have been made of 'BBH' Crown plate. It seems quite probable that 'BBH' is merely a transcription error of 'BBB' (or Best Best Best). Lowmoor plates were all categorised as 'Best'. The pick of the 'Best' plates were sold as 'Best

Best' whilst the most superior grade of all was 'Best Best Best'. Hence one supposes that the boiler barrel was of highest grade Lowmoor material.

When exactly the engine was completed is not known as the only date against it in the books is July 12, 1858, when it was delivered to the Royal Show at Chester. Clearly it must have been completed and tested some weeks, at least, ahead of that date. The inventory catalogued in Stock Book A taken in May, 1858, included (p.39): two connecting rods for 12 horse loco; and again (p.49): 12 horse traction engine saddle. Other references in it related to parts for what is called 'traction engine' without positively linking them to the 12NHP engine, whilst components for an 8NHP self-mover are listed elsewhere in the book. The 12NHP was described in the Show catalogue as 'a new implement'. The price attached to it was £400.0.0. as a self-mover or £340.0.0. as a plain portable. In the description it was claimed that the engine 'would propel itself and draw the combined machine after it over ordinary farm roads.' Elsewhere, however, it was conceded that the chain drive was meant to assist rather than to supplant horse draught. Perhaps, by that time, progress reports on the Australian journey of the Boydell from Morpeth to Clerkness had filtered back to Leiston and had dampened expectations of chain driven self-movers. The engine was named *Locomotive,* possibly a somewhat ambitious title in view of its obviously limited capacity for haulage. No buyer for it came forward, and after a while it was converted to a portable, in which guise it was shown at the Crystal Palace, Sydenham, and finally sold to Easton & Amos of Erith. The Works number allocated to *Locomotive* was 5. If, in fact, three Garrett Boydells had been built, No.252, already mentioned, would have been the fourth self-mover which would have made *Locomotive* the fifth. However, I do not know whether 252 bore the number 4 in its self-moving form, nor do I know if *Locomotive* received a number in the portable engine series after its conversion. Further complications of numbering began on the appearance of the first of the next class of self-propelling engines when another arbitrary set of numbers came into being.

There was one further chain engine, a 7NHP, built at this time, bearing the No.275. This left the Works on November 27, 1858, for delivery to Mr. T. Sage, Heath Farm, Alresford near Colchester, Essex. Sage gave £307.17.3 for it, paid in instalments. Other details are completely lacking. One must not overlook, however, the possibility that it was the 8NHP engine shown in the inventory redescribed as 7NHP. All we know is that unlike the two earlier engines it did not return to the Works. At this point it seems to have been realised by the partners that their design of self-mover was not commercially viable, and production was halted after these three. Five years elapsed before they again built a self-propelling engine, and when the next did appear the design was from another source.

It should, perhaps, be mentioned that the Garretts, father and son, were on good terms with Thomas Aveling, a cordiality that was to continue down the generations. Trade rivals, in any case, were not necessarily personal enemies, but the Garrett-Aveling relationship was on warmer terms than mere civility to a fellow maker. In 1861 when Thomas Aveling developed his first design of true traction engine he had only limited production facilities at his disposal, and found it convenient to license other firms, of which Garretts were one, to manufacture engines to his design. The engines thus produced were the subject of a royalty payment to Aveling and it was the custom in the Aveling engine records to refer to the Rochester Works number as the 'Royalty number', a practice that endured until the end of production there. All the engines built by other firms under licence appeared against their royalty number in the Aveling record books.

Thus the first of the Aveling type engines to emerge from Leiston bore the royalty number 82 and an arbitrary Garrett number of 3, separate from the portable engine number series, suggesting that Nos.252 and 275 were looked upon as 1 and 2 in the traction engine series. After 3/82 the Garrett part of the numbers went in numerical sequence until 14 was reached, whereafter all numbers were in the same sequence as portables. All that is recorded of 3/82 in the Garrett books is that it was of 10NHP and was despatched on August 29, 1863, to a Mr. Hardy of Hartlepool, after having formed the firm's exhibit at the Worcester Royal Show in 1863. In the Show catalogue it was described as:

> A Locomotive Traction Engine for Common roads, invented by Mr. Aveling of Rochester, improved and manufactured by the exhibitors.

The only dimension recorded is the cylinder bore (10"). The cylinder was in the upper part of the smokebox; Aveling's patent pilot steering was fitted; the engine was single speed, and the final drive was by pitch chain. It was stated that a friction brake was fitted and, as there was no differential it may be that this denoted a device for locking, or freeing, the undriven wheel to the revolving axle in the manner of some early Fowler ploughing engines. The wording of a testimonial suggests that the boiler pressure was 50 p.s.i. References as to whether or not it had rubber springs, i.e. blocks of hard rubber interposed above the main axle bearings to give a little resilience, are inconclusive. The second, 4/83 of September 23, 1863, an 8NHP, was recorded as having 'wrought boxes for axle carriages' and rubber springs for certain. The third (5/89 of October 10, 1863) again had rubber springs.

The fourth engine in this series (No.6/93) was again an 8NHP, sent away at some time in October, 1863, though the name of the purchaser is not recorded. It is tempting to conclude that the orders for these engines were taken as a result of the Worcester Show. The surviving dimensions are tabulated below.

Engine Number	Cylinder	Flywheel Diameter	Length of Rear Axle	Diameter of Rear Axle	Diameter of Crankshaft
83	9" x 12"	4' 6"	7' 5"	4¼"	3"
89	10" x [?]	--	7' 11¼"	4⅞"	--
93	9" x [12?]	4' 6"	7' 4¼"	--	--

As to boiler design the meagre information available is contained in a catalogue, undated but of about the same period, which says that thirty-seven tubes of 1¾" diameter were fitted. Although offered as 8, 10, 12, or 14NHP, only eight and ten horsepower engines were built.

There followed a pause in traction engine building until No.114, a 10NHP, came out in May, 1864. In this the cylinder was 10" diameter by 12" stroke. Against the entry in the Leiston books is the note 'saddle, cylinder and coarse gear wheel and pinion off Aveling's patterns not made here'. The piston, however, was cast from the pattern used for the Garrett 10NHP fixed engines. Almost certainly the cylinder was steam jacketed in accordance with Aveling's patent of 1861 (No.1295). On this engine the tank had a cast iron flanged top, bottom, and ends, with wrought iron sides which were carried forward and riveted to the firebox side plates. No.121 followed it in September, 1864, the engine book containing the note 'home made cylinders [!] fitted to Aveling's lengths and with cast iron funnel stand'.

This pattern of engine, although modifications had taken place between the first and last of the series, had effectively been rendered obsolete by the improved design which Aveling had exhibited at the 1862 Great Exhibition. For a while Aveling seems to have held off his licensees from building this improved design, but with No.122, an 8NHP, he appears to have relented, at least as far as Garretts were concerned, for this conformed to the new lay-out. That is to say it used a cylinder casting bolted to the boiler barrel clear of the smokebox. This engine was sold on October 7, 1864. No.123, also an 8NHP, was sent to the Vienna Show in 1864. It may well have been sold from there for there are no subsequent references to it in the Leiston books. A 10NHP engine (No.246) was sold to Pilter, the long standing agent of the Garretts in Paris, Bordeaux, and, later, French North Africa. The books record it as having been completed on October 27, 1866, but do not say when it was shipped. The next engine numerically (No.247) was an 8NHP noted as being 'first with jacketed cylinder', possibly meaning it was the first 8 horsepower engine so equipped. This was one of the rare exports to North America, being shipped on March 31, 1868, to W.S. Taylor of Toronto. Prior to shipment it had been sent for exhibition at 'the Paris Show', i.e. the 1867 Paris Exhibition, perhaps the venue where Taylor had decided to buy it. From Garretts' point of view it was not an advantageous transaction as they had severe problems in getting money from Taylor who eventually defaulted on the final balance. Although 246 and 247 were probably completed at or near the same date their private Garrett numbers, allocated upon the date of sale were 11 and 13 respectively. Their construction was followed by that of another pair (Nos.261 and 262) an 8NHP and 10NHP respectively which became 12 and 14 in the Garrett sequence. The first of them is also noted as having been at the Paris Exhibition and was sold to J. Shaw & Son of Wolverhampton, leaving the Works on September 9, 1867. In the case of No.262 it was sold to Pilter, being sent on December 2, 1867. This group of four engines seem to have been double cylindered.

At this point the practice of using the Aveling Royalty and allocating a private Garrett number was abandoned. From thence forward the traction engines were numbered in with the general sequence of portable and fixed engines which sequence, by a process of inflation involving skipping over batches of numbers at intervals and leaping from 998 to 1999 was then running in the two thousands. Only one more Aveling type engine was sold after this change of numbering policy from which one is tempted to infer that the licence to build expired with the Royalty number 262, though documentary evidence on this is lacking.

The patterns for these engines were kept for some seven years more. The pattern for the 5' 6" diameter by 16½" wide 'hinter travelling wheels' (as the *Rough Entry Book of New Patterns* called them) was broken up on Frank Garrett's instruction at the end of July, 1874. Virtually all others, both 8 and 10NHP were outed by his orders on May 15, 1876. As shown below the items made away with are interesting and throws some light upon the construction of the engines as a group, though not, of course, upon individual examples:

> cylinder and covers, saddle, crankshaft and plummer block, governor bkts., wayshaft, reversing gear,
> 8HP TE slide, name plate covers, pump, guide bar bkt., slide jacket and slide, pump plunger, exhaust pipe and bend, funnel bottom, square axle box, fifth wheel, chain wheel 48".
> 10HP TE cylinder and covers, piston, slide, guide bar bkt., name plate for cyl., pump, slide, saddle, crankshaft plummer block, reversing slide rod bkt, way shaft bkt, brake wheel 24"by 5", chain wheel 51", 12 chills, crankshaft bkt steerage 15½" by 4½", bkt for hand wheel, pump, steerage wheel, steerage sweep, etc., axle carriage, fifth wheel, sq. axle box, round do., funnel bottom, governor pulley, exhaust pipe bend, plate 56½" x 37½" for tank, nave 16 spokes for large travelling wheel.

The decision not to continue as Aveling licensees may, however, have come entirely from the Garrett side as at the time of the cessation of the work under licence the firm had just launched a new design of self-moving engine of their own devising which must have been in gestation at least since Summer 1866, and which reverted to the notion of the self-moving portable. This enabled components of the current design of 8NHP portable to be used to some extent. No drawings of these engines survive, and our ideas of what they must have looked like have to depend on an illustration and description of one of them which appeared in *The Engineer* of July 16, 1869. One assumes that the initial pair (Nos.2017 and 2040, sold in September and December 24, 1867, respectively) would have been similar in their main particulars. No.2017, the first to be sold, though not necessarily the first built, as Works numbers were generally allocated at the date of delivery, had Aveling type steering, either because of a specific request from the customer or because of a thrifty desire to use up the parts. No.2017 was special in a second respect in that it is noted as having two road speeds, though how this was accomplished was never recorded. The introduction of a further intermediate shaft seems inevitable, but where or how it was arranged is difficult to envisage. However, No.2040 had the new Garrett design of steering. This was still worked from the front and employed a vertical steering wheel by which a vertical shaft was actuated through a worm and worm wheel. At the foot of the vertical shaft was a chain sprocket. A length of pitch chain was arranged round it, and from either end of the pitch chain steering rods ran to the front axle. No tensioning arrangements were shown, and one supposes that if the wear in the chain and the various bearings became sufficient eventually the chain would have simply dropped off the sprocket. It would have been fairly simple, however, to have made provision for tightening the chain when necessary by means of long threads and back nuts where the chain couplers passed through the front axle, and no doubt this was done, even though the engraving does not make it clear. Despite the fact that the whole arrangement looks vulnerable, in reality it must have been durable as engines of this type had long lives. For instance, No.4032, delivered to William O'Neill of Athy, Ireland, on July 24, 1871, for a client named Smith, had a new firebox, smokebox, chimney base, and crankshaft in August and September, 1898, and lesser parts were being supplied as late as 1907.

The general appearance of the type is apparent from the engraving from *The Engineering Times* (Fig.12) which shows the small manstand with a tank beneath and tool box behind. Possibly a separate tender was meant to be drawn to carry more coal and water but I have found no mention of it. Link motion reversing gear was fitted and the throttle lever and back plate was of the same pattern as that shown on the Boydell Garrett of eleven years before. The cylinders were placed over the firebox and the crankshaft was carried in brackets bolted to the boiler barrel. From a sprocket on the near-side end of the crankshaft, between the flywheel and the bracket, a pitch chain drove a larger sprocket on a countershaft carried in brackets upon the boiler front. This carried at each end a pinion which could be clutched into or out of mesh with an annular gear bolted to the rim of the adjacent wheel. This arrangement must have been subjected to rapid abrasion by mud and slush from the road or ground over which the engine passed and at risk from pebbles or stones carried up with the mud.

No brakes are visible in the engraving. The wheels were of malleable iron with wrought iron spokes. The boiler was fed by an eccentric driven pump, and there was a single, unprotected gauge glass with a pair of trial cocks as standby. So far as one can see from the engraving there was no bottom cock for blowing down the glass. There was a spring loaded safety valve and a second valve loaded by spring balance near the manstand. A Bourdon type pressure gauge was fitted.

Between September, 1867, and July, 1869, seven of these 8NHP engines were built, numbered 2017, 2040, 2058, 2065, 2167, 2199, and 3309, the latter number explained by another sudden leap of a thousand in the Works sequence between June 14 and 15, 1869. Engine No.2302 came out on the first date and No.3303 on the second. No.3309 was noted as 'seventh to this pattern; original No.2040' thereby confirming that 2040 slightly antedated 2017 though sold and numbered, in consequence, after it. The first two engines of the class, Nos.2017 and 2040, were sold, respectively, to Charles Doubleday of Outwell, Wisbech (spelt 'Wisbeach' in the Garrett books) through the agency of J. Davey of Lynn Road, Wisbech, and William Jewell of Court Lodge, Orpington, Kent, later of Ivy House, Horton Kirby, possible through the agency of Balls Garrett, a younger brother of Richard Garrett III of Leiston, who had set up business in Maidstone. Jewell had a threshing machine to go with his engine, but both were returned in September, 1869, though what became of them is not recorded. No.2065, a later member of the series, dating from August 27, 1868, was bought new by Nathaniel Dring of Over, Wisbech, but returned on January 18 the following year in exchange for an 8NHP portable.

In the Winter of 1867/68 a 10NHP version was introduced. The surviving *Rough Entry Book of New Patterns*, which runs from February 3, 1868, to September, 1881, contains an entry of new patterns for parts of the 10NHP in February, 1868, though these are only for the 'reversing gear bracket and slide rod'. The corresponding patterns for the 8NHP design were renewed in May, 1868, and again in January, 1869. By 1870 five of the 10NHP engines had been built, followed by another in 1872, and a further six in 1874/75. Of these No.7060 and subsequent engines were modified in that cross slabs in the form of strakes were cast onto the driving wheels, whilst the front wheels were cast off the patterns used for the fronts of the Aveling type engines. The steering was transferred to the tender, still with a vertical shaft but with worm and rack on the steering axle and a 6'10" long horizontal shaft thence to the upright steering shaft. This arrangement was used also in 8NHP No.7536 (September 25, 1874). In another 10NHP built in April, 1875, the annular gear was cast in one piece and turned to fit the rim of the wheel. This engine was in stock for some while, finally receiving the number 8924 when it was sold at the end of the year. Another 1875 modification was to No.7940 which was fitted with an exhaust steam feedwater heater. The performance of the chain drive was improved in 1869 by fitting a mortice bracket to the boiler barrel to enable the chain to be tightened after wear, the material of the links being changed at the same time to steel. The first so equipped were No.3358, an 8NHP, and 3386, a 10NHP. Nevertheless the use of all gear drives was gaining ground by the early seventies, marking down those manufacturers who continued with chain drives as having failed to move with the times. Notwithstanding these changes and improvements, by 1875 the day of the self-mover was running out, at least as far as British manufacturers were concerned. Home clients were looking for a more developed form of traction engine though the chain propelled self-mover continued to be in demand on the Continent until the 1920's or later.

On the whole this group of Garrett self-movers was sold to home buyers, six of them through the agency of Balls Garrett in Maidstone. It is rumoured, however, that No.7428, bought by Brassey, the railway contractor, through Balls Garrett, was used by him abroad. Engines known to have gone abroad were No.2167 (8NHP) which went to O. Kohan of Odessa, Russia, and No.4068 (8NHP) for General von Sederholm, The Fortress, Kertch, South Russia. This latter went with winding gear and other sundries suggestive of use by artillery units. A third 8NHP which may have gone abroad was No.4160 sold to Ernst Reuss & Co. of London and Manchester acting on behalf of a client named Obach. Garretts supplied a creosoting apparatus 'with carriages etc.' to go with it. The entries against No.7536 at one time led me to suppose it had been exported, though the name and address on the invoice - Charles Cass of Presdale near Ware, Herts - does not suggest an exporter but again, since colonial customers, such as Clerk, spent some time in the home country selecting their purchases, that could have been the case here.

The Garretts reacted to the obsolescence of the chain drive engines by producing a new design of 8NHP two speed engine but still with traces of the old self-movers. The cylinder, 9" bore by 12" stroke, was sited on the boiler barrel and the crankshaft was carried in cast iron brackets on the firebox, the use of the brackets removing any suggestion of infringement of Aveling's hornplate patent of 1870. A much higher boiler pressure of 150 p.s.i. was used and, as the boiler provided almost 200 square feet of heating surface, this must have enhanced performance a great deal. By an odd reversion to self-mover practice, however, the driving wheels were carried not on an axle but on gudgeons fixed in castings bolted to the sides of the firebox, as in a portable. In their catalogue the makers described the gear drive arrangements in the following terms:

> It is provided with an ingenious arrangement for **two speeds**. The motion being transmitted to the **rims** of the travelling wheels by means of spur-gearing direct from the crank-shaft, by which arrangement a great saving in friction and wear and tear is secured.
>
> For rounding corners an arrangement is provided for throwing the travelling wheels out of gear by means of a simple striking lever on either side, and without recourse to the most objectionable "Jack in the box" differential gearing, which has been proved so productive of unnecessary friction and consequent breakages.

The use of the phrase 'direct from the crankshaft' is meant to convey only that the engine had an all-gear drive, without the interposition of a pitch chain. It was laid out on the four-shaft arrangement. The first such engine was No.9380 supplied on August 11, 1876, to Mr. G. Goodyear of Markyate Street near Dunstable, who paid £425.5.0. for it. It never strayed far from the area, and new gear parts were supplied for it in August, 1900, to George Brown of Dunstable. Another 8NHP that had a longish life was No.9740, the fifth geared engine to be made, and bought on December 22, 1876, by B.H. Sturgeon of Norton, Bury St. Edmunds. Though Sturgeon had it for only three years the engine continued under subsequent owners for many years more, and new gear parts were supplied for it in 1901.

When the designing of this new type of engine was begun cannot be dated with certainty. The first batch of patterns for it is recorded as arriving in the pattern store on May 10, 1876, so that the preparation of the drawings probably ante-dated that by at least six months, placing the commencing date at not later than some time in December, 1875. For its time it was not progressive and lagged behind the products of, for instance, Charles Burrell & Sons Ltd. at Thetford, who had already tried and discarded a similar design after building four examples. It is a great pity that no drawings have survived from that period, and one is forced to rely a good deal upon such detail as can be gleaned from a virtually valueless engraving used as an illustration in the firm's catalogue. This is reproduced in Fig.13. It will be seen that it is practically impossible to deduce anything useful from it concerning the gearing save that the final drive was to a shrouded ring of gear bolted to brackets forming part of the wheel rim casting, a method that added to the complication of the wheel casting though admittedly saving weight. An important point is that the whole arrangement was repeated on the nearside of the engine. The front wheels also are shown as castings, the spokes to both front and rear wheels being of wrought iron.

It is suggested that the two speed gearing was arranged between the crankshaft and first intermediate shaft and that the arrangements, probably of gears on keys, for putting the rear wheels into and out of drive were on either end of the second intermediate shaft. That the gears were varied as experience of use occurred is made clear by notes in the memorandum book. Thus against No.9728 (the fourth made) it says:

> Large pinion on crankshaft 19 teeth, old pattern. Double speed intermediate wheel 24 and 32 teeth, old pattern. Single intermediate 24 teeth.

By contrast, in referring to the sixth engine, No.9800, the entry reads:

> Large pinion on crkshft 19 teeth with small 11 teeth and large intermediate wheel 32 teeth, small 24 teeth. Main driving pinion(s) for travelling wheels 12 teeth. Travelling wheels 13 inches on sole.

The seventh engine in the series, No.9804, was noted as having the crankshaft saddle 'as first pattern'. By inference the next made, No.9884, would have had an extended saddle, though it is not noted to have been thus equipped, as the entry against the ninth engine, No.9916, confirms it by saying 'second engine with saddle projecting 4½" on flywheel side more than first pattern to suit Barford & Perkins plough tackle'. The use of Barford & Perkins' tackle is treated in Chapter 5 and therefore will not be referred to further here.

When No.10072 came to be built it was again noted as having the wider saddle. It was updated in that the ' countershaft in front of firebox' (i.e. the third shaft) was of Bessemer steel, the travelling wheels were 18 inches wide, and that it had a 'circular end tank' and guards over the gears. It was said of it that it was:

> First engine with driving gear to travel faster. Quick speed pinion on crankshaft, smaller intermediate wheel on [*or possibly 'over' as the handwriting is difficult to read*] double pinion and at the other end of countershaft.

With No.10512 this information was supplemented somewhat when it was recorded that the 'quick speed' on the crankshaft had 22 teeth and the slow 12 teeth; that the 'double speed wheel' on the first countershaft had 32 and 22 teeth on its respective sides; and that the pinion on the flywheel end of the countershaft had 22 teeth. On No.14040 (the last) the countershaft was 4 inches in diameter and the engine had 'plummer blocks fixed on tender for countershaft', supposedly instead of on the firebox front.

On the first ten out of the total of twelve built, the front axle was set back beneath the boiler barrel and steered from the footplate by chain and bobbin, with the steersman on the offside. In the last two engines, Nos.10512 and 14040, it was placed under the smokebox. The persistence in the use of malleable iron wheel rims was flying in the face of the best contemporary practice, and was slated by no less a critic than the correspondent of *The Engineer* when he found that Garretts' exhibit at the 1879 Royal Show at Kilburn was so equipped. By contrast, in some other respects the engines were very advanced. From somewhat tentative beginnings the Leiston boiler shop had made great strides, and by the mid 1870's was a thoroughly up-to-date establishment using machine flanging throughout and making boilers entirely of steel, with all seams rivetted and no joints fire welded, a point which earned praise from *The Engineer* when it observed that the boiler of the Garrett engine at Liverpool Royal in 1877 was probably the first traction engine boiler made from end to end without a weld. It was, moreover, the first to be equipped with the famous Garrett sine curved firebox crown, dispensing thereby with crown stays. Although often referred to as 'the Garrett patent firebox' it was, in fact, never patented, for the reason that any attempt to do so could have been overturned on the grounds of prior application. Garretts themselves had earlier made use of the Horton & Kendrick firebox in which deep ribs were formed in the heating surfaces acting, in some ways, as thermic syphons. The Horton & Kendrick firebox was discarded because of the way in which it multiplied rivetted seams and got in the way of tube expanding. The mechanisation of the Garrett boiler shop had enabled both objections to be overcome. The sine curve shape of the crown was shallower than the ribs of the Horton & Kendrick firebox, and was pressed in without extra seams. Various forms of stayless crown were experimented with by the Garrett drawing office and boiler shop, encouraged by Frank Garrett who had taken the initiative in the matter and, doubtless, took a leading part in the technical discussions. Though not a practical man with a 'hands-on' attitude to the same degree as his eldest brother, Richard IV, or his father (the third Leiston Richard), he had, nevertheless, a thorough grasp of engine building as after leaving Rugby School he had studied engineering in Stuttgart. Richard III (1807-1866) had four sons, Richard IV (b.1829), John (b.1831), Henry (b.1841) and Frank (b.1845). John, for reasons explained in detail in *Garrett 200*, had withdrawn from the firm in 1860, Henry, a somewhat dissolute character, was expelled from it in 1878, leaving Richard IV and Frank as the surviving partners who were in control at the time of the introduction of the corrugated firebox. Richard IV himself died in 1884 leaving Frank as sole principal.

How design was managed in the 1860's and 70's, or where the drawing office, if it existed separately from the general office, was located is not known with certainty. Richard III certainly took part in the design of both portable engines and threshing machines though it is likely his impetuous temperament and the pressure upon his time would have meant that most of the actual drawing board work was delegated to others. Though research has disclosed much concerning the personnel of the drawing office in this century much less is known about those who peopled it in the last century. By the end of it the chief draughtsman was Emerich Schmach, an engineer from Austria-Hungary. He joined the firm in 1884, probably introduced by Charles Remy. Remy, who was German, entered Garrett employment as a 'foreign correspondent' in 1882, became the friend and confidant of Frank Garrett, rose to having oversight of the firm's Continental sales organisation and in 1907 was given a seat on the board of directors of the limited company that had been formed in 1897. Though Remy had no direct influence upon design except by relaying the requirements of clients to the Works, Schmach, even though he may not have been chief draughtsman from the very beginning of his Leiston career, undoubtedly had considerable effect. Before him there had been at least three Continental engineers on the design staff. The earliest of these was a German named Eugene Keppler, who was appointed in March, 1872, and stayed until 1880, to be followed by a twenty-seven year old Dane, Thomas Sodring, who hanged himself the following April. His successor, another Dane, was Ernest Boutard from Copenhagen who gave place to Schmach in 1884. Boutard was the inventor of a single eccentric reversing gear used on some Garrett portables.

Less than sixty traction engines of all types were built and sold by the firm in the quarter of a century up to the end of 1881 and, indeed, No.14040, the engine sold in 1882, had been in stock for three years when it left the Works. The already sluggish sales situation had been made worse by the onset in the late seventies of the agricultural depression that was to last for some twenty years. Free trade policies allowed foreign grain to enter the country without hindrance so that as railways opened up the potential wheatlands of the American Middle West and, a little later, Australia, grain from these fresh sources undercut home produce in price, a situation made worse by a series of very poor summers and bad harvests. All the English traction engine builders suffered a set-back in sales from this cause. The sales record of Garrett traction engines was already poor, and the partners, Richard and Frank, decided voluntarily to abdicate whatever niche they held in the home market and to concentrate instead upon export sales of portable engines and machines.

Only one more traction engine was built at Leiston before 1890 and this was an 8NHP chain engine subcontracted to the Works by Thomas Cooper of Great Ryburgh, Norfolk, later to be the builder of the Cooper diggers and a fair number of portable engines. Allocated the Leiston Works No.17073, it was built in 1887, and was finished in time to be exhibited at the Royal Show of that year, held at Newcastle-upon-Tyne. The boiler was conventional though little else was. As to the engine, it was a compound, when such were a rarity. Link motion reversing gear was rejected in favour of shifting eccentric gear giving no facility for expansive working. The speed when working on the belt was 170 r.p.m. which contrasted with the 270 r.p.m. required to maintain the advertised single road speed of 4 m.p.h. The engine was connected to the driven axle by Cooper's own design of chain, fabricated from stamping of ¹/₁₆" thick saw-blade steel with ⁷/₁₆" diameter pins at 1¾" centres. Twenty-six stampings went into each link. A differential was fitted, by no means a common facility at that date. The small rear manstand provided limited space for a coal bunker but water was carried in a belly tank. The engine was steered from the manstand by a long, nearly horizontal shaft, probably working via a worm and sector. The low steering position gave a very poor field of vision for the steersman.

The engine was submitted to a practical test at the Newcastle Royal, and the published results of the trial contain an abstract of the salient dimensions which are given in the table below, together with the assessors' verdict on the coal consumption per brake horse power hour.

NHP	8
Cylinders	6" and 9" by 11"
Flywheel	4' 0" by 6½"
Pressure	125 p.s.i.
Tubes: Number	22
Diameter	2½"
Heating Surface: Firebox	23.0 sq.ft.
Tubes	98.3 sq.ft.
Smokebox	3.6 sq.ft
Grate area	3.67 sq.ft.
Coal burned per b.h.p. per hour	3.746 lb.

The Foden compound traction engine that took part in the same series of tests gave a consumption result of only 1.977 lb. of coal per brake horse power hour. Notwithstanding this reverse Cooper did manage to sell further engines, though he did not turn to Leiston Works to build them. Nevertheless he remained on amicable terms with the Leiston partners who later supplied him with boilers for some of his diggers.

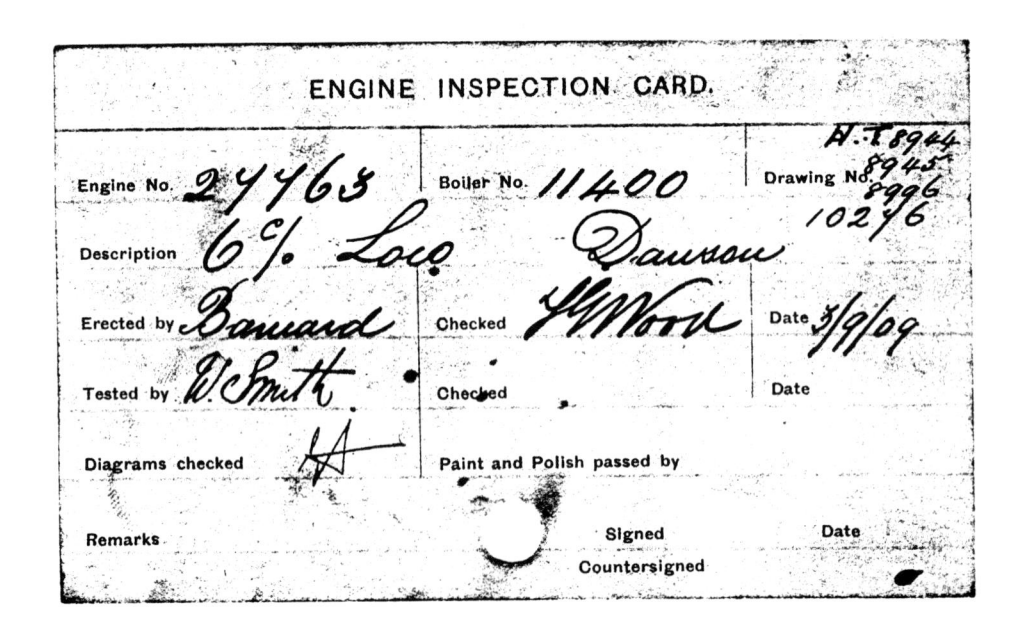

Fig.13. *This view of the 1876 design of 8NHP geared traction engine, is not, perhaps, to be taken as authentic in all respects. The piston rod, for instance, looks to be off-centre of the cylinder and, so far as can be seen, the valve gear seems unworkable. Mounting the ring of gear of the final drive upon the brackets cast integrally with the rims of the rear wheels may have saved weight but at the cost of greater complication in the casting.*

Fig.14. *No.17073 (1887), the 8NHP Cooper engine, the last chain drive traction made at Leiston. Cooper's design of chain was an improvement upon the earlier pitch chains but lost out to roller chains.*

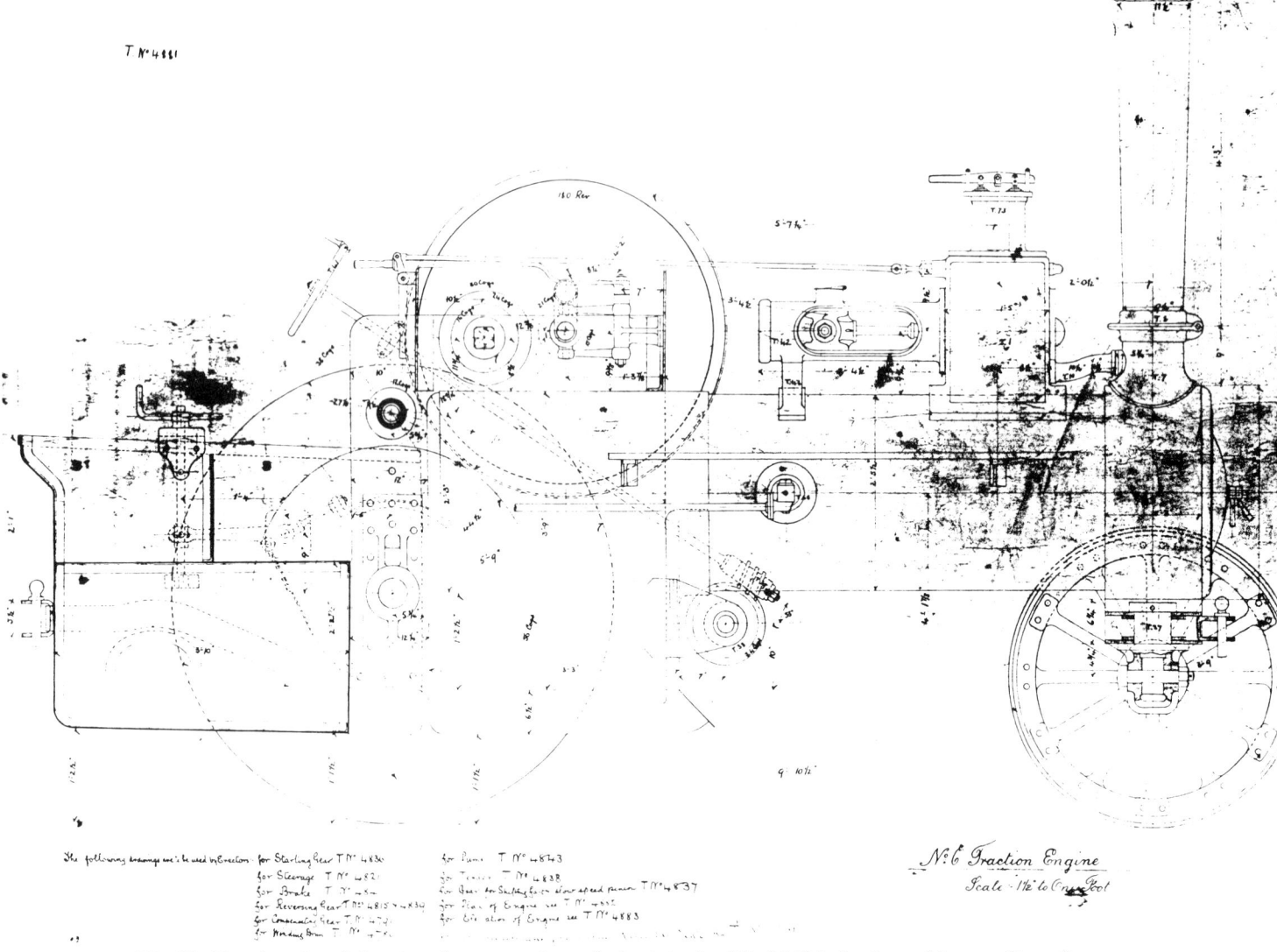

Fig.15. The elevational drawing, from a much marked original, of No.20485, the first of the new line of Garrett traction engines, representing an entirely fresh start.

Fig.16. No.20485 as turned out in Royal Show finish for A. Henninger, the company's agent in Darmstadt, Germany. The picture was taken not later than May, 1896. This engine was fitted with the Garrett Schmach differential lock.

Fig.17. (right) and Fig.18 (centre). The elevation and plan respectively of the Garrett shifting eccentric valve gear applied to No.20485. This was drawn by John Butler from a Works drawing too soiled for direct reproduction. The weakness of the gear was said to lie in the rapid wear of the fulcrum pin and the consequent loosening of the lever arms upon it.

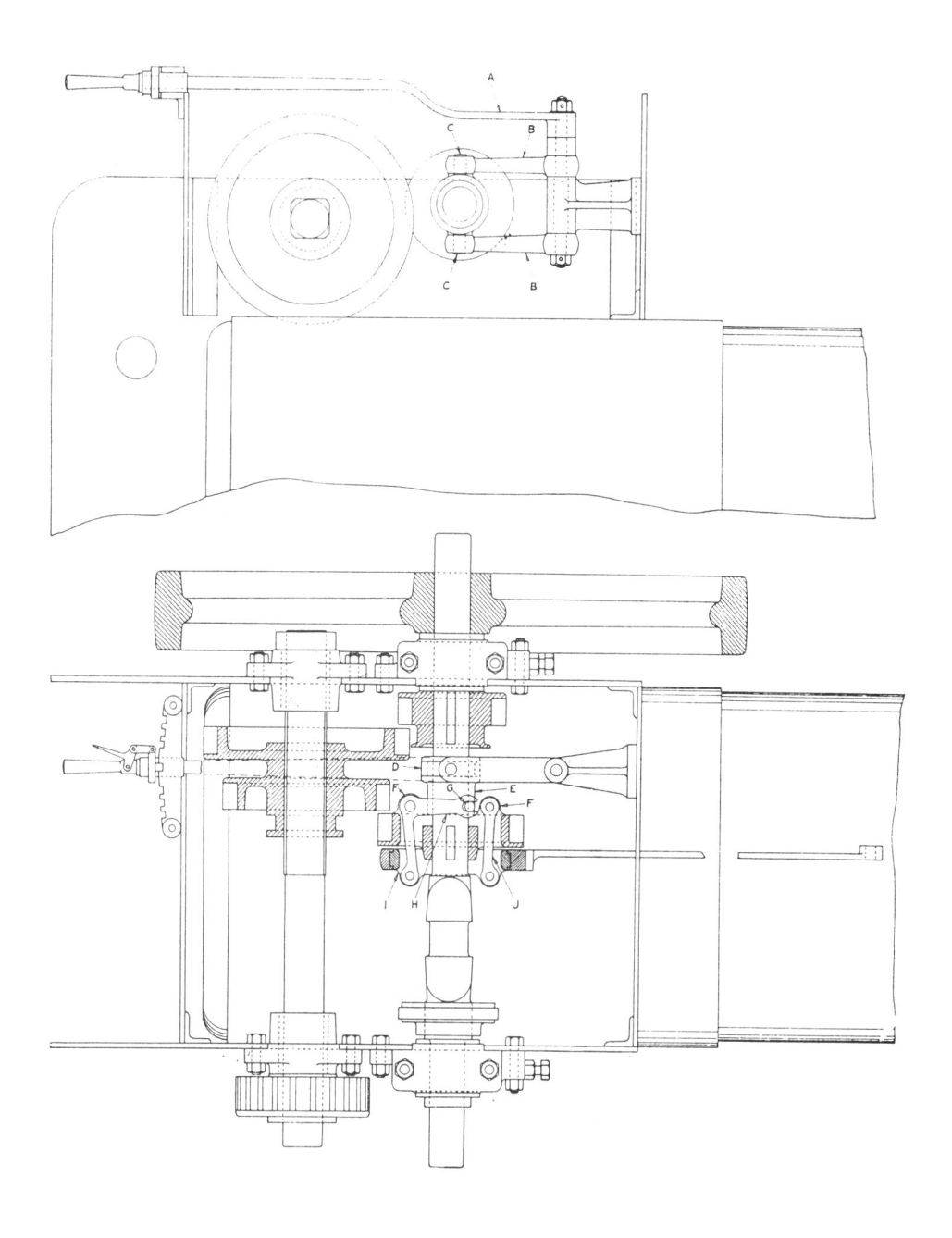

Fig.19. The 6NHP single No.23021, completed July 31, 1900, as the Works crane engine, standing in Waterloo Avenue, Leiston, near the White Horse Hotel.

Fig.20. 6NHP single No.23992 (Nov. 13, 1902) in its latter days when owned by Taylor Bros. of Bildeston, Suffolk. Note the long stalk by the chimney, which carried a driving mirror when the engine was on the road.

[R.G.Pratt]

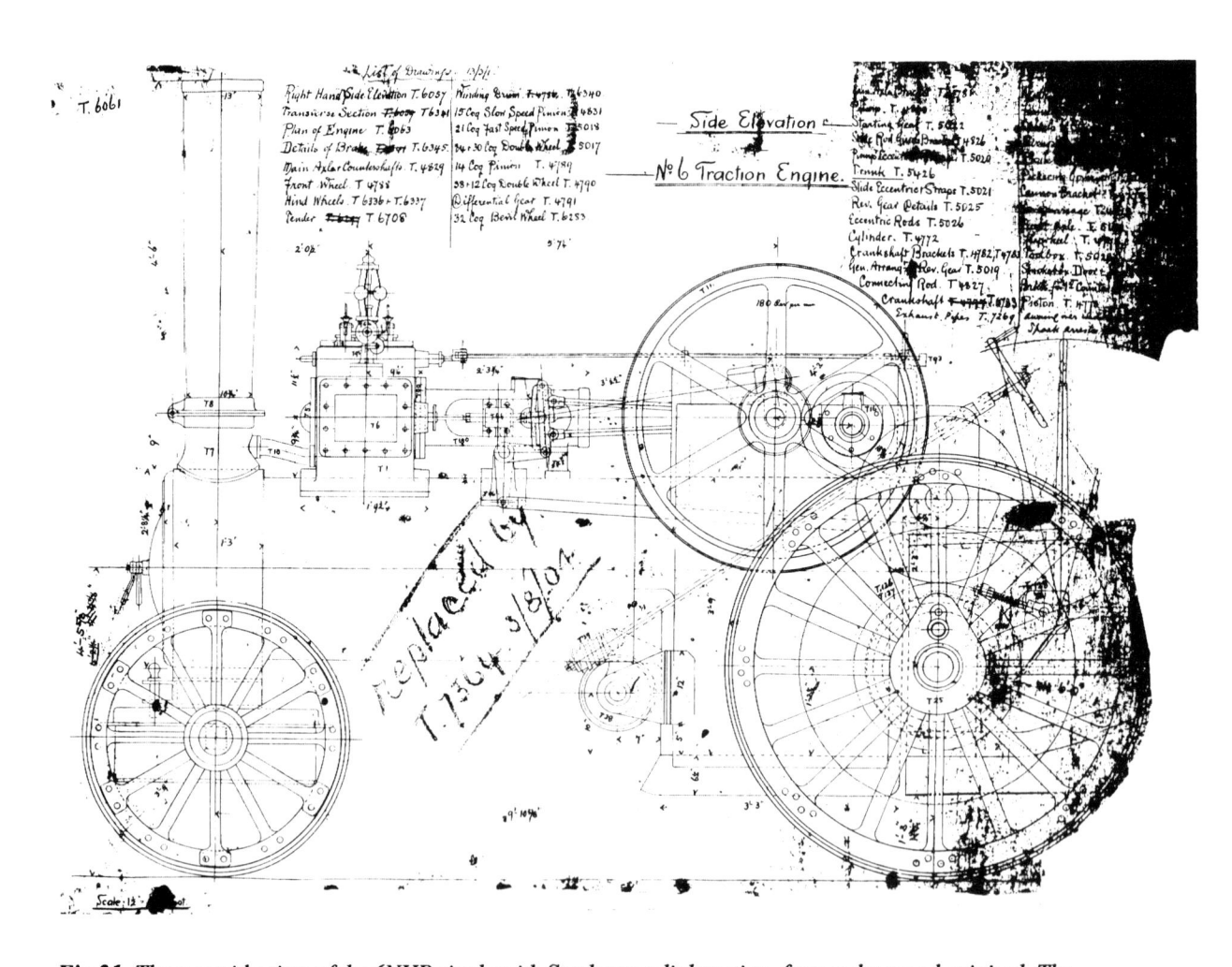

Fig.21. The nearside view of the 6NHP single with Stephenson link motion, from a damaged original. The alterations to the figured dimensions illustrate some of the sundry amendments that led to the elevation being redrawn in 1904. One of the larger changes on that revision was the positioning of the manhole on the nearside a little to the rear of the motion bracket.

Chapter 3

Traction Engines Recommenced

The death of Richard Garrett IV in 1884 had a profound effect upon his younger brother and partner, Frank (1845-1918). The two had been very close, as in many ways Richard had acted as a father figure to Frank, standing in place of their often absent parent who had, in any event, died whilst Frank was a young man of twenty-one. The two were not at all alike. Richard had been denied much formal schooling and his by no means negligible level of culture had been reached by his own efforts, not least by extensive reading. Richard had been born in the Works House, so the Works had formed the background of his childhood, and from the age of fourteen he had been actively engaged in its working. Handy with his fists, muscular in his physique, and powerful as to his voice he had held his workmen in thrall to his personality. He represented the kind of figure that many of them, had they come to enjoy his level of worldly riches, might have aspired to be. Frank, by contrast, was of a quieter and more reserved character. Whereas Richard would have shouted and cursed at a miscreant, and then allowed the incident to be forgotten an hour later, Frank rarely lost his temper but would cut down an opponent to size with quiet and bitter sarcasm that often rankled. This made him respected but not loved. His education, too, was very different from that of Richard, for by the time of his schooldays his father had become a very wealthy man, able to send him to Rugby for a public school education. Despite the contrast in their personal characteristics the two brothers were deeply attached to each other and made a very good pair in their business association. Together they had weathered the rift with their brother John which had resulted in his departure to Magdeburg, from which base he conducted a venomous campaign against them, a depravity compounded, at least in Richard's eyes, by his having taken into partnership James Smith, the suitor who had supplanted Richard in the affections of his Cousin Louisa. Together they had seen the ignominious departure of a second brother, Henry, as a result of personal conduct which each of them had regarded as infamous. In consequence Frank was deeply affected by his brother's death, becoming more sombre and aloof, and less susceptible to fresh ideas.

For the six years that the affairs of the firm remained in his hands alone after the death of Richard things jogged along pretty much unchanged, focused mainly upon the overseas trade in portables, threshers, and agricultural machines. During this time technical progress was not neglected though confined, in the main, to existing fields of manufacture, but there seemed no desire to explore new types or classes of machine. In any case he had little faith in the home market as the basis of a business, having witnessed the outset and progress of the twenty year agricultural depression from the second half of the seventies onward. As might have been expected his frame of mind resulted in the firm entering a phase of corporate hardening of the arteries - culminating in the onset of decline. This state of affairs, however, was arrested by the fact that he had four sons, all intent upon entering into the family firm. The eldest son, Frank Junior (1869 - 1952), after being educated at Rugby, was sent for four years to study engineering at the works of Dehne, the German agricultural implement manufacturers at Halberstadt. On his return in 1890, nominally as Works Manager, he found that the number of men on the pay-roll had declined from something in excess of 600 to an average of only 445 for the year 1890. Over the next four years this level increased to 588 but then began to decline again. Soon after his return Frank (Junior) had concluded that permanent betterment could be achieved only by expanding the range of staple manufactures, although his persuasion unaided was insufficient to bring about wide changes. Only after his younger brothers, Alfred and Stephen, had come into the company did a marked change of emphasis occur.

The first visible result of the campaign for expansion came with the launching of a new 6NHP single cylinder traction engine in 1894-95. Leiston Works had no continuous tradition of traction engine building. As was shown in the previous chapter the making of traction engines had petered out fifteen years earlier with a design that was well out-dated by the time it was abandoned. Emerich Schmach, the head of the drawing office though a very competent engineer, was not a traction engine man, and it seems likely that Thomas A. Jones, who was responsible for many of the subsequent drawings of traction engines in this century, was recruited for the task of designing the new project. Since William Fletcher had inaugurated traction engine building at Wallis & Steevens, few designers had had such an unrestricted chance to produce a new design unfettered by vested interests in the Works or opinions of superiors. On the whole, the result produced by Schmach and Jones was not a pace-setter, not rising much above the commonplace.

On February 8, 1895, an order was secured from A. Henninger of Darmstadt, Germany, one of Remy's established customers, for a 6NHP traction engine. Whether the design was produced entirely from that date onwards or whether design work was in hand and was merely given impetus by the order is a 'chicken and egg' question to which I do not have an answer. Certainly, however, Victor Garrett was of the opinion that the drive that launched the project came from Frank (Junior) with the backing of his brother Alfred. The beginning of the project cannot be dated with certainty but the general arrangement elevation drawing No.4881 is dated April 5, 1895. The engine was completed and despatched to Henninger on September 4, 1895, as No.20485, in what the books called 'local show finish', i.e. superior to the ordinary production run but not equal to 'Royal Show' which was the bane of apprentice boys' lives, involving as it did a mirror finish to many steel components, even to the extent of burnishing the fairlead rollers. The recorded details were as follows:- cylinder 8" x 12" stroke; crankshaft 3" diameter; main axle 4½" diameter; flywheel 4' 2" x 6½"; speed 180 r.p.m; rear wheels 5' 9" x 16"; front wheels 3' 9" x 8"; road speeds 1¾ and 3½ m.p.h; total heating surface 119.5 sq.ft; grate area 4.75 sq.ft; working pressure 120 p.s.i.

In its general configuration No.20485 conformed to the four shaft traction engine convention of the period but had Continental type spring balance safety valves and the firm's own design of shifting eccentric reversing gear instead of Stephenson link motion. An essentially similar gear was used on engines built by Mann & Charlesworth of Leeds. This was not the result of coincidence but of collaboration. Sydney Charlesworth had been deputy to John Sherwood, the Works Manager at Leiston, in the period 1885-1888, leaving to join James Mann in the Leeds partnership but returning as full Works Manager from 1899 to 1901. The use of this valve gear seems to have been experimental for in all subsequent traction engines straightforward Stephenson link motion was fitted. One must assume from this that the single eccentric gear was deemed to lack practical advantages or customer appeal. A feature perhaps worthy of mention is that a Holden & Brooke No.3 injector was fitted.

The second engine of the series, No.20548, must have followed closely on the progress of the first through the shops. Built as a speculation it passed from the Works to the stockyard on December 1, 1895, though it was not sold until August 28, 1896. This was fitted with a rear wheel brake, applied by a hand-wheel and vertical shaft on the left (driver's) side. The abandonment of the shifting eccentric valve gear in favour of Stephenson's link motion necessitated minor dimensional revisions to the crankshaft but otherwise the first and second engines were the same. Also noted were a water lifter, injector, and winding drum. Unlike No.20485 it stayed close to home all its life. Its first owner was Samuel Bull of Wood Farm, Hitcham, near Ipswich, followed by Joshua Coe of Bulmer, Essex, and later still B.W. Death of Lavenham, Suffolk. It was last licensed in 1947, thus achieving a life of 52 years, not a discreditable span for a pioneer.

A third example, No.20800, was taken into stock on December 1, 1896, in time to be sent to the 1896 Smithfield Show. This engine did have Royal Show finish and duly appeared at three important shows during 1897 - the Bath & West, the Suffolk, and the Royal, though the level of interest by the trade press and the public was very low. On August 8, 1897, it finally left the Works for Brook Farm, Romsey, Hants, having been bought by George E. Coleberd. During its life it wandered to Somerset, Gloucestershire, and finally to County Durham where it was last licensed in 1939. It had a winding drum and 50 yards of wire rope, a water lifter with the 25 feet of 1¼" suction hose allowed by the AEA price fixing convention and, again, a Holden & Brooke No.3 injector. However, when the engine returned from the Royal Show the axle was replaced by a new axle $4^{7}/_{8}$" in diameter and all succeeding examples were so fitted.

In No.21315, the 1897 Smithfield Show exhibit, the boiler pressure went up to 125 p.s.i. On this engine a Gresham & Craven injector replaced the Holden & Brooke used on the earlier examples. By the time No.23021 was shown at the 1900 Smithfield Show the boiler pressure had been increased further to 130 p.s.i., perversely stated as 9 atmospheres. It remained at this figure for some years.

The first three of the 6NHP tractions were erected by the gang of Billy Vale, one of the leading figures in the erecting shop whose brother George was foreman of the pattern shop. My late friend Jack Simpson, who, as a lad, knew both of them, described them as men of impeccable standards in both their working and their private lives. As he put it, anyone encountering William on his Sunday afternoon walk, clad in a dark blue suit, stiff collar, neck-tie, hard felt hat, and highly polished black boots, and carrying a cane, might have believed himself to have met the local bank manager. From No.21126 onward the erecting of the traction engines was taken over by Walter Rogers, a younger man who, in due course, earned himself the same measure of respect and regard as Billy Vale enjoyed. To him were entrusted such tasks as the erecting of the early overtype wagons, the first electric wagon, and the making of the working models of wagon rear axles now in the Long Shop Museum. A year or two later H. Peskett became involved, first with steam rollers, then with the traction engines. He was an incorrigible practical joker, a trait which palls quickly on one's companions. Then, or soon afterwards, Tom Barnard, who had been in the erecting shop since the 1860s also began to play a part.

Only twelve Garrett 6NHP traction engines were built and sold in the years 1895-1900 inclusive, and half of these were for export. One of those that did remain in this country was used by the Works as its crane engine. This was No.23021, delivered into the stockyard on December 1, 1900, an engine with a faintly curious history. No intending purchaser was mentioned and the fact that its working pressure was stated as 9 atmospheres instead of 130 p.s.i. suggests the Continental market may have been in mind, a conjecture given weight by the fact that it had a large manhole in the nearside of the boiler - a feature stipulated by Henninger on engines supplied to him, commencing with the second made for him (No.21126 of 1897) which he requested should have a manhole 'as Fowler's pattern'. Soon after completion it was shown at the 1900 Royal Smithfield Show, for which purpose it was fitted with a brass cap to the chimney. No purchaser being forthcoming, an order was issued on February 1, 1901, for its adaptation to a convertible though no subsequent record exists of the roller parts ever having been added. Instead it was equipped with a fixed jib stayed back to the hornplates, as shown in Fig.19, the hoisting unit of which was a winding drum between the chimney and the jib, taking its power from a horizontal shaft on the off-side of the engine, driven by bevel gears from the crankshaft. In this guise it lost the brass topped chimney, doubtless set aside for the next Show engine. Like the earlier 6NHP engines No.23021 had a long life and survived until the end of 1946, latterly in the hands of B.W. Death of Lavenham.

Despite the poor sales as a traction engine during the early years after its appearance the 6NHP did form the basis of a heavy steam roller, not dealt with in this book, and the starting point for a line of vertical drum ploughing engines described in Chapter 5. As Frank Garrett's sons took increasing control of the Works, a shift of emphasis was adopted towards the United Kingdom market. This might be said to have had its first stirrings in 1897, when the firm was reincorporated as a limited company, but burgeoned with the coming of the new century, when a more positive approach to home sales became apparent. E.J.C. Ballam was appointed to establish a system of agents to promote sales and handle spares, following the lines of the organisation built up by Remy for overseas sales, and to create a home sales department at Leiston. At first, in reality, this consisted of Ballam plus a clerk but it grew with time.

Figures taken verbatim from a notebook kept in Ballam's office show that in the period of twenty-one years from 1898 to 1918 the combined efforts of these two sales forces resulted in sales of self-moving vehicles (tractions, rollers, tractors, and wagons) as tabulated below :

YEAR	ENGINES	No. MADE
1898	2 Tractions, 2 Road Rollers	4
1899	1 Traction, 3 Ploughing Engines	4
1900	2 Tractions, 2 Ploughing Engines, 2 Road Rollers	6
1901	5 Tractions, 2 Ploughing Engines, 3 Road Rollers complete, 2 ditto less rolls	12
1902	7 Tractions, 2 Ploughing Engines, 9 Road Rollers, 2 ditto less rolls etc.	20
1903	11 Tractions, 3 Road Locos, 8 Road Rollers, 9 ditto less rolls etc.	31
1904	14 Tractions, 2 Road Locos, 11 Road Rollers, 4 ditto less rolls, 8 Ploughing Engines	39
1905	24 Tractions, 2 Ploughing Engines, 1 Tractor, 23 Road Rollers	50
1906	22 Tractions, 2 Ploughers, 14 Tractors, 27 Road Rollers	65
1907	19 Tractions, 4 Ploughers, 11 Tractors, 29 Road Rollers, 1 Road Loco, 1 Col. Traction	65
1908	21 Tractions, 8 S/B ditto, 18 tractors, 33 Road Rollers, 3 Road Locos, 2 Lorries	85
1909	30 Tractions, 2 Ploughers, 38 Tractors, 30 Road Rollers, 4 Road Locos, 1 Lorry	105

1910	41 Tractions, 2 Ploughers, 14 Tractors, 23 Road Rollers, 6 wagons	86
1911	43 Tractions, 17 Tractors, 17 Wagons, 24 Road Rollers	101
1912	31 Tractions, 18 Tractors, 54 Wagons, 40 Road Rollers	143
1913	29 Tractions, 25 Tractors, 66 Wagons, 18 Road Rollers	138
1914	15 Tractions, 41 Tractors, 72 Wagons, 23 Road Rollers, 1 50-BHP Ploughing Engine	152
1915	3 Tractions, 40 Tractors, 86 Wagons, 3 Road Rollers	132
1916	3 Tractions, 42 Tractors, 80 Wagons, 1 Road Roller	126
1917	5 Tractions, 32 Tractors, 80 Wagons, 2 Road Rollers, 1 E.V.	120
1918	5 Tractions, 104 Tractors, 21 Wagons, 2 'Suffolk Punch'	132

Plans to extend the range to include an 8NHP unsprung single were afoot as early as 1896, suggesting that such an engine may well have been in mind from the recommencement of traction engine building. For instance, the elevations of the engines were dated in February, 1897, but not put to use for another three years. Building of 8NHP engines in fact began with the vertical drum ploughing engines designed and built for Rudolph Sack of Leipzig, as narrated in Chapter 5. Thus the cylinder, trunk, piston, piston rod, crosshead and the relevant covers, slide valve and mountings designed for the 8NHP traction came to be first used on the ploughers. The cylinder pattern U1, made during the construction of the ploughers and used on all subsequent 8NHP singles, had been designed for the 8NHP tractions in 1896/97. Two of the draughtsmen who worked on the 8NHPs were Arthur Girling and Thomas Jones. The third man involved, whose initials were 'W.H.', has so far eluded identification. Arthur Girling was the son of Ishmael Girling, foreman of the threshing machine erecting shop, and had been with the firm from boyhood. Tom Jones had been recruited to the drawing office in the mid-nineties but nothing is known about his career prior to that beyond that he was said to have come from one of the Lincoln firms. In design the eight was a strengthened version of the six, the 8 inch cylinder bore of the latter being increased to 9 inch in the larger engine, and the flywheel diameter going up from 4' 2" to 4' 6" though as a corollary the governor speed fell from 180 to 165 r.p.m. Use was made of drawings and patterns made for the 8NHP ploughers and tractions in a roller convertible to a traction engine supplied as No.23375 to Th. Pilter of Paris which was despatched on April 26, 1901. The first produced as a traction engine, No.23423, was despatched on December 21, 1901, to C.G. Miles of Alburgh, Norfolk. About 1911 it passed to T. Phillips of Swanton Abbot and by the mid-twenties was owned by Tyler Brothers of South Repps. It existed at least until mid-year in 1947 but thereafter was lost sight of. Nevertheless a working life of 46 years was not a bad one for an engine that was first of its type and, from this point of view, the Garrett 8 NHP single must, therefore, be rated as one of the firm's successes. As a commercial venture, however, it was a complete loss. Besides No.23423 only eight other 8NHP singles were sold in the home market. The first of these, No.23641, was completed in June, 1902, as the Show engine of the year but not sold until December 17 when it went to A. Kelly of Writtle, near Chelmsford. Later in life it migrated to Yorkshire, and its last recorded owners were Herbert Steel & Sons of Ardsley near Barnsley. The following year the sequence of events was more or less repeated with No.23785, which, too, was built as a Show engine and taken into stock on June 1, 1902. Among the shows it attended were the successive Suffolk Shows in June, 1902, and June, 1903. Finally it was sold to J. Drake of Winsor, Totton, Hants, with whom and his successors it remained until 1946.

As a consequence of this disappointing level of sales, which probably reflected the fact that the average English threshing contractor found an 8NHP rather larger than he required unless consistently on double work, not the rule at that time, the No.8 was dropped from active production in favour of a new 7NHP single, again mainly from the boards of Arthur Girling and Tom Jones, completed in time for the December, 1903, Royal Smithfield show. In the first example, No.24600, the general principles of the 6NHP were followed, having the same cylinder casting bored out to 8½" with a boiler pressure of 140 p.s.i. Ample heating surfaces and a moderate boiler pressure made it a comfortable engine to handle, even if not as economical with coal and water as it might have been if pressed to 180 p.s.i. The No.7 proved to be a more saleable type of engine, and a hundred or so were sold up to the advent of the AGE combine in 1919. Most were sold in East Anglia or the South and South-West of England with a handful distributed in Scotland and the Welsh Border. Only the occasional example was exported, though of these Muscate, the agent in Danzig, had two (Nos. 24755 and 25608) and Henninger of Darmstadt had three (Nos.28284, 28288, and 28998) plus a further 7NHP of his own special design.

Muscate's first purchase (No.24755) was, in fact, only the second 7NHP single to be built though it had been in stock since December, 1903. Several minor modifications had to be made to it to suit German law and the purchaser's own requirements, such as the substitution of spring balance safety valves, the grooving of the flywheel, and the fitting of a guard to the end of the crankshaft. Thus amended it was sent away from Leiston on April 25, 1904, its first duty being to appear on Muscate's stand at the German Royal Agricultural Show. No.28998, shipped to Henninger on June 3, 1911, was sent in Royal Show finish for exhibition at the German Royal Show of 1911, held that year at Cassel. The last 7NHP single that he bought, No.31378 (sent on April 22, 1913) was fitted with an entirely new design of cylinder block, in which a piston valve replaced the slide valve. This was the only 7NHP so equipped which might make it seem to be a very expensive machine from the constructor's point of view. In practice, of course, this was not entirely so as the 7NHP block was the same as that for the 6NHP but bored out a half-inch more in the diameter. It differed also in that it was equipped with a Graham type spark arrester, the invention of Paul Graham of Stockholm, designed in the first instance to permit the safe burning of brown coal, but subsequently used also on engines intended for straw or wood firing.

The French firm of Th. Pilter of Paris who, by the turn of the century, had branches in Algiers and Tunis in addition to the long-standing office in Bordeaux, was the customer for five 7NHP singles, Nos.27838, 30096, 31508, 31581, and 32146. The first of these, shipped to Algiers on June 15, 1909, differed only in having spring balance safety valves and other fittings to suit French law and in being provided with an awning over the manstand to protect the driver from the North African sun. The subsequent engines for Pilter were all ordered with Schäffer & Budenberg injectors. Nos.30096, 31581, and 32146 were ordered, for a reason now unknown, with the steering chains secured to an angle ring on the top of the spud box instead of direct to the axle as was standard. No.31581(shipped on June 3, 1913) was special in more ways in that it was fitted with an extended smokebox and dynamo stand, a Pickering governor, and guard plates over the motion. One supposes this might have been intended for a French travelling showman but, tantalisingly, no details survive of its working life.

The decade from about 1893 to 1903 saw the controversy between the advocates of the three and four shaft arrangements at its height. The debate, often in the most heated and intemperate terms, raged through the length and breadth of the world of traction engines. It is perhaps worth observing that a threshing engine spent such a high proportion of its time on belt work, where the transmission system was of no consequence, that the loss of power in a four shaft engine or the benefits alleged to accrue by its having the change speed gears 'indoors' or between the hornplates had no great economic impact. In engines consistently used for haulage the case was, perhaps, different. Here Fowlers stood as advocates of the four shaft, and Burrells of the three. As in politics those who took part in the discussions did so with the intention of overwhelming the opposition rather than of conceding conversion themselves. At the conclusion of such exchanges, therefore, most persisted in holding the same convictions as when the arguments began. By contrast Garretts struck no postures in the matter, preferring to offer what they believed the consensus of customers wanted. Thus in the traction engines for the home market they conformed to the four shaft convention although they did design and build three shaft tractions for export. These are described in Chapter 7. When steam tractors were added to the range of products on offer these were all three-shaft.

The success that had been enjoyed in sales of compound portable engines, particularly in the larger sizes, led to the launch of compound versions of the 6, 7, and 8 NHP traction engines. The sales results achieved with compound traction engines were, however, extremely disappointing. Only nineteen of the 6NHP compound traction engines were built up to 1919 of which twelve went abroad. The sales of the No.7 compound were even worse. Five were built, of which only one stayed in Great Britain. When it came to the 8NHP's fifteen were built prior to 1919, all for export. How to evaluate these bare statistics concisely is more challenging. It could be demonstrated by actual dynamometer tests that, size for size, a compound on belt work would give a fuel consumption 20% less than its single cylinder version. However, it cost some 12½% more to buy, took more cleaning and oiling each day and, of course, consumed more lubricants. There were, besides, more wearing parts to be kept in repair. On the other hand the compound had behavioural advantages over the single. It had a quieter exhaust less prone to disturb horses it might meet, and threw fewer sparks, a useful attribute in an engine that spent its working moments amidst inflammable straw. Nevertheless, the threshing trade remained very coy concerning compounds. Many owners took the view that it was difficult enough finding drivers who would look after a single decently, let alone the extra complication of a compound. Probably it would be true to say that while all manufacturers found compounds hard to sell Garretts found it harder than some. They had the disadvantage of coming relatively late to the market and of finding their competitors well established in it. However, for evidence that there was little to fault in their product one may look to the first 6NHP compound (No.24900) as an example. This was built in the Summer of 1904 with laminated springs to both front and rear axles, and finished to Royal Show standards in Midland Railway crimson lake, set off by polished copper pipework, brass boiler bands, and a copper top to the chimney. In addition it was equipped with a 1½ pint Crosby sight feed lubricator. Up to then the lubricator favoured by Garretts had been mainly the Mollerup, liked on the Continent but never popular in Britain. The engine attended the 1904 Devon Show and appears to have caught the interest there of Henry Arden of Heavitree, near Exeter, to whom it was sold on October 31, 1904, and named *SIR ROBERT*. If one is to find a fault with it, it is that the working pressure was only 160 p.s.i. whereas 180 p.s.i. would undoubtedly have been more economical of fuel and water. Arden did not keep it long and in mid-summer 1907, via the agency of Dingle & Son of Stoke Climsland, it passed to J. Tamblyn of Pillaton, and finally, in 1916, to Cornwall County Council with whom it remained until scrapped in 1949. This is hardly the record of an inadequate machine, and the only conclusion one can draw from such a history is that it was a well constructed and useful engine.

The second engine of this type (No.25816 of July 27, 1906) was also sprung but with the additional refinements of a third speed, a belly tank, balanced crankshaft, and motion plates. The customers were Crawley Brothers of Linton, Cambridgeshire, who soon afterwards developed the Crawley Agrimotor, early examples of which were built for them at Leiston (see *Garrett Diesel Tractors*). Later owners were J. Taylor & Sons of Fulbourne, Cambridge; Brown Brothers of the same place; W. Wood of Hambro Hill, Rayleigh, Essex; and finally John Keeling of Crays Hill, Essex. The third example (No.26517 of September 18, 1907) was actually built for stock earlier in 1907, and was again a special in that it had right hand steerage, two pins on the driving wheels, and a spud-rail instead of the usual pan. This, too, was a three speeder, but with a special *low* speed. All in all it smacks somewhat of the engines supplied to Grimaldi and Pilter for direct ploughing, dealt with in Chapter 5. The last No.6 compound built in pre-AGE days was 33068, which survives in preservation. Supplied on June 6, 1918, to the Norfolk Motor Transport Co. Ltd, it was turned out with the accoutrements of a road locomotive though still only basically a traction engine. It was sprung on both axles, was fitted with rim brakes to the rear wheels, had a 105 gallon belly tank, a plated flywheel and motion covers, was provided with a three quarter length awning and 7" nameboards, and had an extended coal rack on the tender. Because it was intended for round timber extraction and haulage it was ordered with a 100 yard long and ⅝"diameter wire rope on the drum, and also with a 35 feet long water lifter hose. It was one of the first Garretts to be fitted with a Manzell double feed oil pump. Although the 1914-18 war was in its critical final stages when it was built it was ordered and delivered with show finish and gold lettering. The actual engine colour was standard green. After some three years with Norfolk Motor Transport it was sold and had a succession of owners until 1942 when it was bought by S.J. Philp & Sons of Castle Hedingham, Essex, by whom it was owned until 1996.

Sales of No.7 compounds in the home market amounted to one engine only, No.27333, which was delivered to A. Kelly of Writtle, scene of the earlier adventures with the first Boydell. He had it less than two years before it came back into the hands of Garretts by whom it was converted to a showman's engine and then sold to Swales Bolesworth, the London showman. Two other 7NHP compound general purpose engines were sold new to showmen and all three of these engines are discussed at length in Chapter 6. If the sales of the No.7 compounds in the home market were scanty those of the 8NHP were worse - none were sold at all!

Four 7NHP compounds were, however, sold through the agency of Grimaldi of Turin, two of which, used for direct ploughing, are discussed in Chapter 5. The other two, Nos.30111 and 30112, were intended for Societa Italiana Ernesto Breda of Milan who probably used them for road haulage as they had motion covers, rear wheels 18" wide on the treads and fronts 9" wide. It was Grimaldi, too, who sold five 8NHP compounds out of the fifteen made. Three of them (Nos.28771, 28772, and 28773) were expressly for direct ploughing but the first, No.27109 (shipped June 6, 1908), was a more or less standard engine whilst the last, No.29035, August 2, 1911, was probably for road haulage, being sprung, fitted with an awning over the manstand, and having not only a wire top to the chimney but also a spark grate in the smokebox. Particular attention was paid to cylinder lubrication in that two brass displacement lubricators were fitted plus an Imperial mechanical oil pump. The trading connection between Grimaldi and Garretts was of very long standing, tracing its origins to an English emigré, named Whitmore, in Milan in the 1860s. Soon the firm became Whitmore & Grimaldi, and so continued until Whitmore's

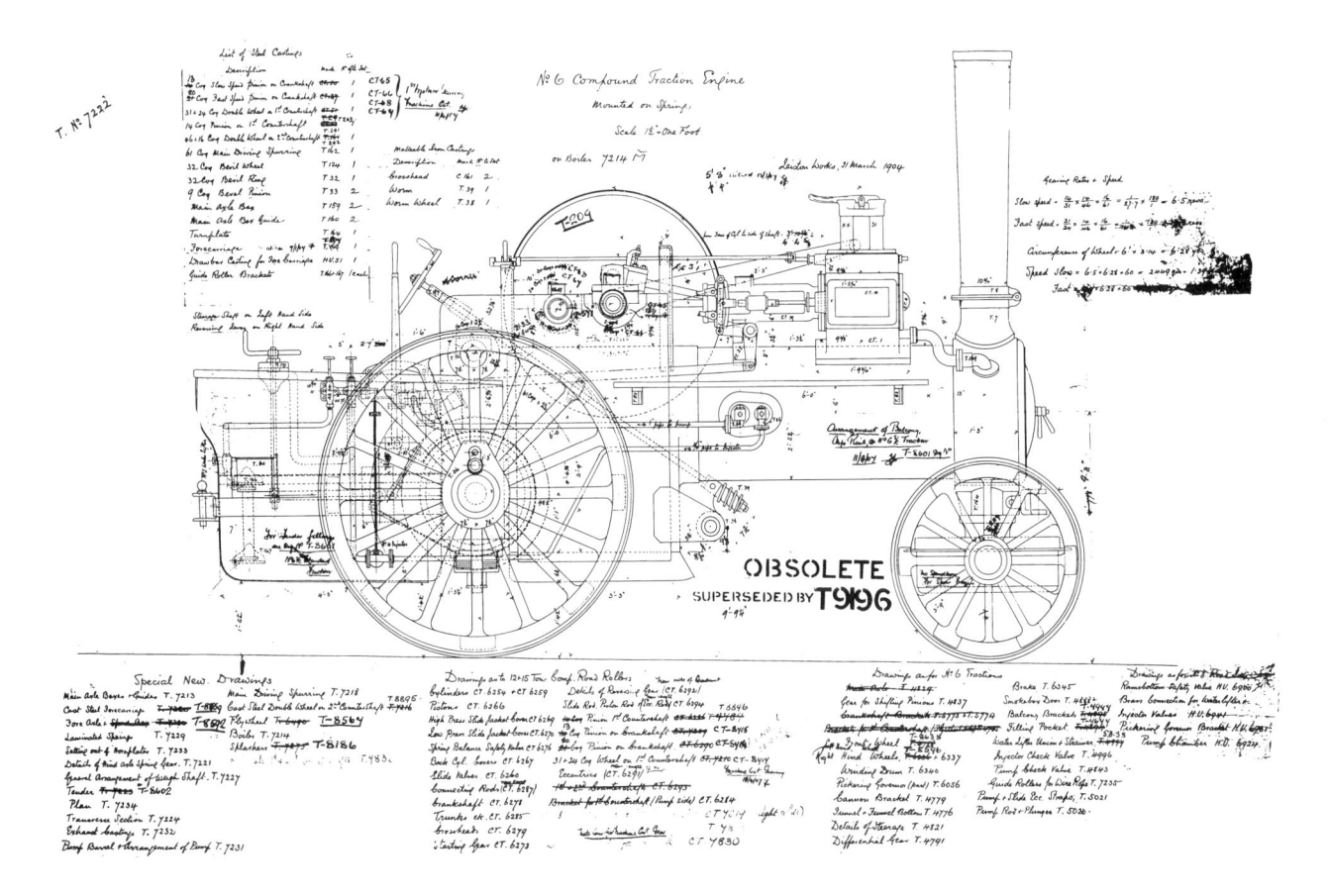

Fig.22. The compound version of the 6NHP traction.

Fig.23. No.25816, the fourth 6NHP compound made, built for Crawley Bros. of Linton, Cambs, was a superior engine in other respects also, being sprung; three speed; fitted with motion plates and a belly tank; and having a balanced crankshaft. Bob Pratt caught it on June 26, 1935, when owned by Brown Bros. of Chesterford, hauling Clayton & Shuttleworth No.34818 through Cambridge, probably on its way to Duce's scrapyard. No25816 itself survived until 1947.

Fig.24. Although designs for an 8NHP single were begun very soon after the launch of the 6NHP none were built until 1901. The third 8NHP made, No.26694, left the Works in 1907 for Wiseman & Silcock of Oby, near Yarmouth, and stayed in Norfolk all its life. Its last owner was S.H. Witham of Erpingham, who still owned it in 1947 when this picture was taken. [A.J. Martin collection]

Fig.25. Sales of the 8NHP were very slow, mostly because owners preferred the 7NHP such as No.27162, for R.H.Draper of Shrewley, Warwickshire, despatched on June 23, 1908. The first 7NHP came out in 1903 and rapidly became a favourite. [SRO]

death in March, 1895, after which it continued under a new agreement in the name of Filippo Grimaldi alone until 1903 when a further revised agreement between F. & L. Grimaldi and Garretts was signed on October 31. By that time the firm had an additional office and depot in Turin.

In 1912, almost at the end of the limited production of 8NHP compounds, the design was modified and updated to incorporate as standard a number of the changes that had been made to suit individual customers in the nine years since its inauguration. Mostly the changes were minor, such as moving the pump and injector delivery clacks nearer the smokebox - the pernicious practice of putting them on the side of the firebox having already been left behind. The most visible change was in the fitting of a 23" wide smokebox where previously 15" had been used, and at the same time the larger pattern of smokestand devised for the 10NHP ploughers was fitted. The crankshafts of the compounds were webbed though the singles retained the plain forged crankshaft.

The first engine of the updated type was No.30369 shipped to Lisbon through the agency of Whitehead, Sumner, Harker & Co. Ltd. on July 25, 1912. Fitted with a so-called colonial boiler pressed to 12 atmospheres (180 p.s.i.) this had, besides, four pinions in the differential, the wider gears already used in 8NHP ploughing engines, and a 6¼" diameter rear axle, where previously 5¼" diameter had been used. Out of deference to the powerful sun of Portugal an awning was fitted over the manstand. It was followed on May 7, 1913, by No.31132, an identical engine. Both were turned out in 'Local Show finish'.

After having tested the appeal of compound tractions to potential purchasers and found the response wanting the company set out to ascertain the market's reaction to superheating, another subject that had engaged the attention of the management for some years. Experiment had established that a smokebox superheater achieved measurable economies when applied to portable engines or to semi-stationary power plants, and it was resolved to construct a traction engine so equipped. To a certain extent superheating of traction engines had been given a trial canter with No.26446, a 6NHP single with piston valves built for Henninger in 1907 in which he had had incorporated a smokebox superheater of his own invention and manufacture using banked coils in a large flat topped smokebox. The Henninger design of superheater was a failure but other items designed for the engine found a use, either as originally drawn or with minor modifications, after a new form of smokebox superheater had been devised in the drawing office. In the late Summer of 1909 work was put in hand on another 6NHP superheated piston valved traction, using the Leiston pattern of superheater, with the intention of having it ready for the Smithfield Show. It was indeed finished on time, being taken into stock on December 1, 1909, turned out in Royal Show finish, but it did not go to Smithfield. Why it did not go is not clear, but it may have been because of problems with clearances in the cylinder. The diameter was especially noted as two thousandths of an inch oversize and the piston eight thousandths undersize i.e. a clearance of 10 thousandths made. Even with the modest amount of superheat imparted this clearance may have posed a lubrication problem. Whatever the facts of the matter it did not go to the Show or find a home customer, ending up by being sold to Henninger for whom spring balance safety valves and German type boiler fittings were substituted for those on it. By the time it was ready to leave, (May 7, 1910) it was deemed expedient to replace the original Works number of 27950 with the number 28272.

Notwithstanding the firm's generally favourable leanings towards technical advances originating in German speaking countries they elected not to take up the use of the smoketube superheater, such as the Schmidt, which was applied with considerable success to railway locomotives, adopting instead a home designed smokebox superheater. Avoidance of patent royalties otherwise payable may have been the whole explanation of this attitude of mind, which was shared by Fowlers, but there may also have been other cogent commercial and technical reasons behind the decision, bearing in mind the fact that the application of superheating to portables and locomobiles was expected to outnumber those to tractions and rollers by more than ten to one and, moreover, ante-dated them. When superheat was first applied it brought with it serious problems in the carbonising of the cylinder and valve lubricating oils then available, resulting in damage by seizing or scoring. Since this problem intensified as the temperature of the superheated steam rose it is possible that Garretts looked for a system in which the temperature of the steam averaged perhaps 550 - 600° F at 150 p.s.i. rather than possibly 100°F (or more) higher in a Schmidt type superheater. Perhaps they also sought a method that would leave the main body of the boiler essentially unaltered and have a lower initial cost. To suit all these postulates the choice lighted upon a superheater housed in a smokebox raised above its midpoint into a boxing square on plan with a flat top embodying the smokestand. The superheater itself consisted of two cast steel header boxes extending virtually the whole width of the boxing, their long axes parallel to the tubeplate. The lower was placed a little above the top row of firetubes and the other near the top of the housing, the two being linked with twelve banks of 1" internal diameter (1⁵/₁₆" external) solid drawn steel tube - a total of 141 feet - bent into flat coils and expanded into the headers. Saturated steam was fed into the lower header and superheated steam was taken from the upper one, having taken superheat mainly in its passage through the banks of coils which were in the path of uprising flue gases. Thus there was some 48 square feet of external tube surface exposed to the hot gases.

To enable the coils to be kept clean of soot a live steam lance was provided but notwithstanding its use the efficacy of the superheater declined progressively from the commencement of work after one cleaning until a stop was made for the next. Nevertheless in dynamometer trials with portables, run for long periods on full load, useful economy of fuel and water was achieved. Convincing the potential purchasers that the pros outweighed the cons proved difficult, however. Few cared for the piston valve which necessarily replaced the slide valve on a superheated engine's cylinder; many were scared off by the problems of lubrication which were only gradually conquered; more distrusted the higher capital and maintenance costs. In consequence sales were disappointing, particularly insofar as traction engines were concerned.

The next traction engine to which superheating was applied was a 6NHP single, No.28375, designed and built during the first half of 1910. The preparation of the drawings extended over a lengthy period. The boiler drawing (No.10227), for instance, went back to mid-summer, 1909, but the completion of the drawings probably occurred in March, 1910. The drawing list, marking the end of drawing production, was finished by Tom Jones on March 21, but by that time many of the drawings were already in use on the Works. The actual erection work was put in hand on June 17, 1910, entrusted, like many such jobs involving new or radically altered designs, to Billy Vale. It was sufficiently different from the general run of 6NHP singles (the drawings for which had the prefix 'T') for it to have a prefix 'BT' of its own. Whereas most 6NHP single cylinder tractions were being turned out to run at 140 p.s.i. No.28375 was pressed to 180 p.s.i. which pressure, taken in conjunction with the benefit derived from the superheater - probably not vast - gave it a sufficiently enhanced power output on the belt to justify the flywheel diameter being increased to 4' 6" (as on a No.8) with the governed speed dropped to 165 r.p.m. The engine was noted in the books as completed on July 28, after which it was sent to the Dumfries Show and then to Allan Meikle of Mount Vernon, Glasgow.

To what extent the design of No.28375 arose from Meikle's ideas is now impossible to determine. He was well-known to the firm and acted as a stockholder for engine spares. He was, moreover, of an investigative disposition and an experimenter by nature, anxious to be in the forefront of engine design. Certainly the many special features beside the smokebox superheater and the piston valved cylinder block suggest that he must have been closely involved. For instance, it was at Meikle's express wish that a circular smokebox door was used rather than one with a square top such as might have given improved access to the superheater coils. The engine was sprung both front and rear. It had a belly tank, motion plates, rim brakes to the rear wheels, and a full length awning. It had also what the order book described as 'Scotch hind wheels' shod with 3" x 1" strakes. Incidentally, it was one of the first - if not *the* first - Garrett engines to be fitted with a Manzell mechanical lubricator and a Penberthy injector. Unusually the rope guide rollers were 1' 8" long, suggesting that it was intended for roping work in difficult situations. Belt rollers, to the design for the 4 CD tractors, were sent subsequently for fixing to the top of the belly tank. It also had the ingenious differential locking system devised by Emerich Schmach. This is described in Appendix 2. As delivered the engine had all the outward appearance of a road locomotive, though it remained at heart a general purpose traction engine. Meikle gave it the name *BONNY JEAN*. The illustration (Fig.33) shows it hauling a marine boiler on a characteristically squat low-wheeled boiler trolley. A similar superheated 6NHP single was built later in the year for Alexander Wilson of Bridgend, Forglen, Turriff, turned out in Royal Show finish with copper pipework, the so-called 'Scotch' strakes, and an awning over the manstand but without the other extras and/or refinements bestowed upon *BONNY JEAN*. This engine was despatched on March 27, 1911. As it was last licensed in 1943, having worked for 33 years, one may reasonably presume that it was a useful engine. Latterly, at least, it worked at timber hauling on the Baltimore Estate in Argyllshire. The next was No.29024 shipped to Henninger in June, 1911, and exhibited at the Cassel Show in Royal Show finish. Lastly came No.29764 sent on August 10, 1911, to Raymond J. Colcombe, The Grove, Sellack, Ross. This engine is preserved and has had its superheater reinstated after having been without it for many years.

Following closely on these latter 6NHP superheated engines were two 7NHP engines with almost the same configuration. The first of these was No.30802, a fully sprung engine with full length awning, rim brakes, and a belly tank, supplied to M. Constant Randon, a client of Pilter's Paris office, who was situated at Rinxent in the Pas de Calais, just about as near to England as it is possible to be whilst still in France. The second was equally interesting being a 7NHP version of *BONNY JEAN* and for the same purchaser, Allan Meikle, though in this instance his address was entered as Tollcross, Glasgow. This engine, No.31063 was sent on November 11, 1912, and carried the name *DREADNOUGHT*. As a closing note to this mention of 6 and 7NHP superheated engines it is perhaps worth recording that when, a little later, Henninger ordered 7NHP piston valved single No.31378, he laid down the stipulation '*NO* superheater'. Evidently he liked the piston valve arrangements but had had enough of superheaters. Incidentally, superheating was never tried on an 8NHP traction engine.

The Agricultural Engineers' Association, the price fixing ring to which all manufacturers belonged, had rules that they all paid lip service to whilst doing their damnedest to circumvent them. These were loaded against the selling of 5NHP engines except at virtually the same price as a 6NHP. The cylinder diameter laid down for a 5NHP was 8", which made it a 6NHP under the RASE rules, although the stroke was 10" instead of 12". Although information fed back to the Works from agents suggested that a 5NHP engine might find a potential market if substantially cheaper than a 6NHP all the time the firm abided by the AEA ruling this could not be offered, and interest in the idea was allowed to lapse. However, in 1909 Ed. Zehder, the Garrett agent in Riga who supplied engines to the Baltic area of Russia (now the Baltic States), sent an enquiry for a 5NHP that revived the idea of adding such an engine to the Leiston production range, since AEA rules did not apply to overseas orders. By that time the No.4 single cylinder tractor was already in production, and what the Works produced for Zehder was No.27855, effectually a No.4 single with a colonial firebox, unsprung and having the cylinder bored to 7" diameter instead of 6½". This was given Royal Show finish and despatched to Riga on August 12, 1909, with obviously satisfactory results as a steady flow of orders for engines of this design, or developed versions of it which Garretts called 'the Continental traction', continued until the outbreak of the 1914-18 war. Their story is detailed in Chapter 7.

The success of this venture prompted a renewal of efforts to market an engine of a similar basic configuration in the United Kingdom. Drawings were put in hand between perhaps October, 1909, and March, 1910, mostly from the hands of Arthur Girling and Gordon Thomson. These were scheduled in Specification No.65 dated March 11, 1910. Three were put in hand, subsequently allocated the numbers 28257, 28382, and 28756. The No.5 thus produced borrowed more than a little from the No.4 single cylinder tractor but was a somewhat longer engine having a boiler barrel 5' 1³/₁₆" long compared with 3' 10³/₁₆" in the tractor. The working pressure was 180 p.s.i. as in the tractor, giving the new design an advantage in power output, relative to size, over the range of larger traction engines, working at 140 p.s.i. Being based upon the No.4 tractor the 5NHP engines were three shaft. The change-speed gears were on the offside end of the crankshaft outside the hornplates, with the higher speed tight up to the bearing, in this respect resembling a Burrell - not so much by deliberate plagiarism as because the position was dictated by sound engineering practice. The omission of the second countershaft and its gearing helped in the reduction of overall weight and probably helped to gain the 5NHPs their reputation for good power output on the road. They had a 7" diameter cylinder and a 10" stroke, which, taken with the higher boiler pressure, meant that they were capable of a 25 brake horse power output under continuous load, compared with 27 for a 6NHP. According to the AEA rules these engines should have been sold at a list price of £435.00 (compared with £460.00 for a 6NHP). In fact they were offered at below £335.00. According to the late Leslie Cooper, who owned and worked 5NHP Garrett No.34045 at threshing for some years, it was a very brisk and economical engine, compact and handy into the bargain. The first of the trio was sold to the Irish Agricultural Wholesale Society for their customer Patrick Fenelon of Shangary, Myshall. Co. Carlow, to whom it was sent on August 8, 1910. The second, No.28382, went on September 21, 1910, to a more domestic destination being sold to Edward Cheney, who lived at Mill Farm in Kelsale, an adjoining parish to Leiston. These two sales were in flagrant breach of the AEA agreement. Victor Garrett once told me that his eldest brother Frank had very little time for the cartel, characterising its objectives as the protection of the manufacturers already in the market, no matter how inefficient they might have been in their methods, against firms attempting to enter it, as exemplified by Richard Garrett & Sons Ltd. Victor went on to say that the sale of the two 5NHP engines was noted and reported to the AEA who took his father and brothers to task over the alleged breach. The board of directors, probably influenced by Frank (Senior), decided not to rock the boat of price maintenance by persisting in the sale of 5NHP engines in the United Kingdom, at any rate for the time being.

As a consequence of this decision No.28756, the third engine of the initial trio, was not offered for sale but was retained at Leiston and used as a Works hack. The idea of smaller traction engines was left, so to speak, on the table until revived in the PV1 series at the time of the 1914-18 war. The building of a simpler version of the 5NHP and of the 4NHP traction engines for use abroad was not affected by the attitude of the AEA. After this brush with the AEA the firm concentrated more effort upon the manufacture of the overtype wagons, the story of which was set out in *Garrett Wagons - Part 1* and the 4NHP compound steam tractor which it is hoped to describe in a future volume.

The idea of building engines in a lighter and cheaper version for export reflected in some degree the lessons to be learned from the American traction engine manufacturers who, notwithstanding the fact of their having to pay the highest wages in the world to skilled artisans, nevertheless managed to produce engines at competitive prices, almost entirely by ruthless economy of finish and by simplification to the point of crudity. Many American single cylinder engines had overhung disc cranks instead of crankshafts, and where a crankshaft *was* used it was rarely webbed or balanced. Even after conceding the fact that a fair proportion of American engines fell into the category of self-moving portables there remained a solid core of them performing duties comparable with the average British threshing outfit. In finish and accoutrements, however, they were very different. Absence of lagging, open gear trains, flywheel clutches, single eccentric valve gears, wire spoked wheels, engines on Corliss frames, and the use of piston valves instead of slide valves marked them apart as did the low level of paint finish. British makers, such as Garretts, who found themselves in competition with the American firms abroad were forced to compete by making engines simplified to the same degree. This led on to the additional question of how much of American practice it was worth attempting to use in production for the home market. As far as Leiston was concerned the market had rejected shifting eccentric valve gear so that the use of piston valves appeared to offer the next most promising economy. Furthermore, in superheated engines their use became a necessity.

The design of Leiston-built engines underwent some changes as the influence of the younger Garretts waxed and the resistance of their father diminished. It was not necessarily that he agreed with their methods but was prepared increasingly to let them have their heads though their habit of table thumping debate jarred upon him. It was partly to impart a steadying influence upon these noisy discussions in the board-room that his old friend and colleague Charles (Carl) Remy was appointed a director in 1907, perhaps in the hope that he would be a mellowing influence as all the younger Garretts liked him, particularly Stephen who was the family member then involved in sales promotion, and hence most closely in contact with Remy day by day.

Under the altered regime changes were made in the methods used upon the Works and in the drawing office. In 1905/06 the use of blueprints was instituted in place of the old system of using boy tracers to replicate drawings. Third angle projection was made standard about the same time. A useful by-product of these reforms was the introduction of drawing lists, or specifications, in which all the drawings to be used in the production of a given type of engine were set out in prearranged forms on tracing linen from which blue-print copies were made. These were gathered together in sets between card covers for the use of the various Works departments. In the Works new machine tools were introduced, not the least important of which was gear hobbing machinery. Frank Walker was appointed, nominally to have charge of testing but in addition to advise the directors on the Works methods. Walker was a shrewd engineer of a social and educational standing compatible with their own and had no axe to grind when evaluating proposals put before the board by the Works departments. Chestertonian in build, comfortably off in his personal circumstances, skilled at handling cars, capable of piloting an aircraft, he was able to foster numerous changes for the better, not the least of which was to institute a programme of standardisation of components. Hitherto each new type of engine or machine had been designed more or less *de novo* by the draughtsman in charge. Walker advocated standardisation, and to secure its enforcement the board appointed a new member to the drawing office staff, Francis Xavier Thoburn. By about mid-year 1913 his work was complete.

Under Alfred Garrett, a dedicated administrator, such innovations as an internal telephone system, the introduction of typewriters and, after a while, lady typists, the use of loose-leaf books and of printed books for engine memoranda all made an appearance. It was Alfred who organised the minute books of directors' meetings and arranged set paths for the dissemination of information between departments, establishing where the channels of command lay and upon whose authority work was taken on and put in hand. During this period of reform the old butty system of paying hands, by which, for instance, a smith was paid the wages for his whole gang and then paid out his strikers and labourers himself, was abolished, to the irritation of many of the senior hands who had been quietly appropriating a proportion of the wages which had been entrusted to them for distribution.

As the work load in the drawing office increased under the expansion of the range of products additional draughtsmen were recruited. One of the more senior and enduring of these was Fenton Gordon Thomson - he always used his second Christian name - who joined in 1909 and whose first major undertaking was to design the 5NHP traction engines. Four years later Maurice Plane who was later to become head of the drawing office was taken on.

On the workmen's side efforts to unionise began, against the strong disapproval of the directors. This led to a week-long lock-out of workmen in March, 1912, after which the men were re-employed selectively excluding known firebrands. The way in which this policy was implemented led Ishmael Girling to protest to the senior management and in the atmosphere of strained tempers he was sacked. After tempers had cooled this action was regretted but never rescinded. Frank Garrett Junior, as managing director, held back from cancelling Girling's dismissal, fearing that in so doing unprompted he might be seen as admitting to excessive hastiness and thereby lose face, whilst Girling, for his part, was too proud to be thought to be pleading for reinstatement. Faced with this situation his son Arthur, who had had, as has been noted, a prominent part in the design of the traction engines, left out of sympathy, thus robbing the Works of two of its most reliable and knowledgeable men.

The design side of traction engine building was less affected by this hectic period of change. Probably the most significant revision was the raising of working pressure which had been 140 p.s.i. for singles and 160 p.s.i. for compounds to 160 and 180 respectively, a change made without wholesale redesigning of the boilers and accomplished over a period of about a year in 1909. Changes in the gear arrangements on the crankshaft came about as circumstances demanded rather than as part of an overall scheme of amendment. Thus, from 1896, the standard 6NHP traction engine had the low speed next to the bearing at the flywheel end of the crankshaft and the higher speed adjacent to the eccentrics. This layout was carried over into the 7NHP and also into some of the earliest 8NHP singles such as No.25858 for G.F. Townsend of Exning near Newmarket. In the compound version the same arrangement was again employed though it involved an outward set in the hornplates to give sufficient space between the bearings. Incidentally it was also used in the No.6 compound road locomotive (see Chapter 6) but with the higher speed being next to the bearing. In the 8NHP two speed singles a differing scheme prevailed. In them the higher speed gear was inside the crankbox next to the flywheel bearing and the lower speed outside the crankbox on the offside.

In this period of design amendment (c.1909/10) this arrangement was applied to 6NHP compound traction engines, thus obviating the outward set in each hornplate. It was earlier applied to the 8NHP compound road loco (see Chapter 6) but still required the hornplate to be set outwards. The application of a third speed to a 6NHP single traction engine (such as Meikle's *Bonny Jean*) was achieved by lengthening the crankshaft so as to carry the highest speed outside the bearing. There was just sufficient room between the bearings to allow the pump eccentric to be inside the crankbox. This was used also on at least one 7NHP three speed single (No.28748) supplied to W. Adamson of Hunter Hall, Glencarse. The problem of putting a third speed on the 8NHP road locomotive is referred to in Chapter 6. The provision of a third speed on a 6NHP compound traction engine was tackled by substituting for the usual spoked flywheel a disc flywheel with a longer boss on the bearing side. This boss was turned and the highest speed pinion was pressed onto it, thus allowing the standard straight hornplates to be kept but requiring a longer second shaft.

So few three speed engines were made that the ability to use a standard boiler rather than to have to manufacture one with offset hornplates was a useful economy measure, enabling the boiler to be from stock and obviating the lengthening of delivery time that would have been incurred had it been purpose made. Boilermakers liked their products to spend a month or two in the stock field to give time for the formation of rust to ensure total water-tightness.

One might have expected, in this period of change, an improvement in the method of springing the traction engines but this was another feature which was not altered, probably because the level of demand for sprung engines was so low. Of 230 traction engines of 6, 7, and 8NHP built during the period under review (i.e. from 1895 to 1918) only 50 were sprung. The system used throughout gave no more than a slight cushioning against the harder shocks, no more movement, in fact, than was permitted by the depth of the gear teeth. In practice this probably meant ⅜" to ½". It was secured by placing two eight leaf springs transversely beneath the rear axle to which they were connected by a compensating lever and hangers. The rear axle brackets were extended downwards to carry the weight onto this arrangement. If springing was ordered to the front axle it was accomplished by placing an eight leaf spring through the carriage jaw to bear upon the axle. To allow movement the holes in the carriage jaw which accommodated the horizontal securing pin were elongated vertically. When the rear axle of an 8NHP was sprung it made an unpopular feature of the boiler even more disliked. About 15" below the firehole door there was a mudhole, access to which was troublesome at the best of times but on a sprung engine bordering on the impossible. It is difficult to see how it could have been removed without someone getting wet. Yet in another way the No.8 boiler was in advance of the others in having a rectangular firehole with lever operated sliding doors. It might have been expected that the unsatisfactorily positioned mudhole would have disappeared in the general programme of upgrading the traction engine designs but, on the contrary, it remained until the end.

As a matter of policy, the physical dimensions of the boilers of compound engines were slightly less than those of singles, as will be seen from the table (Appendix 1), but the working pressure, of course, was higher. The first No.6 engine (No.20485) had no manhole, but at least from No.21126 (1897) onwards a manhole was fitted, though the position of it was varied - sometimes below the cylinder block but at others below the weighshaft bracket, the latter becoming standard. After the initial engine with single eccentric valve gear the majority of Garrett traction engines had the steering on the left and the reversing lever on the right but numerous engines were made in which this disposition was reversed, usually to suit the customer's preferences. Thus, for example, the 7NHP singles Nos.26045 and 26046 supplied in October, 1906, to Isaac Sheldrake of Bunwell, near Wymondham, Norfolk, both had the steering wheel and reversing lever transposed. An interesting feature of the Garrett steering wheel was that it had cast on it an arrow pointing anti-clockwise and lettered 'left'. In recent times this has attracted a certain amount of derision, but the wheels were cast from a metal pattern (No.T 41) which was in use unchanged for many years, and might well have survived from the days when tank steering, with which the wheel was turned left to turn the engine to the right, was still met with, though not on Garrett engines. In this setting a reminder that anti-clockwise movement of the steering wheel turned the road wheels *left* was not untimely.

The flywheels used in the traction engines were somewhat heavier in the rim than some of their contemporaries but not otherwise noteworthy. Bored trunks were used to carry the crossheads. The crankshafts were forged and turned, usually on the Works although when output of engines outstripped the capacity of the smithy cranks were bought in from outside suppliers, mostly from Clarke's Crank & Forge Co. of Grantham with which firm Leiston had a good relationship. Clarke's was managed for many years by Louis ('Greyhound') Smith, sometime works manager of Leiston Works, later knighted for his work on munitions manufacture in the 1914-18 war. The gearing was cast steel throughout - the castings bought from outside suppliers and finished on the Works. The differential, fitted with three bevels, was on the offside, the winding drum being on the nearside. Spring loaded safety valves were used on all home orders but a high proportion of overseas boiler regulations required the use of spring balances. Pressure gauges were Schäffer type as standard, and the single water gauge glass fittings, as a rule, came from Dewrance, supplemented by the customary two try-cocks. As has been noted already, from the beginning cylinder lubrication was by a mechanical lubricator, with, in addition, a displacement lubricator on the front of the cylinder block.

Differences with the AEA did not stop at the 5NHP engines. Signature of the agreement required participants to observe strict rules concerning trade discounts (restricted to 10%); discounts for cash (limited to 2½% with onerous qualifications); and the rates of interest on hire purchase agreements. The names of agents and representatives had to be registered with the AEA, and they were forbidden to share their trade discounts with their lay clients, the offence of doing so being counted as a breach of the rules by the manufacturer for whom they were acting. Signatory firms were required to deposit with the AEA a

Fig.26. 6NHP single No.23378 belonging to W.Wilson of Darmsden, Suffolk, photographed by the late Derek Stoyel at Darmsden on Sept. 7, 1938.

Fig.27 (below). The 7NHP single had most adherents among English threshing contractors. This is No.25890 (1906) working for H. Challand & Sons, Rippingale, Bourne, Lincs, on Sept.20, 1935.   [B.D. Stoyel]

Fig.28 (below). The 8NHP compound was a poor seller. The eight examples made were all for export. This is either 27115 or 27204, but probably the former, at work in Queensland in 1908, having been sold through the agency of Clark & Fauset. The roof was added in Australia to save bulk and weight in shipping.

Fig.29. Two 7NHPs and a tractor in R..W. Portway's yard at Radwinter in June, 1936. On the left is No.28410 (Oct.2, 1905), centre is No.32323 (July 5,1914) and right No.4CD tractor No.33513 (May 16, 1919).   [A.J. Martin collection]

Fig.30 (centre). A further 7NHP single, No.28747, in the yard at Redbourn, Herts, of the late George Taylor, dealer, repairer, and reluctant scrap-man (Aug.8, 1935). New to G. Cooper of Ashwell, it had a double drawbar for direct ploughing. Taylor sold it to Edward Welcher of Doddington who had it until c.1947.
[A.J. Martin collection]

Fig.31 (below). The first Leiston built superheated traction was No.26446, a 6NHP for A. Henninger of Darmstadt, to take his patent superheater, made in Germany and fitted at Leiston. It was shown at the 1907 Dusseldorf Exhibition but pronounced a failure.

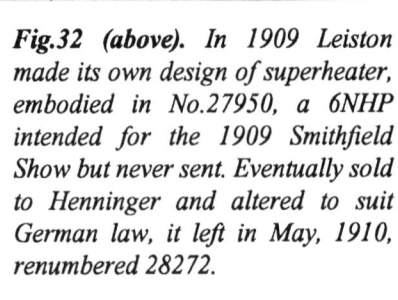

Fig.32 (above). In 1909 Leiston made its own design of superheater, embodied in No.27950, a 6NHP intended for the 1909 Smithfield Show but never sent. Eventually sold to Henninger and altered to suit German law, it left in May, 1910, renumbered 28272.

Fig.33. Allan Meikle's Bonnie Jean, *a 6NHP, (No.28375 of 1910), still a superheated single, but with differences to 27950 - third speed (visible outside the hornplates) circular smokebox door, and belly tank. The marine type boiler behind it is by Bow McLachlan & Co. of Paisley, who themselves essayed at least one traction engine.*
Fig.34. Bonnie Jean *is shown here threshing, but in 1912 Meikle bought 31063,* Dreadnought, *a 7NHP of similar characteristics, probably a little more useful at the job.*

Fig.35. One source of Garretts' tussle with the AEA was the 5NHP single No.28382, sold in 1910 to Edmund Cheney of Kelsale (the next parish to Leiston). Despite the hassle over the price-fixing agreement the engine had a long and fairly placid life in the district, latterly with William Easey of Theberton. (See Fig.36 overleaf).

45

a maximum of £400.00. An offence against the rules could result in a fine, the amount of which was to be deducted from the deposited sum and then to be distributed to the other signatories deemed to have suffered loss as a consequence of the transgression. After the brush with the AEA over the 5NHP engines in 1909, the Garrett board turned attention away from the selling of traction engines in the home market as they considered that the only way in which they could have generated useful sales was by competitive pricing, either in the form of direct reductions in the selling price or by throwing in, free of charge, extras requested by the clients, such as enhanced tool kits, extra lifting jacks, an additional road speed, or more elaborate painting schemes. As a consequence of this change of emphasis only three compound traction engines and fifty-five singles, made up of 21 of 6NHP, 33 of 7NHP, and 1 of 8NHP, were sold in the home market between 1909 and the amalgamation into AGE in 1919.

Fig.36. *The nearside view of No.28382, very probably with the same threshing drum, in the late 1930s. Note how much higher the manhole was placed than those of the 6 and 7 NHPs.*
[A.J. Martin collection]

Fig.37. The Works crane engine (No.23021) driven by Jack Newstead entering Main St. from Gas Hill, Leiston, c.1910. In the right background is the old Works gas holder, and behind the engines is Howe's grocery shop, soon to be demolished for the building of the new Tool Room etc.

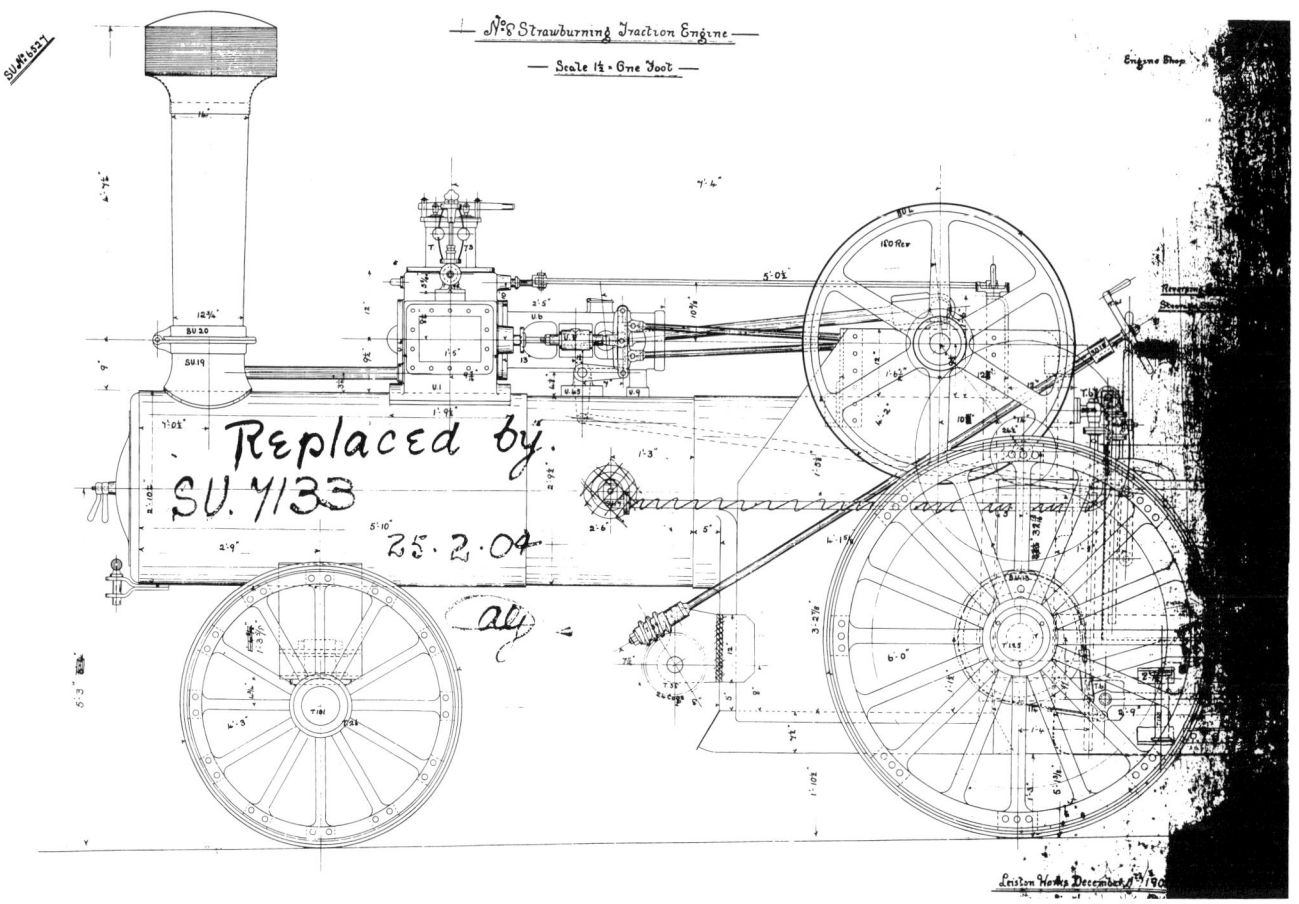

Fig.38. The 8NHP strawburner of 1902, as exemplified by Nos.24001 and 24316 exported to the Roumanian agent Eugen Behles in Bucharest.

Fig.39 shows the arrangement of the firebox in these engines and illustrates the baffle that bridged the front of the box, forcing the gases to rise over it on their way to the tubes and thereby creating - or so it was hoped - an intense swirl of flame onto the firebox plates. Having the baffle pivoted made it relatively easy to get rid of the fly ash carried over and dropped between it and the tubeplate.

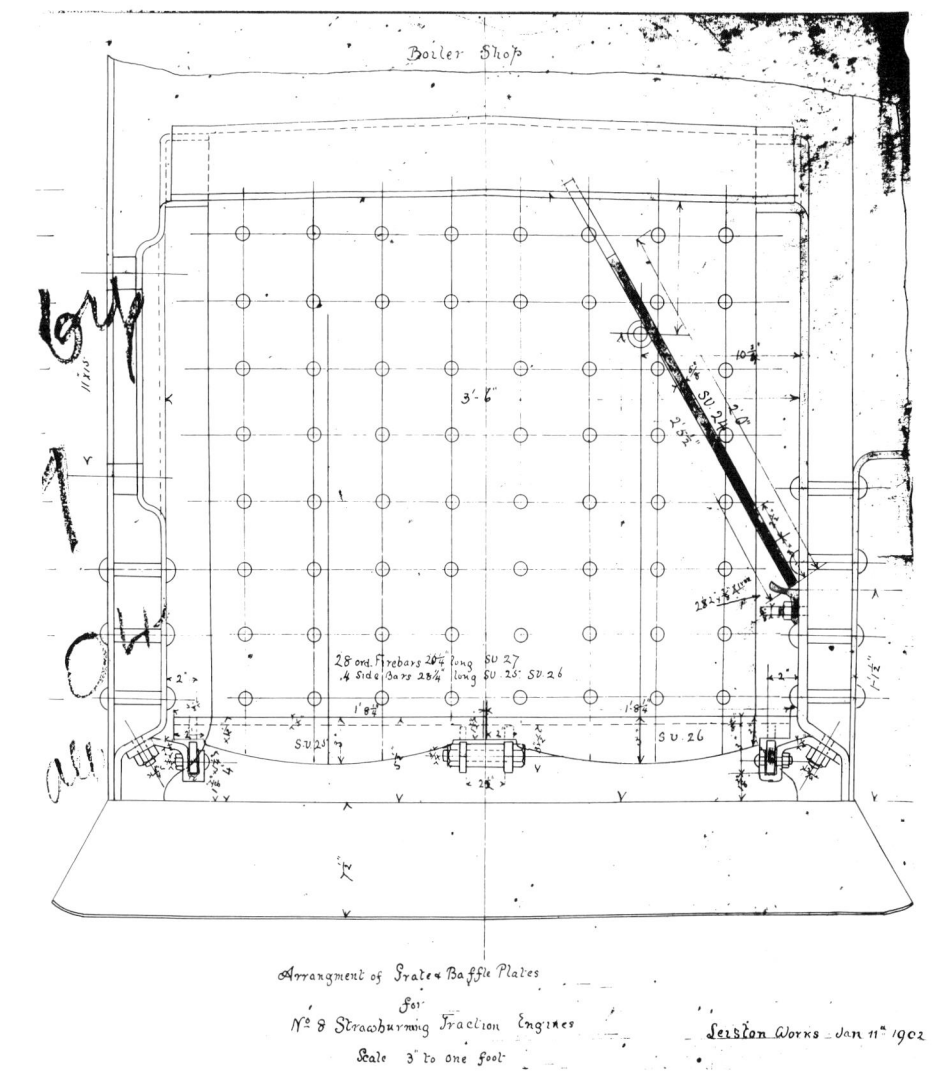

47

Fig.40. *The newly completed 10NHP strawburner No.25060 threshing at Knodishall Hall on test, October 10, 1904.*

Fig.41 (right) *shows the side view of the second type of 10NHP strawburner developed for M.E. Mattos of Buenos Aires, modelled on United States practice.*

Fig.42 (below) *shows a three quarter rear view. Peep holes were fitted on each side of the fire box to enable the space between baffle and tubes to be inspected and the tube ends brushed.*

Figs.43 and 44 (below) *show the flywheel clutch and the method of mounting the gear rings upon the road wheels.*

Chapter 4

Strawburners

In the nineteenth century Garretts' trade in portable engines for Hungary, then a vastly larger country than now, was conducted mainly through the agency of a Hungarian engineer, Paul Kotzo, who had an office and warehouse in Budapest where he held stocks of Garrett engines and machines which he sold on the firm's behalf. This establishment was referred to in the Leiston books as 'the Budapest warehouse'. The arrangement with Kotzo was both enduring and cordial. One outcome of their co-operation was a patent (dated November 15, 1871) for a system of strawburning as applied to portable engines. Burning straw was important in the agrarian economy of Hungary, so much so that Riley, the Californian authority on steam threshing, writing in the *Pacific Rural Press* of 1876, noted that there were upwards of 200 strawburning threshing sets in use in Hungary of which about a quarter were by Garretts. Under this Garrett/Kotzo system of strawburning the water legs of the firebox were made somewhat deeper, and provision was made for two positions of firebars, a higher one for use when coal was being burned and a much lower one for straw. Each level had its own firedoor, the lower of the two being provided with a chute to enable the straw to be thrust through the door more easily. When set up for threshing and the use of straw fuel a pit was dug under the firebox to receive the ashes, enabling the ashpan to be dispensed with, loose plates banked up with the excavated earth being placed around the firebox to control the entry of air. This apparently happy-go-lucky system, derided by the makers of more elaborate and, hence, much more expensive apparatus for the same purpose, seems to have worked satisfactorily enough. Subsequently it was modified by the introduction of a transverse division, topped by an iron baffle or a firebrick wall over which the products of combustion had to pass. The Schemioth power operated straw feeding gear was later applied to many portables. Once steam was up it enabled straw to be fed to the fire without the constant presence of a fireman and, notwithstanding the increased initial cost, was preferred by a significant minority of purchasers.

Because straw had less calorific value weight for weight and enormously less volume for volume than even the relatively low grade coal and briquettes available in rural Austria and Hungary, it was necessary to burn a larger volume of it to maintain the same heat output. This was achieved in part by the greater rapidity of burning but also by the much enhanced firebox volume. Straw fires were as prone to clinker formation as those burning the available coal and, moreover, tended to produce a spiders-web of filmy clinker strands over the tube ends thereby reducing the draught. In the early days the engine fireman brushed these away using a besom broom inserted through the upper firehole door, the degree of success depending upon his aptitude, but in the later fireboxes the introduction of the firebrick wall was designed to prevent these cobwebs of clinker from forming and growing.

At the beginning of the present century the portable engine continued to be the predominant power source for threshing sets throughout the Austro-Hungarian empire though the proportion of Garrett sets had declined in the face of much enhanced competition from locally manufactured machines. The use of straw-burning traction engines to power threshing sets had increased somewhat in Germany but not so significantly in Austria-Hungary wherein Garretts never won an order for such an engine. The first strawburning traction engine built by Garretts was one of a pair of 8NHPs begun in 1901, seemingly as a speculation, and was given the number 23652. Drawings were begun during Autumn, 1901, with Arthur Girling as the draughtsman in charge. Drawing No.6493, the general arrangement of the offside and cross-section, was dated December 4, 1901. By that date the 8NHP vertical drum ploughing engines for Rudolph Sack (see Chapter 5) had already been drawn and were in production but because the three shaft arrangement was adopted for the strawburners only limited numbers of the existing drawings and patterns could be fitted into the new design. Nevertheless, the cylinder, trunk guide, guide bracket, and weigh shaft bracket were all cast from the existing 8NHP patterns, whilst the crosshead pattern was that (No.CE 190) used for 8NHP portables. These items apart, the majority of the castings were to new patterns with the prefix SU. However, Girling was able to use the differential, the steering wheel, steering worm, wormwheel, and forecarriage jaw from the 6NHP traction. The boiler was 2' 10¼" in diameter with a circumferential joint just clear of the cylinder block, the smokebox being rolled in one with the front ring of the boiler. The boiler pressure is unknown, but if in accordance with contemporary policy would have been 140 p.s.i. The firegrate was 2' 3½" wide x 3' 6" long (i.e. a grate area of 8 sq. ft.) and a pivoted baffle plate bridged the front of the box so that gases had to rise and pass over it before entering the tubes (Fig.39). Interestingly there was no foundation ring, the bottom of the firebox inner plates being stepped outward to meet the outer wrapper as in a portable.

The engine was designed to run at 180 r.p.m., compared with the 165 r.p.m. in the 6NHP tractions. The single speed road gearing was on the offside, outside the hornplate. The gear on the crankshaft was of 15 teeth (or 'cogs' as Arthur Girling described them) at 2" pitch meshing with 62 teeth on the intermediate shaft, where a further 18 tooth gear engaged with 68 teeth on the differential spur ring. There was a small water tank under the manstand but otherwise no tender, and the driver/steersman's position was raised up a further 6" by wooden floorboards and bearers on top of the tank. Boiler feed was by an eccentric driven pump and an injector. Which type of injector is not recorded but Holden & Brooke were the reigning favourites at the time. Conventional 6' 0" diameter rear wheels of a design specific to these engines were used, and a winding drum was fitted.

This first strawburner was accepted into the stockyard as a finished engine in the Spring of 1902, figuring in the stockyard list dated April 1, 1902. It was sold to Pilter's Paris office for shipment to Algeria, the name of Billiard & Cuzin being put onto a nameplate. Alterations requested were the provision of a tender water tank, the removal of the strawburning grate and the provision of bars for coal-burning. Thus fitted it left Leiston on May 16, 1902, having apparently been re-numbered 23737. The second, which appeared on the stockyard list of December 1, 1902, received the number 24001. Whilst this had been under construction an order had been received, supposedly via the network of contacts which Carl Remy had in South East Europe, from Eugen Behles of Bucharest, Roumania, for two strawburning traction engines. No.24001 was allocated to be one of these and was sent off on April 3, 1903, to be followed by a sister engine, No.24316, on May 29. Thus, because it is dubious if No.23737 ever worked as a strawburner, Nos.24001 and 24316 represented the only two of this 8NHP design to have done so, as no further examples were made.

A second and more promising start, however, took place soon afterwards. Richard Garrett & Sons Ltd. had well established dealings with both the Argentinian importing firm of M.E. Mattos, who had an office at 299 Calle B Mitre, Buenos Aires, and their representatives in London, Torromé & Co. Ltd. of Lawrence Pountney Lane in the City, who enquired for the supply of a 10NHP strawburner with the prospect of recurring orders if the initial example proved satisfactory. They required a relatively light-weight and very cheap engine moulded upon North American practice, to which reference has already been made in Chapter 3. Thus, in a number of major respects, the design was leading the drawing office onto new ground. No one there had ever been involved with nor had anyone, it is believed, even seen an engine constructed on these lines, the nearest being some of the colonial engines produced by other English firms such as, for instance, Clayton & Shuttleworth. There William Fletcher, the chief designer, had made a study of American traction engines sufficiently detailed to lead him to write his book *'English & American Steam Carriages & Traction Engines'* as a spin-off. Whether or not any of the Leiston drawing office staff went into the subject to a comparable degree seems improbable for what was produced there in the initial stages of fulfilling this order was in some respects like a 'stretched ' version of the Eugen Behles' 8NHPs, albeit reverting to use of the four shaft layout with two road speeds. In fact the plan drawing (SU7198) produced for the first example was initially labelled '8NHP', crossed out and altered to '10NHP'.

Since there was no 10NHP traction engine design then in production at the Works the building of this first example, which left as No.25060 on October 20, 1904, entailed a considerable number of new patterns. The change speed gears were on the offside end of the crankshaft, outside the bearings. Instead of being upon a first intermediate shaft the driven gears were mounted on a stub shaft. The cylinder was 10" bore x 12" stroke. Unlike that of the 8NHPs the smokebox was rolled separately but the boiler shell still had a circumferential lapped joint. The boiler worked at 140 p.s.i. and, in the search for economy in weight, the longitudinal rod stays through the steam space were replaced by triangular gussets fixed with angles, three at each end. By a slightly curious economy the front axle and wheels of the No.6 traction were used though the rears were of new design albeit of the conventional form. Water was carried in a 220 gallon belly tank instead of under the manstand, which was reduced to a 1' 3" wide cross platform with a guard railing on its nearside and rear. Access to the driving position was up two steps from the firing point which was formed with an open cratch for straw. These arrangements are best understood by reference to Fig.40. The engine was given a practical test at threshing on John Sherwood's Knodishall Hall Farm near Leiston where it was said to have worked well enough. There can be no doubt, though, that it was much heavier than Mattos had intended it to be and consequently, although it was accepted, it was not repeated and the design was entirely revised to follow more closely American practice before further strawburners were supplied. In order to strip off weight radical departures had to be made from what the Leiston and most other English drawing offices would have regarded as good practice. Firstly the typical English traction engine wheel had to go in favour of a bar spoked tension wheel. In this, ⅞"round spokes of Lowmoor BB iron were threaded at each end. One end was screwed into tapped holes in the hub at an angle and secured with a cast iron tapered washer and back nut. At the other it passed on the rake through the steel tyre. On the inner face there was another cast iron tapered washer and a back nut. On the outside, however, a flat was machined onto the outer ring of the wheel at right angles to the centre line of the spoke and a fixing nut on a lock washer was tightened down onto this. Strakes gave way to echelon pattern grips.

To suit this light pattern of wheel the differential was moved to the single intermediate shaft from which double drive was used to rings of gear bolted to pressed steel spiders on each of the wheels (Fig.44). In a further concession to North American practice a flywheel clutch replaced the primary drive pinion. Where the first intermediate shaft would have been there was an idler pinion on a stub shaft, the second travelling speed necessarily having been another sacrifice to this relentless process of lightening and cheapening. This altered gear train was on the nearside of the engine. The steering position remained on that side using the same components as before. The belly tank was kept but the iron straw cratch was discarded.

The purpose of the changes was not only to save weight but also to save cost, a cause advanced further by the engines being classed as 'black' i.e. no machining, fettling up or polishing being done where not essential to the fitting up and running of the engine. The painting standard was also reduced but I do not have the details. Five engines (Nos.25406, 25407, 25408, 25409, and 25410) were despatched to Mattos in 1905 on September 25 (the first two) and October 2 (the remainder) followed by another five (Nos.25575-25579 inclusive) in the second half of November.

Further modifications were still called for and the drawings were revised once more in 1906, though this time the amendments were mainly of detail rather than in principle. The four engines of this design (Nos.25936-25939 inclusive) supplied to Mattos in September, 1906, were followed by a further batch of five (Nos.27176, 27177, 27179, 27180, and 27181) supplied to him in September/October, 1908, for the Ministerio Obras Publicas in Buenos Aires and a final group of three sent in October/November, 1908 (Nos. 27353, 27354, and 27355). These engines were equipped with a fire fighting hose connected to the Moore's steam feed pump with which they were provided. After delivery of No.27355 the arrangement with Mattos seems to have ceased. Meanwhile, however, two of the 10NHP strawburners had been sold through Osias Ausschnitt of Galatz into Roumania. These were Nos.25742 (April 7, 1906) and 26145 (sent on March 14, 1907). The final example to be sold was No.32317 sent to Eugen Behles in Bucharest on April 16, 1914.

Before the line of 10NHP engines had petered out, however, there had been a further and smaller design produced in response to an enquiry for a 6NHP strawburner from Palmer Graham & Co., the firm's long-standing trading partners, mostly in portables and threshers, in Rostoff-on-Don. For this the drawing office used a similar arrangement to the first layout of the 10NHP i.e. with the sliding pinion rather than the flywheel clutch in the primary drive. The cylinder and trunk guide patterns of the 6NHP ordinary traction engine were used as was the unfailing steering wheel to pattern T41, in this case telling uncomprehending Russian drivers, in a language and alphabet they did not understand, to turn anti-clockwise for left and clockwise for right, as it had done already for drivers speaking Roumanian, Spanish, French, and Portuguese. Only in the firebox and ashpan area was the engine remarkable. In the firebox, which, unlike the 10NHPs, had a solid foundation ring, the first 1' 4" forward from the firehole door was a sloping dead plate, with deep firebars in the front part of the box. The dead plate could be replaced by bars when used for burning coal or wood. There was also a very elaborate baffle plate to deflect rising fragments of burning straw back over the firebox before entering the tubes. This again was removable for burning other fuels, being hung on studs projecting from the firebox sides, about which it pivoted for cleaning. In the use of the baffle and the dead plate the design was following American experience. Straw, on the whole, required less air for combustion than coal on a volume to volume basis, since its density was so much lower. Providing the necessary air at the front of the grate caused flame to impinge on the baffle and to be deflected backwards before entering the tubes, thereby restricting spark emission to a minimum whilst keeping an intense source of flame in contact with all of the heating surface in the firebox. The firebars for straw were thinner and more closely spaced than those for wood.

The ashpan was fitted with a watertight open-topped trough in front of the forward damper, another idea borrowed from the Americans, so that ashes could be raked out into water and quenched. These aspects of the firebox and ashpan reflected a very healthy apprehension of the risks of fire involved in working a strawburner, surrounded as it was by its fuel and the debris of threshing. How these features, as incorporated into this design, worked in practice is not on record but as no repeat orders ensued No.28373, which left the Works on August 16, 1910, remained the only example of its class. Thereafter the building of strawburning traction engines languished for a decade and a half until, under the AGE regime, it was revived by an order from Argentina as narrated in Chapter 8.

Fig.45. *The last pre-war design of Garrett strawburner, of 6NHP, designed for Palmer Graham & Co. of Rostoff-on-Don.*

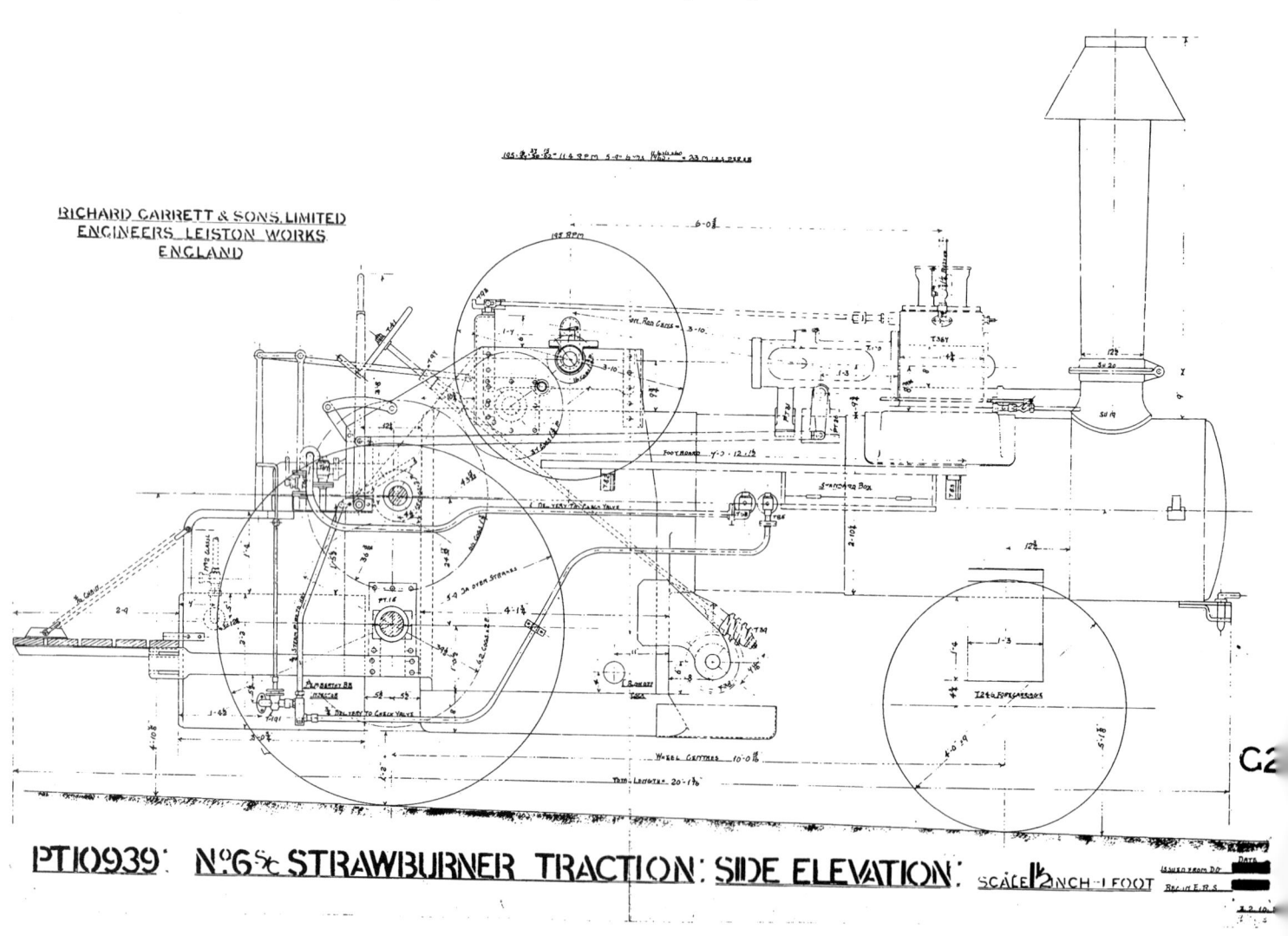

Fig.46. *Garretts' first involvement in steam cultivation albeit an oblique one. Halkett's guideway system (1855), used on his farm at West Hill, Wandsworth, was powered by 6NHP Garrett portables. Too involved for practical use the invention was soon abandoned.*

Fig.47. *Though roundabout tackle was time-consuming to set up it had a low capital cost and the advantage that it worked effectively.*

Fig.48 (below). *The patent drawing of the Savory plougher, examples of which Garretts sent to the 1864 Newcastle trials.*

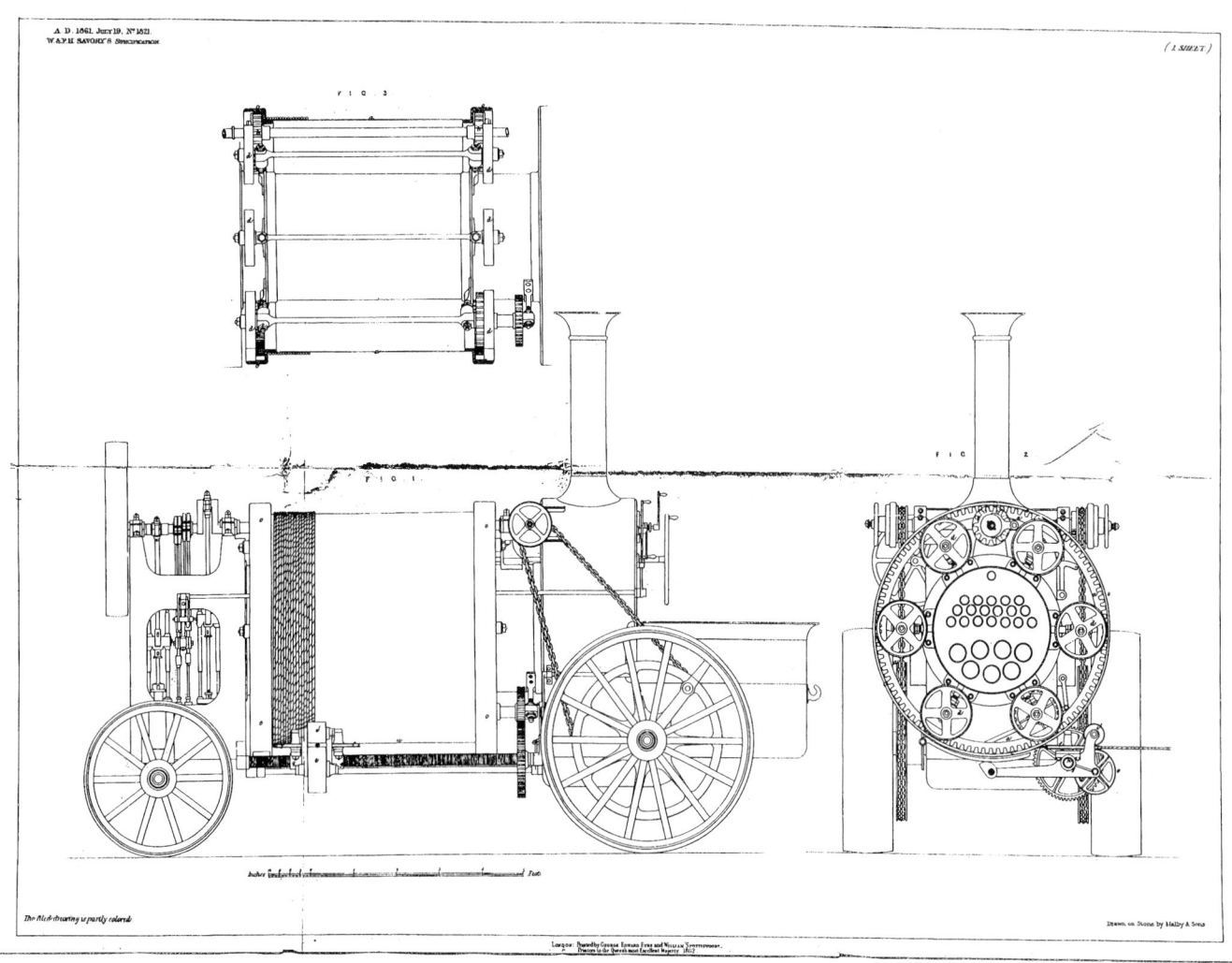

Fig.49. The Rudolph Sack system of steam ploughing as first applied viz. on a portable engine. [Stadtarchiv Leipzig]

Fig.50 (below). The same system applied to a self-moving portable engine.
[Stadtarchiv Leipzig]

Fig.51. The third step in the progression - the Sack system on a 10NHP traction engine- from an engraving, no photograph being traceable. The Sack official history described this as 16 horse-power! [Stadtarchiv Leipzig]

Fig.52. As early as 1896 Sack had designed and built an internal combustion engined cable ploughing set. In this he was a pioneer.
[Stadtarchiv Leipzig]

Figs. 53 and 54. The elevation and cross-section (from a damaged original) respectively of the 8NHP ploughing engine designed for Sack and sold under his name.

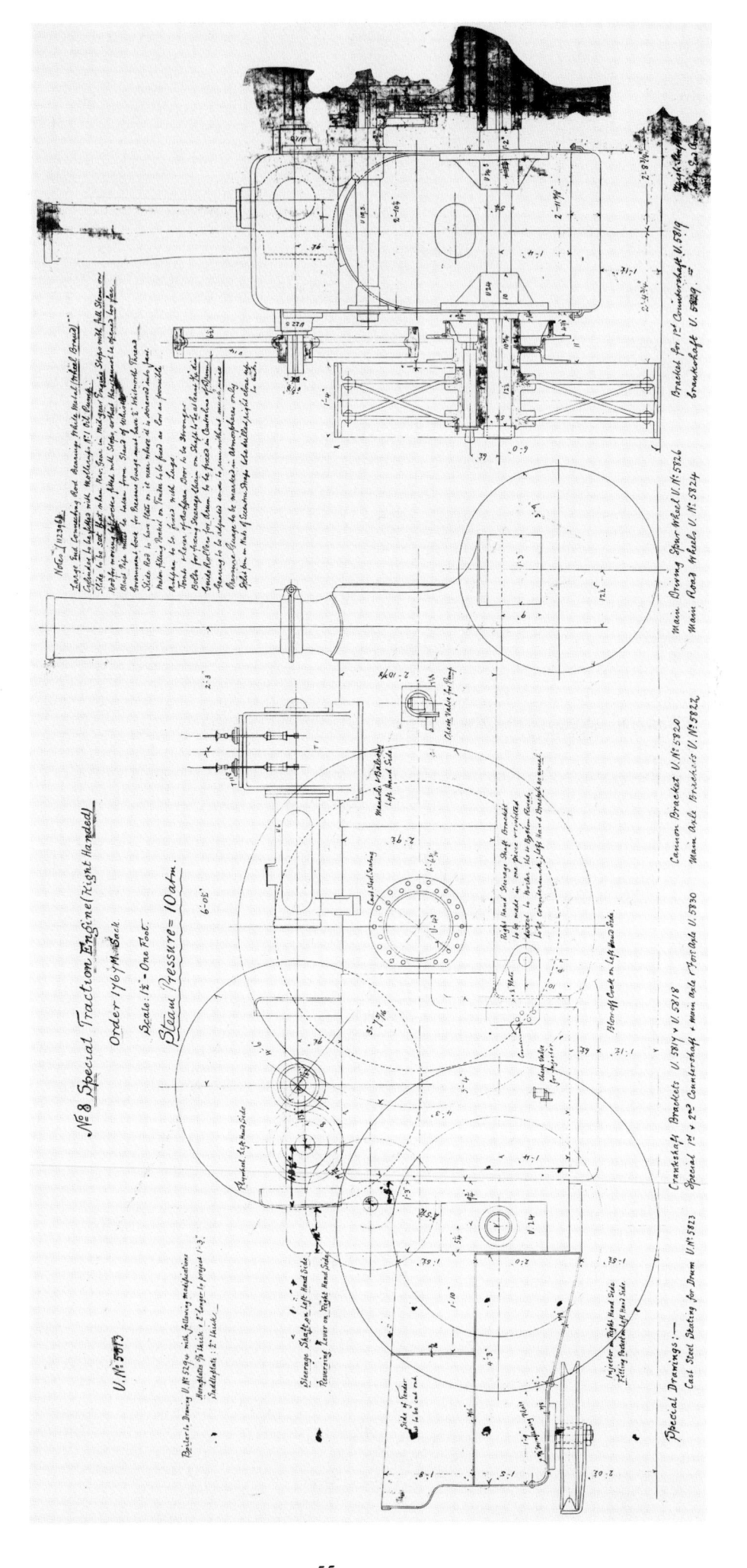

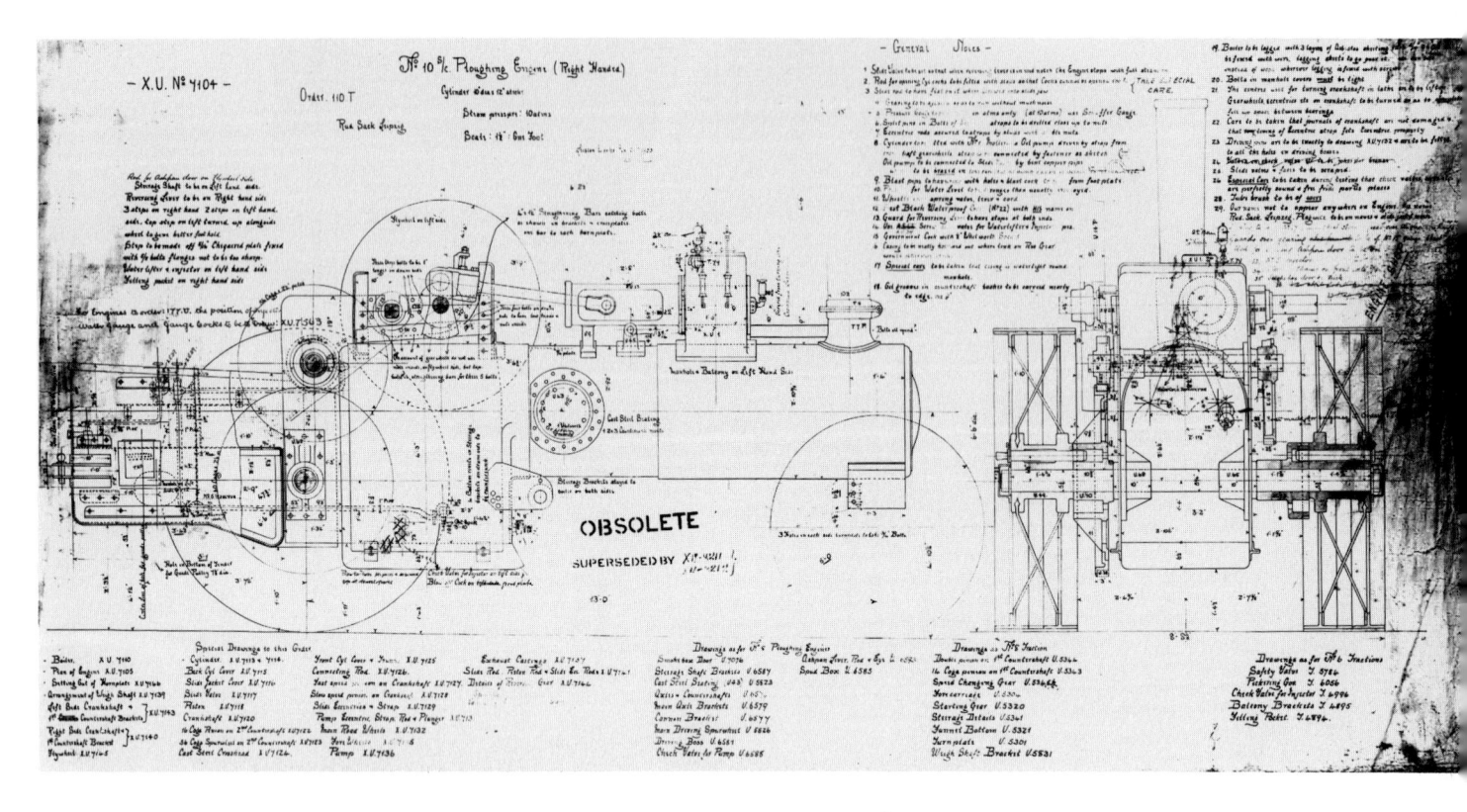

Fig. 55. *A 10NHP Garrett/Sack ploughing engine of the penultimate design.*

Fig. 56. *The summary of results of the Newcastle Ploughing Trials 1864. Column 'A' included 12½% for wear and tear and 5% for interest per annum divided over 200 working days. The ploughing was 7 inches deep.*

Maker	Price	Time to raise steam	Working pressure p.s.i.	Time to set down tackle	Soil moved per acre tons	Nature of work	Working time h. m.	Fuel consumed c. q. lb.	Work done a. r. p.	No. of acres —day of ten hours	Cost of coal per acre at 1s. per cwt.	Wear and tear and interest on capital per day	Labour and oil per day	Total cost per acre
Fowler Two - 7 h.p.	£1,034	50 min.	70	—	775	Cultivation	3 47	5 1 0	5 0 22	13.58	1s. 2d.	18s. 1.1d.	18s. 0d.	3s. 8d.
do.	£1,066	do.	90	12 min.	—	Ploughing	5 28	7 3 25	4 2 36	8.64	1s. 8.3d.	18s. 7.8d.	18s. 0d.	5s. 11.1d.
Garrett Two - 12 h.p.	£1,028 10s.	56 min.	73	—	691	Cultivation	2 49	11 1 14	5 0 1	17.77	2s. 3.3d.	17s. 11.9d.	17s. 6d.	4s. 3.2d.
do.	£1,175	do.	90	6 min.	—	Ploughing	5 35	13 0 20	4 3 16	8.69	2s. 8.6d.	20s. 6.2d.	17s. 6d.	7s. 1.1d.
Savory One - 12 h.p.	£726	50 min.	100	—	749	Cultivation	Time not taken due to accident	—	4 3 20	—	—	—	16s. 0d.	—
do.	£785	do.	100	47 min.	—	Ploughing	4 58	8 3 25	3 0 27	6.38	2s. 9.9d.	13s. 8.8d.	16s. 0d.	7s. 5.5d.
Fowler One - 14 h.p.	£875	1 hr. 19 min.	105	—	920	Cultivation (digging)	6 3	9 2 14	5 0 10	8.37	1s. 10.7d.	15s. 3.6d.	16s. 0d.	5s. 7.5d.
do.	£875	do.	100	40 min.	—	Ploughing	5 29	6 0 25	3 1 2	5.34	1s. 10.8d.	15s. 3.7d.	16s. 0d.	7s. 2d.

'A'

Chapter 5

Ploughing Engines and New Zealand Tractions

In Chapter One I quoted the somewhat dismissive words on rope haulage systems of steam ploughing spoken by Richard Garrett after Fowler's paper on the subject had been delivered to a meeting of the Royal Society of Arts on January 30, 1856. Richard stated a preference for Boydell's ideas on direct traction but looked forward to a system of implements mounted on the actual engine, a method that a hundred years later carried the day though not, it is true, with a steam engine as the motive power.

As the double engine system had yet to be brought into use his comments upon rope haulage were aimed at the so-called 'round-about' system then practised, in which a portable engine provided the power for a double drum windlass, moving the implement by hempen ropes to the respective drums on the windlass, the ropes passing through fixed and movable anchors and being supported by rope porters. The method did not require the portable engine to be reversible. Changing the direction of pull was done by disengaging the drive pinion from one drum and engaging it with the other. Practical success attended this arrangement by the mid-1850s. In 1855 Fowler patented a system in which the engine and the double drum windlass were on the same frame, though not self-moving. Working independently, William Smith, a farmer of Little Woolston, Bucks, designed a system in which a cultivator, made for him by James & Frederick Howard of Bedford, was hauled by a windlass of his own design powered by a Ransomes portable engine. Smith, who did not believe in the use of the plough, preferring the cultivator, patented his system in 1857 and thereafter many sets of such equipment were made by the Howards, who did believe in ploughs, being noted makers of that implement. This involved them in wordy disagreements with Smith, who was also at odds with Fowler whom he accused of pirating his ideas.

Notwithstanding the senior partner's lack of conviction concerning the method a number of Garrett portables were sold for working with tackle of this type. Garrett catalogues offering roundabout tackle gave purchasers the options of Howard ploughs, Coleman cultivators, or Steevens ploughs, the latter a double ended implement, carried on a pair of main carrying wheels amidships and single land wheels at each end of the frame. At each reversal the shares of the Steevens plough were raised and lowered by worm and rack. It is likely that initially only the portable engine of such an outfit was built at Leiston. When a similar selection of items was shown at the 1862 Royal Show at Battersea the catalogue description contained no suggestion that Garretts had made any part of it save the engine but, on the other hand, the report in the *Mechanics Magazine* of December 12, 1862, (page 375) on the Garrett exhibit of a portable engine and Howard type plough at the Royal Smithfield Show that year inferred that both were built at Leiston.

Knowledge of who had portable engine ploughing tackle is only fragmentary. In a ledger entry in 1865, for instance, a charge occurs to W.B. Chandler of Sutton, near Woodbridge, (formerly of Hacheston) for 'ploughing engine parts'. Later that year I.H. Hutchinson, 27 Craven Street, Strand, London, was invoiced for 'Steam cultivating apparatus £485.0.0' - plainly for use elsewhere. In November, 1865, Thomas Nunn of Constantinople bought a 10NHP portable engine, together with a 'steam plow and harrows' for which he was charged £323.19.5. The freight, insurance, and shipping charges amounted to a further £66.4.10. Nothing more is known.

A group of ledger entries which I find very intriguing occurs in 1867 and 1870. The earliest records the sale, in August, 1867, of a 'Patent cultivator to design £400.0.0', followed by a second invoice in September for 'Completing cultivator'. The consignee was Colonel B. Christoforoff of Nickopol, Odessa. What the cultivator was, and whether or not it was self-propelling remains unknown. Christoforoff paid by instalments, the two earlier ones in April (£60.0.0) and June, 1867 (£40.0.0), whilst the building of the cultivator was still in progress, and the balance by degrees over the next year. In 1870 a second Christoforoff cultivator was made and shipped, this time invoiced, under the date March 10, to His Highness Prince Woronzow in Odessa at a cost of £304.2.0. The amounts charged for these cultivators suggest they must have been elaborate mechanisms as at that time an 8NHP portable engine cost not much over £200, whilst an implement alone scarcely ran into three figures. Therefore it seems at least possible that they were self-propelling though the information that survives neither confirms nor denies this. In the same way it has proved impossible to establish the degree to which the Garretts were involved in building the prototype of Lieutenant Peter Halkett's elaborate guideway system of cultivation, patented in 1855, and installed on his farm at West Hill, Wandsworth, Surrey. They are known to have supplied the 6NHP engine, or engines, but no more can be determined about the transaction. Richard III's comments on engine mounted implements might have been interpreted as referring to Halkett's experiments though it seems improbable that their complication would have appealed to his critical and analytical mind. Although Halkett's name does not recur in any matters connected with the Works the name of Colonel Christoforoff and his machine come up again in September, 1876, when 'axle cranks' for it were invoiced at a cost of £60.0.0, a sum incidentally that was never paid and which had to be written off as a bad debt in 1882. Though this formed an inglorious end to what seems to have been an interesting association it does establish that the machine had a life of at least ten years.

Even after the double engine system had become well established as the principal method of steam ploughing, roundabout tackle had a long life perhaps helped by the onset of the agricultural depression. Indeed a well-known set of such tackle, powered by a McLaren traction engine, worked for the Checksfields on Romney Marsh until nearly the end of commercial steam ploughing. In that case the windlass was driven from the end of the engine's crankshaft by means of a connecting shaft with a Hooke joint at each end. Barford & Perkins of Queen Street Ironworks, Peterborough, - the Barford part of which had connections by marriage with the Garretts - were still offering roundabout tackle at the beginning of the twentieth century, worked by either a windlass powered by a portable or traction engine or by vertical drums mounted on a traction engine. At least two Garrett 8NHP traction engines (Nos.9884 and 9916) were supplied for this use which involved driving the windlass by pitch chain taking its motion from a sprocket on the offside end of the crankshaft. To accommodate the extra loading thus applied the saddle carrying the crankshaft was made 4½" wider on the flywheel side. No.9984 was sold on June 21, 1877, to Johns Brothers of Swindon from whom it went to a purchaser named Stratton in the August of that year. No.9916 was supplied via Balls Garrett of Maidstone, the Garrett partners' uncle, to a client named Godwin, leaving the Works on April 14, 1877, i.e. well before No.9884. Though Balls Garrett never aspired to the level of affluence or social standing of his nephew Frank and remained a bluff unaffected Suffolk countryman, albeit an expatriate, all his days, he was much loved by his Leiston nephews, great nephews and great nieces. Victor told the story, which he had heard from his older sisters, of how Uncle Balls, visiting Aldringham House, the home of Frank (Victor's father), for dinner, was served with the traditional Suffolk summer soup made from pea pods. 'Whoi Emma' he exclaimed, turning to his wife with a beam of delight, 'pea-shuck sup - thaas what oi've been a-wanting for years!'

Richard (IV) and Frank Garrett never pursued their father's professed interest in engine mounted implements but their brother John, after he had left Leiston in 1860 to set up in Magdeburg, designed a steam digger which he patented in 1879. The Garretts remaining at Leiston Works after his departure had, however, followed a somewhat different path having become interested in the system devised by William & Paul Haines Savory of High Orchard Ironworks, Gloucester, for double engine cable ploughing. The Savorys had developed their system from Collinson & Hall's, patented in 1859. Collinson & Hall used a large spirally grooved drum, long enough to accommodate the whole of the winding rope in a single layer. Their patent also referred to such a drum being placed around the boiler of the engine though the actual positioning was not the essence of the patent. By contrast, the Savory patent specified that the drum should be around the boiler, detailed the methods employed to drive the drum and the mechanism for guiding the rope onto and from it, the spiral groove being already covered by Collinson & Hall. This Savory patent (No.1821), dated 1861, was the one which attracted the interest of the Garretts who acquired the patent rights and the copyright in the second design of Savory ploughing engine early in 1864. The rights in other Savory patents remained with the patentees.

A return tubed boiler formed the basis of the machine. In this the smokebox was situated over the firebox at the manstand end. From the firebox a group of seven large smoke tubes, perhaps 4½" in diameter, ran forward to a smoke header at the far end of the boiler, in which the flue gases rose, to return via a bank of eighteen tubes of about 2¾" diameter to the smokebox above the firebox outer crown and thence to the chimney. The winding drum, which was a 5' 3" diameter wrought iron construction, was placed around the boiler barrel. At the ends of the drum were annular rings, toothed for part of their width to take the drive and smooth for the remainder to ride upon the locating rollers fixed to brackets carried on the boiler shell. The drum was driven by a double cylindered crank-overhead engine placed at the front of the machine. The stroke of this engine appears to have been 12". As it was rated at 12NHP on the RASE system the cylinder diameter would have been of the order of 7¾". The 90° crankshaft was part of a long shaft, about 3" in diameter, extending as far as the smoke box where it terminated in a bevel. Two pinions slid upon this shaft and could be clutched into or out of drive with the toothed sections of the annular rings. The flywheel was placed transversely across the engine at the extreme front. The drive to the road wheels was by a cross shaft driven by the bevel, already noted, on the end of the main drive shaft, the final drive to the wheels being by pitch chain. A small, almost inadequate, man-stand and bunker with a water tank beneath were fitted. The drum could take 550 yards of rope in a single lap and the coiling was controlled by an ingenious arrangement of two vertical and two horizontal pulleys fixed into a small traverser block moved by a lead screw which was powered by three pinions and a short shaft off the toothed annular ring at the footplate end. Savorys' patent catered for two separate drums on the same engine, if required, to enable the roundabout system to be used, but this was not taken up by Garretts.

Work was commenced on building a pair of engines for exhibition and competition at the Newcastle Royal Show of 1864 but they were not completed in time for the event. The engines that were sent to the Show instead of them were a pair of 12NHP engines built by Savorys themselves (or at least assembled by them), delivered in 1863 to Benjamin Bomford of Pitchill, Warwickshire. This meant that the Garretts were competing with engines made in the ordinary course of commerce rather than 'racing engines' built solely with performance on the trial ground in mind, a type of machine increasingly in evidence at the practical tests conducted by the Royal Agricultural Society of England and which tended to defeat the objectives of the trials. At Newcastle the Savory engines worked with a Steevens plough, a Howard plough, and a Howard cultivator. Independently, the Savorys had entered an engine of their own build to work as a single engine with roundabout tackle but this has no bearing on our narrative.

The two classes in the practical trial were for engines of less than 10NHP and for engines of 10NHP and over. The Garrett entry came into this second group and was thus in competition with a Fowler 14NHP single engine set and a pair of his 7NHP engines working with an endless rope and his controversial clip drum system. They were tried on a field of medium gravelly soil on the farm of Mr. Jamieson. Garretts engines worked with the Howard plough and cultivator with which they were offered for sale. They actually worked again on a second trial solely to demonstrate the Steevens plough, but this second appearance is not really relevant to this narrative. The panel of judges were D.K. Clark, H.B. Caldwell, J. Coleman, C.S. Read, and F. Sherborn (Junior). The times made by the entrants were tabulated and are shown in Fig.56. The alleged cost per acre of the work achieved is shown in the final column and would have weighed against Garretts' entry on economic grounds had the basis of calculation been sound. In fact it was fallacious and the costings, therefore, were not valid. The farming members of the panel of judges criticised the ploughing as 'untidy', and were not over-impressed by the quality of cultivation, complaining that the implement moved too fast, did not penetrate deeply enough into the soil and missed some low spots altogether. These observations were legitimate expressions of opinion and whilst the Garrett/Savory team might have not necessarily have agreed with them there were no grounds for taking exception to their having been spoken or written.

When it came to costings, however, the judges had made certain assumptions as to the cost of the overheads due to wear and tear (which heading, one supposes, comprehended both repairs and renewals and depreciation) and on capital respectively which were open to serious exception. For the former 12½% and for the latter 5% per annum distributed over an assessed annual total of two hundred working days were assumed. No fault can be found with the interest figure but the percentage for 'wear and tear' was open to grave objection under several heads. First it was applied arbitrarily to all entries without any attempt having been made to assess their probable useful working life. Secondly it made the tacit assumption that the annual repair bill for a cheap engine would be less than that for a dearer engine, an assumption so manifestly flying in the face of probability as to need no further consideration. Thirdly it made no attempt to assess the relative reliability of the entries and their proneness or otherwise to mechanical upsets.

The fallacy underlying its application is amply demonstrated when the case of the prize-winning pair of 7NHP engines is considered. These were purchased after the Show by the Honourable A.H. Vernon, one of the Stewards of the Yard, but had a working life of only two years. They were, as events proved, much too lightly constructed for the work for which they were intended and were unable to resist the stresses imposed upon them in day to day work. Ordinary engine drivers, as opposed to the highly trained show team, found it difficult to synchronise their actions and cases occurred of the engines pulling against each other at the end of a pull, sometimes with damaging results. For instance, one engine was brought to its knees by having the forecarriage pulled apart.

How the judges came to appraise the costs in such an ill-conceived fashion is difficult to understand. David Clark was an immensely experienced mechanical engineer involved in the design of both railway and road locomotives. For such a man to have resorted to rule of thumb to evade assessing the cost of maintenance, liability to breakdown, and probable length of working life appears to border on the ludicrous. In the judges' assessments of costs Garretts' entry was second to the Fowler 7NHP double engine set. Had the allowance for depreciation and repairs to the latter set been corrected to a realistic figure, for even an assumed life expectancy of five years would have flattered their actual lives, their running cost would have been increased by some two shillings per acre making their work the most expensive in the Show. It may be objected that the judges could not have been expected to display second-sight, but it needs to be remembered also that practical men contemplating the purchase of steam ploughing equipment might reasonably have looked for observations from the judges on the likely soundness of the exhibits relative to one another couched in language that would have assisted them in deciding which equipment to buy. The failure of the judges to deliver such advice led Richard Garrett to make a spirited protest to the RASE, which was followed up by a letter to the Editor of *The Engineer* published in the issue of October 14, 1864, and worded thus:

THE STEAM PLOUGHING TRIALS AT NEWCASTLE-ON-TYNE

SIR,- You did us the favour voluntarily to insert in your columns our protest against the awards of the judges in the steam cultivating classes, at the meeting of the Royal Agricultural Society of England, in July last; may we now beg you to kindly insert this letter in review of the report of the judges of steam cultivators, which has just appeared in the second part of the 25th volume of the Journal of the Society more than two months after the trials took place?

We competed with a pair of engines on Savory's principle, of our own manufacture; but these engines not being completed in time for trial, we exhibited a pair of engines which were manufactured last year by Messrs, Savory, for Mr. Bowford [sic.] of Pitchill, near Evesham; on the 8th of July we informed the secretary of the Royal Agricultural Society of England, by letter, that the engines we had sent were not of our own manufacture, stating, at the same time, that if this circumstance would disqualify the engines should they be found worthy of a prize, we were desirous of withdrawing from the competitive trials. We received no reply to our communication before leaving for Newcastle, and on our arrival there we at once represented the case to the Society's officials, by whom we were requested to proceed to trial. We mention this because we have been accused by one of the leading agricultural journals of sailing under false colours! We protested against the awards of the judges, at Newcastle, as soon as they were published, because we considered that in making those awards, they 'took no notice of the main points in which our engines and tackle are manifestly superior'; a careful consideration of their report has confirmed us in this opinion. We were well aware that competing as we did with engines manufactured in the ordinary course of trade, and which had been through some six months work, in Mr. Bowford's hands, we should not stand in a good position with reference to the consumption of fuel, when compared with the performance of 'racing engines', manufactured expressly for competition.

Our experience in steam cultivation has, however, shown us that 'consumption of fuel' is by no means the most important point to be considered by employers of steam cultivating machinery, and we were rash enough to anticipate that some other elements would be taken into consideration by the judges in arriving at their final decision. We believe the question of 'wear and tear', with reference to the means employed for hauling the implement, stands uppermost in the minds of those men who have had any lengthened practical experience with steam cultivating machinery, and we are convinced that the capability of performing a large amount of work in a given time will be considered a very important point before steam will be generally adopted in preference to horse labour in the cultivation of the soil. A careful perusal of the judges' report will show that, in making their awards at Newcastle, they were mainly guided by the consumption of fuel; thus reducing the whole trial to a simple test of the engines and boilers; no attempt was made to arrive at the comparative merits of the various systems brought under their notice in other more important points.

With regard to the 'wear and tear' a paragraph attached to the tabular statement in page 397 of the Society's journal speaks for itself:

'The same figures were adopted for 'wear and tear', and interest as in the Worcester report, viz., 12½ per cent. for 'wear and tear', and 5 per cent. for interest, divided over 200 days'.

With the following competitors before them, viz.: 1st, Fowler's well-known system, with 14-horse power engine, and self-moving anchor; 2nd, Fowler's double engine system, 'the chief novelty of the show'; 3rd, Savory's engines, with two winding drums and self-moving anchor, the first engine made on this principle. And, 4th, our double engines on Savory's principle, introduced at the Worcester Show; the judges surely cannot wish it to be understood that no one had the advantage in this most important point.

Did the simple rule of three, adopted at Worcester, apply to all equitably and justly? If so, the matter might have been settled by simply taking the selling price at which each apparatus was entered in the Society's catalogue without going through the farce of a trial.

> Do the consulting engineers of the Society endorse this? We are under the impression that the judges did not feel competent, with the opportunities afforded them, of forming an opinion on the subject, and, consequently, they got out of the difficulty by applying to 'novelties' they had never before seen, 'the same figures as in the Worcester report'. Can anything be imagined more unjust to the competitors, or more likely to mislead the public?
> With reference to the capability of getting over a large amount of work, we are aware that to make good-looking work with the plough, it must not travel beyond a certain speed. With the cultivator the case is different, and we see no reason why twenty to thirty acres of land may not be cultivated in a day with Savory's engines.
> On reference to page 401 of the Society's journal it will be seen that we were working at the rate of 17.77 acres per ten hours with two 12-horse power engines, the price of which was £1,028 10s. Fowler's two nominal 7-horse power engines costing £1,034, worked at the rate of 13.58 acres in the same time: while Fowler's ordinary 14-horse power engines, with travelling anchor worked at the rate of 8.37 acres per day. Should this count for nothing? The judges think it ought, and, instead of giving us any credit for this performance, they say, in a paragraph on page 402 of their Journal, 'Notwithstanding the excessive pace, the consumption of fuel was enormous' (not so much, however, as with Fowler's single engine system), from which we gather that, with the excessive pace, they expected a reduced consumption! This is scarcely to be credited in these days of blockade runners and limited mail trains. We still adhere to our protest, and maintain that the judges at the Newcastle trials did not ascertain the relative merits of the competing systems of steam cultivation, as regards wear and tear; that they did not give due consideration to the capability of performing a large amount of work in a given time; nor to the facility for moving the tackle from place to place, and setting down to work; on which points we also contend that Savory's patent engines, as manufactured by us, are manifestly superior to any others.
> The judges' awards, as the reports clearly show, were based on the consumption of fuel alone, thus; and on this point, as we have explained, we were at a manifest disadvantage, but have no fear as to what the result would have been, if we had been working under the same conditions as our competitors.
> The judges awarded us a 'high commendation' for 'improvements in double engines', which, under the circumstances well-known to the Society's officials, we were clearly not entitled to, the engines being Messrs. Savory's own manufacture. This 'high commendation card' we returned to the Society with the best grace our feelings would allow, and notified our intention of finally withdrawing from the competitive trials of the Royal Agricultural Society of England, under the conviction that the system, as at present carried out, is productive of no benefit to the manufacturers or the employers of agricultural machinery.
> We tender you our best thanks for the opportunity thus afforded us of bringing our case before the public, and with this explanation we are quite satisfied to abide by their verdict in the matter at issue between us and the Royal Agricultural Society of England.
>
> R. GARRETT AND SON
>
> Leiston Works, Suffolk, October 10, 1864.

Critics of the Savory design made much of the speed at which the implements were worked. With the gear ratios used by Savorys (14 to 104) and an engine speed of 165 r.p.m. the resultant speed of the implement was slightly in excess of 4.m.p.h. whereas the pundits would have preferred not more than 3 m.p.h. As John Haining and Colin Tyler remarked in *Ploughing by Steam* this implied that the critics, the most notable of whom was J.A. Clarke, were condemning the whole Savory principle when all that was in question was the gear ratio. To have amended the ratio, however, would have needed a reduction in the driving pinions to 11 teeth, thus making them dimensionally unsound from an engineering point of view. Conversely, to have reduced the speed of the implement by the alternative method of knocking 25% off the rate of the engine's revolutions would have dealt a serious blow to its power output and restricted the rope haulage capacity in all but the lightest soils. The Savorys were, therefore, in a very real dilemma. They could not placate their critics by altering the gear ratio whilst to have done so by reducing engine revolutions without restricting the capacity for work would have meant putting up the cylinder diameter to 8¾" or thereabouts, an amendment that would have meant considerable redesigning at the front end to make room for the changes. Justified or unjustified, however, the comments of the Newcastle judges gave an immense boost to Fowler and killed any chances of success there were for plant of Savory's pattern. Viewed with hindsight the Fowler double engine system as subsequently developed was superior to that of the Savorys, but the clip drum shown at Newcastle was a failure and should have been seen as such and condemned.

Little further dimensional data or detail of the engines and boilers used on the Savory engines survives. The Leiston Works engine memorandum books had spaces left in them for two pairs of ploughers, but no particulars were entered. At the time that I wrote *Garretts of Leiston* this led me to doubt if they had been completed, but subsequent research in the accounting books of the firm showed that they were. This is disclosed by entries in the *Distant Counties Ledger*. Thus in November, 1865, the Shrewsbury Steam Cultivating Co. were charged for 'guide brackets for ploughing engine drums'; the following April there was a charge to Wm. Savory & Son at High Orchard Works for 'repairing ploughing engine £112. 9. 2.' As to the second pair the evidence comes from the same source for 1871 and 1872 wherein Haughton &

Thompson of Lowther Street, Carlisle, were debited in November, 1871, with 'One pair of Savory ploughing engines, at £886. 12. 9. Again in the *Rough Entry Book for New Patterns*, running from February 3, 1868, to September, 1881, there is an entry for August 31, 1870, of 'New patterns for 12h.p. Ploughing engine', against which is scrawled 'Savory's'. The patterns listed were:

    1 post for steerage
    1 table for do.
    2 brackets for do.
    1 pulley for do 5" di. by 2"
    1 starting gare [sic] slip
    1 24" x 5½" pulley altered to flywheel'

Again on October 7, 1870, an entry occurs thus, under a similar heading:

    1 roler [sic] for rope guide 4" di by 16" long
        strickel to do.
    1 friction pulley 5" di by 2"

In *Journeyman's Ledger No.2* there are a number of relevant entries:

    November 26, 1870   W. Clow; 18 days putting traction engines to work at Carlisle
    March 13, 1871   W. Clow; 14 days putting traction engines to work at Carlisle
        Geo. Ede; 14 days time at Haughton & Thompson's, Carlisle,
            putting ploughing engines to work

In the *General Ledger 7 A-G* (1867) there is a debit to Thomas Corbett, of Castle Foregate, Shrewsbury, for 'coiling apparatus for steam cultivating tackle £22.13.8' and again on page 235 there is an entry dated August, 1869, against Brown Lock & Maude of Shrewsbury for 'worm wheel and pinion for Savory's engine £17. 0. 3', supposedly relating to one of the Shrewsbury Steam Cultivating Co. engines. The Shrewsbury pair does not appear subsequently in a recognisable entry in Garretts books. Haughton & Thompson seem to have failed in their payments, and their engines were repossessed and sold, as in February and April, 1872, ploughing engines at £150 each were sold to D.W. Stanfield, Willow Holme, Carlisle, and Wheatley Kirk & Price of Manchester. How and when the four engines finished their lives is not known to me. With regard to the Pitchill engines that were sent to the Newcastle trial the late Douglas Bomford told me that they did not have a particularly successful career, suffering by comparison with slightly later Fowler sets, and were scrapped early.

With the final disposal of the unfortunate Savory-type ploughers the Garrett interest in steam ploughing came to an end for some years. Its revival came about through a commercial acquaintanceship begun in the 1860s. In 1863 Rudolph Sack, a German agricultural engineer, had established a works for the manufacture of agricultural machines, mainly ploughs and drills, at Plagwitz near Leipzig. His ploughs, especially potato ploughs, soon made a good name for themselves and Sack implements were sold all over Eastern and Central Europe. For a decade or so, from the mid-1860s to the mid seventies, Garretts included some of them in their catalogues for sales in the United Kingdom. As the firm flourished so Plagwitz grew and was finally merged into Leipzig in 1891. The firm survived all the vicissitudes to which German industry was subjected in this century, including nationalisation under the German Democratic Republic, and only finally succumbed in 1993. By the mid-1890s Sack had become interested in double engine ploughing, having designed a vertical drum system based upon portable engines. In this a reversible engine with a wet bottomed firebox (see Fig.49) was equipped with a manstand, tub bunkers, and a water tank below the boiler. The drum, mounted upon a boss studded and nutted to a pad rivetted to the boiler, took its drive via an internal ring of gear from a mating gear on the end of the crankshaft capable of being clutched into and out of drive. Incidentally, for the roundabout method he had also devised a double drum windlass, powered by an internal combustion engine. Both this and the portable steam engine sets were being offered by 1896.

It is possible that the portables were fitted with a winding forward winch to enable them to move themselves along the headland but there is no evidence of such a fitting on the engraving. There is in existence, however, a further and much less precise illustration, in the form of a woodcut (Fig.50) showing a variant of the portable design, and, moreover, the opposite hand, in which straked traction wheels have replaced the carrying wheels under the firebox, and a suggestion of a driving chain appears between the crankshaft and axle.

It is not difficult to see that working the double engine system with Sack's self-moving portables might have had shortcomings sufficient to lead to his being interested in ploughing engines of more conventional type. Exactly how chance brought him into contact with Garretts in pursuit of this end is not so easy to define. The contact was effected through Paul Behrens of Magdeburg who seems to have been an acquaintance of Carl Remy. One assumes that his earlier dealing with the Garretts may have prompted his discussions first with Behrens and then with Remy. Sack required the engine part of a 6NHP vertical drum ploughing engine without the drum or its driving mechanism which he proposed to add in Germany. The likelihood seems to be that he had seen No.20485 and considered that, with modifications, it would suit his purpose. The amendments that he requested to the standard design were such as would provide the space needed for the ploughing gear. The smokebox lower plate was extended forward 8" at the bottom enabling the perch bracket to be set forward by the same amount. As it was to be a right-hand engine the right-hand rear travelling wheel was moved out 3½"further from the boiler centre line and the left-hand wheel by 2 inches, necessitating a longer axle. The crankshaft was lengthened on the pump side by 4" and the end left square, the right-hand crankshaft end brasses being increased to 6" long. A cast steel seating, of Sack's design but supplied by Garretts, was rivetted to the boiler barrel, immediately forward of the joint between the firebox wrapper plate and the barrel, to receive the ploughing drum. This was set with a circle of 1" Whitworth studs, the drum and drum stud being supplied and fixed by Sack in Leipzig.

Sack's system, largely borrowed from the Everitt & Adam's patents, mounted the vertical drum., which was 6' 6¾" in diameter, upon this steel seating. Apart from providing the crankshaft extension on the drum side, with the squared end for Sack to mount the drum drive on, Leiston had no further part in the ploughing gear drive, the clutch mechanism being also put on by Sack. Under the floor of the tender tank Sack fixed a grooved pulley, about 2' 9" in diameter. The wire rope ran from the drum rearward, between the road wheel and the firebox, passed round the pulley, leaving on the nearside of the engine. Garretts' part in these arrangements was limited to increasing the tender plates to ³/₈" thickness, and ensuring a flat surface for the pulley mounting to be fixed to, which entailed countersinking eight of the rivets.

This engine, No.21452, was completed in mid-March, 1898, and sent away from Leiston on March 26. Its price thus modified was £420. 0. 0. After this there was a pause, presumably while the engine was completed in Leipzig and tried, though there is no record of this. How the engine was tested in work is not known for certain. He might have used one of his portable engines at the other end of the field but as there were plenty of Fowler engines in Germany at that time it could equally easily have been paired off to work with one of them. No.22059, the second, i.e. left-hand, engine was duly ordered and was despatched on March 21, 1899. Apart from its being handed it differed only in that it was specified to be without a differential and that Garretts' name was to appear nowhere upon it, Sack's name and city being cast on the rear wheel naves instead.

The conclusion drawn from the results obtained by testing No.21452 in service appears to have been that a rather more powerful engine, i.e. of 8NHP, was needed. Whereas producing the 6NHP ploughers had merely involved the amendment of the traction engines already in production an entirely new design was required to build an 8NHP. It is not clear to whom Schmach delegated the execution of this project. His choice rested between Arthur Girling, Thomas Jones, and a third steam engine draughtsman then in the office, named W.H. Florey. Possibly it was Arthur Girling who ran the project as later drawings for 8NHP ploughers bore his initials. Certainly work on the drawings and patterns was already in hand when the second 6NHP engine was shipped. The boiler plates for the first pair of eights were ordered on December 5, 1898. Although the boiler barrel was longer in these engines, the forward extension of the smokebox was still found to be necessary. These engines and the 6NHPs which had preceded them did not have the dished smokebox door with the central dart fastening as in the traction engines, but the smokebox front was closed by a flat plate, divided horizontally and hinged above the line of the top row of tubes, the opening lower section being secured by two dog catches. This resulted in a very airtight joint which pleased Sack. The single cylinder design was retained, the bore going up to 9", but in other respects the general layout of the 6NHPs was carried through into the larger design. The first pair, Nos.22223 (right-hand) and 22224 (left-hand) were sent off two weeks apart on August 1 and 15, 1899. A further pair followed in late Autumn, 1900, and a third set three months later, whereafter there was a pause until June, 1902, when 23730 and 23734 went, and after another gap the final pair (24612 and 24613) were sent in March, 1903.

Dimensionally the boilers were identical to those subsequently fitted to the 8NHP single cylinder traction engines, already discussed in Chapter 3, and to the details given in Appendix 1. The working pressure is believed to have been 9 atmospheres but this is not certain. The boilers, originally to Drawing No.5294 of 1898, were redrawn several times, first in November, 1900, to 6039, again in February, 1902 (No.6568) and finally, for the last pair, in January, 1903 (Drawing 7066), but the revised drawings often merely represented the formal record of changes made during the work of construction in the boiler shop. Mostly the revisions related to minor changes in the siting of holes and fittings, but that on No.6039, however, increased the length of the smokebox by 6", abolished the projection of the bottom plate, and substituted the dished door with centre fastening for the original arrangement. The boiler pressure was increased to 10 atmospheres in the revision of February, 1902.

In the engine and gearing the bearing brasses on the crankshaft and countershaft were generally 6" wide, but on the drum end of the crankshaft no less than 8¼" wide, the bearing brackets being of correspondingly heavy construction of cast steel. Some problems appear to have been experienced with end float of the crankshaft and flexing of the hornplates as in the 1902 revision 4" x 1¼" steel strengthening bars were arranged horizontally along either hornplate, planed each end to fit over the flange of the cross plates of the crankbox so as to pick up the bolts holding the bearing brackets. A note written on Drawing 7067 of 1903 said:
> Especial care must be taken so that gear wheels and eccentrics completely fill up space between shoulder on crankshaft and bearing.

In the 1903 revision the bore of the cylinders was increased to 9½", the stroke remaining at 12".

The success of these engines led on to an order for three pairs of 10NHP singles in which the cylinder bore was increased to 10", the general arrangement of the engines remaining much the same albeit with a larger boiler, in which the firebox was 6" longer, though the barrel remained the same length. The main change in the barrel was that the smokebox and front ring were rolled out of one plate and that the plate thickness was increased from ½" to 9/16". The working pressure continued to be 10 atmospheres. The engines contained a proportion of components in common with the 8NHP ploughers and 8NHP tractions. Thus the drum seating, axles and countershafts, main axle brackets, cannon bracket, main driving spur wheel and driving boss were as in the 8NHP ploughers as were various lesser components such as the smokebox door and fittings, the steerage shaft brackets, pump check valve and ashpan lever, rod and eye and spud box. The rest of the steering gear, forecarriage and turnplate were as used in the 8NHP traction engines as were the gears on the first countershaft and the speed changing gear. Items such as the funnel bottom and smokestand were common to all the 8NHP engines. A few details, of which the safety valves, Pickering governors and injector check valve are examples, were common to all the traction engines and ploughers. On the other hand the cylinder, trunk, pistons, crosshead, the gears on the second countershaft, the slow speed on the countershaft, and virtually all the Stephenson link motion were new designs as were all the road wheels, and the pump together with the pump eccentric, strap and plunger. A weakness of this and of the preceding 8 and 6NHP ploughers was the positioning of the pump and injector check valves on the firebox sides. The wheels of the 10NHP engines were 22" wide and the fronts were 16" wide. On the drum side both front and rear wheels were set 2⅝" further from the engine centre line than on the flywheel side. The numbers and dates of despatch, in 1904, of the three pairs, giving the right-hand engine first, in each case, were 24835 (May 5), 24836 (June 10), 24869 (July 30), 24870 (August 30), 25076 (December 15) and 25077 (December 30). A further pair were sent in the Spring of 1905, namely 25300 (March 28) and 25301 (April 3). In 1907 two more pairs followed, 26087 (March 4) and 26088 (February 23) with 26411 and 26412 leaving on May 18 and 31. Between the 1905 and 1907 batches the drawings were redrawn on linen to enable Works copies to be made as blueprints in place of the earlier practice of having copies traced onto linen by boy tracers. There had been a more or less continuous series of minor changes, some merely to save money in building the engines, but some marking real improvements such as adopting asbestos packed blow-down valves in lieu of the plain plug cocks on earlier examples. No engines left between May, 1907, and late Winter, 1909.

During this intervening period it appears that a few further minor amendments were made to the drawings, not all of which were to the liking of Sack as will become apparent. The first pair to be despatched after this pause were Nos.27349 and 27350, sent on February 27 and March 25, 1909. These were the cause of an upset with Sack which was a contributory factor in bringing the arrangement to an end. In the Summer of 1909 a complaint concerning these engines, so extraordinary as to be almost unbelievable, reached the Works. The owner of the engines, Herr Eschenbach of Guthop, finding it impossible to keep the tubes tight, had removed a number of them to discover that some had been put in *crossed*. He had called in the boiler inspector who had made a number of other criticisms, and as a result Rudolph Sack were demanding that a responsible member of Garretts' staff be sent to investigate.

Appropriately, the man upon whom the lot fell was George Airey, foreman of the boiler shop. Airey and an unnamed companion were sent at once to Leipzig to look into the matter. Whilst the identity of the companion cannot be stated with certainty he must have been fluent in German as Airey spoke none. It seems probable that he may have been W. Jungclaussen (whose name occurs again in the quoted documents that follow). H. Jungclaussen of Ahrensbök, Germany, was an agent purchasing machinery from Garretts. Garretts made it their practice to have on the Works, as so-called 'gentlemen apprentices', the sons of such agents to whom, it was hoped, they would be able to impart the elements of engine building. It is likely that Jungclaussen Junior was one of these. What Airey discovered at Leipzig is probably best described in his own words:

Report on the 2 Ploughing Engines at Guthop   26.7.09

After an interview with Commercienrat P. Sack at Leipzig we proceeded to Guthop to investigate the various complaints. We found both engines with the tubes partly out, the other tubes being left in so that we could see how they were set in the boiler. We at once proceeded to take out the remaining tubes and also to inspect the tube settings and found that one stay tube was not set in properly. Took this tube out and put in a new one into a different hole at one end. By doing this we was enabled to get all the tubes in quite different than before. All the tubes are now perfectly straight and fairly parallel with the exception of 2 which are also straight but rise at the smokebox end fully 2". On examining the fireboxes we found that <u>both</u> tube plates were bulged in centre of plate just in the area of the bottom tubes between stay tubes. We also found that this bulging was much more in one boiler than the other. After consulting the drawing we found that the pitch of the stay tubes on one boiler did not correspond with the drawing. On this boiler the distance between the lowest stay tubes was one tube wider or about 2½" and after we had moved this stay tube to enable us to get the tubes in straight the distance became 5" wider than the drawing and therefore we decided to put in 2 more stay tubes in the centre of the bottom row of tubes thus greatly strengthening this one boiler. The other boiler was quite in accord with the drawing and the tubes and stay tubes quite straight and fairly parallel. The pitch of the stay tubes in this boiler was much smaller so we did not think it necessary to put in any more stay tubes.

After properly expanding and beading all tubes we tested both boilers with hydraulic to 15 atms. pressure. No deflection or bulging could be noticed on the wood splines which we fixed in fireboxes and the tubes are now all perfectly tight and no leakage could be found or seen on any part of the boilers. After speaking with the engine drivers who told us that they had to clean the soot and dirt out of the smokeboxes every 2 or 3 hours and that even large pieces of coal was drawn through the tubes. After hearing it confirmed our own opinion that the engines must have had too much draught and here we see the real reason of the leakage of the tubes. The engineer on the farm had already taken out the mouthpiece or ferrel of the exhaust pipe but still the draught was too much and therefore we think it advisable to lengthen the exhaust pipe about 15" so that it will go into the funnel base. After persuading the owner of the engines Oberamtmann Eschenback that the engines would be all right after our alterations he said that he would be satisfied if the engines worked without any trouble in the future and if the boiler inspector would also pass them.

But the complaints of the boiler inspector are:
1] Plates too thin - Found these full thickness and were quite able to satisfy the people about this.
2] Not sufficient stay tubes - We altered as described. The other boiler agrees with drawing.
3] Tubes crossed up and down - We altered this very much but was not able to make them quite satisfactory.
4] Tube plates; arrangement of tube holes - This arrangement is not satisfactory as the plates do not correspond with each other and the distance between tube holes is sometimes less than the thickness of the plate and in others more than 1½". This is the chief complaint which was of course impossible to alter without new plates.

<u>Suggestions</u>
Should it be necessary to put in new tube plates I think it would be much better to use the 1909 setting which will mean 4 new plates as Sack is much pleased with this.

George H. Airey

Not unnaturally Frank Garrett, Senior, was appalled. Airey's report was dated July 26, the Chairman's comments the day following. He wrote:

Memo - Sack: Airey's Report

1] I assume there is no alternative to replacing the 4 tube plates as indicated in Item 4 at our own expense?
2] Who is responsible for this very bad workmanship? It seems extraordinary!
3] Will Messrs. Sack's confidence be restored?
4] This experience will be an 'Eye opener' to W. Jungclaussen!
5] A strict account of the cost incurred should be kept. Can an estimate be made?

F.G.
27.VII.9

In the short term the remedial works were put in hand. Airey was asked to make a supplementary report of the amendments that had been asked for by Sack, and he submitted this on August 4:

<u>Alterations Required by Rud. Sack</u>

Oil hole on door of gear guard to be fixed on side instead of in centre at front.

Injector handles too high; these must not be higher than 1½" above tender top.

Stud holes in cast steel seating for winding drum to be tapped deeper. Thread not to be less than 1³/₈" to 1¾" deep.

Injector behind hind travelling wheels to be moved back 6" if possible so as to enable handles to clear wheel.

Old type smokebox door preferred to new one., but if new type is used 2 pins to be fixed in ring with slot holes. for cotters to keep door closed. In Sack's opinion the one in centre is not sufficient. Also 2 small brackets, chain to hold cotters.

Tender draw-bar pins, old type preferred. These are turned, the new ones only rough forged.

G. Airey
August 4, 1909

In the long term the incident must have undermined Sack's confidence as Frank Garrett had feared because only two further 10NHP engines were supplied, Nos.27903 and 27904 sent in April, 1910. As foreman of the boiler shop Airey must have been the man on whose shoulders responsibility for work in the shop rested. By what seems great forbearance, in the climate of the times, he was not dismissed, but the revision of the testing and inspection of engines was taken seriously in hand with the appointment of Frank Walker, already commented upon. Although the underlying reason for the latter's appointment was to provide the board with an informed, yet detached, view of technical questions and policy his nominal duty was to reorganise and oversee inspection and testing, which he did with considerable success. The rapid expansion of output had increased the numbers of skilled men employed more rapidly than could be accommodated by the ordinary channels of recruitment and apprenticeship. Many, therefore, had been recruited from outside. As the traction engine firms, generally, were in the throes of a comparable expansion the number of available artisans was limited. When firms shed staff they tended to do so by getting rid of their least satisfactory employees so that those men looking for jobs in other companies necessarily included many who had been found wanting in their previous situations. The boiler shop was not the only one to suffer in this way. Another of Frank Walker's early tasks was to look over the first of the new design of 5-ton wagon in April, 1910, before it was launched on the market. The plethora of work in 1909 had not only included the new design of 5-ton wagon but also the launch of the range of semi-stationary power plants; the upsurge in the manufacture of steam tractors and the continued production of portables at the rate of nine a week. In short, the firm had grown too fast in the production side for the administration to keep pace with it and this had to be put right.

Although this somewhat inglorious episode may have assisted in the demise of the arrangement with Rud. Sack it was not the only cause. The manufacture of steam ploughing engines in Germany itself had come on apace since Leiston Works had begun building for Sack. Output from the Fowler works at Magdeburg, already in progress when Garretts had supplied their first plougher to Sack, had continued to produce engines for the German market but, in addition, by 1910 Heucke of Gatersleben, who had begun in a small way in 1884, was making some 25 engines a year whilst about 1900 Ventski of Graudenz had also entered the field followed by Kemna of Breslau. The competition had, therefore, increased four-fold and the profit margin, in consequence, had probably gone down in inverse proportion, so the chances are that the upset over the tubeplates represented no more than the last straw that broke down the association between the two firms.

Before turning to another aspect of vertical drum engines made at Leiston for export it is worth looking at an unsuccessful attempt made by the firm to sell vertical drum ploughers in England. On February 24, 1909, they submitted an estimate for a pair of 10NHP ploughers to H. Le Grys of nearby Heveningham. Le Grys himself was well-known to the Garretts and it was to him they had turned, as an experienced threshing contractor, to put their new seed huller to a practical test. The nett estimate they gave him for the pair was <u>£1668. 0. 0</u>. The way in which this cost was calculated was as follows:

One each left and right hand 10 HP S/C ploughing engines as delivered complete to Rud. Sack, without the ploughing drums or ploughing gear......ea. nett	£605 - 0 - 0	
Lamps, firebars, whistle, spuds to both driving wheels, angle rings to front wheels, tube brush - not supplied to Sack and for which allowance	£ 11 - 0 - 0	
	£616 - 0 - 0	£1232 - 0 - 0
	£ s d	
Ploughing drum + parts ex Sack - cost to RG &SL	100 0 0	
Delivery of same from Leipzig to Leiston	10 0 0	

Cost of erecting same on each engine	20 0 0		
Drawings	5 0 0		
Painting of each engine (not included in price to Sack)	5 0 0		
Testing each engine	<u>5 0 0</u>		
	£ 145 0 0		
	<u>73 0 0</u>		
@ nett per engine	£ 218 0 0	<u>436 - 0 - 0</u>	
Nett price quoted to Le Grys for one pair of			
10 HP S/C ploughing engines fitted up complete		<u>£ 1668 - 0 - 0</u>	

Unfortunately Le Grys did not accept the estimate!

Rudolph Sack appears to have been selling at least some of the ploughers to Hungary though it is only with 26087 and 26088 that we can actually link their numbers to a purchaser. These two engines seem to have been sent to Count Alexander Sztary, Nagy Mihaly, Hungary. We do know, however, the location of one more pair, though without knowing more of their identity. On January 22, 1906, new cast steel main spur rings and other materials were sent to Pfeiffer's Gutsverwaltung, Station Beska, Royal Hungarian State Railway, near Esseg, Slavonia.

In parallel with the ploughing engines supplied to Sack there ran an interesting series of ten engines, from 5 to 8NHP, all but one of which were singles, supplied to James Macalister, the New Zealand machinery importer whose head office was Invercargill, and referred to as *New Zealand traction engines*. The first to go, No.25114, left Leiston on June 28, 1905, and the last (No.31157) on November 26, 1912. The total was made up of two 8NHPs (Nos.25113 and 28753); three 7NHPs (28752, 29773, and 31127); two 6NHPs (25114 and 28751); and two 5NHPs (31128 and 31157). The solitary compound was No.31129, an 8NHP. The first in numerical order, No.25113, did not go until August 28, 1905. This had a large vertical drum mounted on the boiler barrel, similar to a Sack plougher, but the rope left the bottom of the drum in a forward direction passing round a large pulley suspended under the boiler barrel (see Fig.57). Though the drum bore a superficial resemblance to those used by Sack it was, in fact, cast from patterns made at Leiston. The centre plate of the differential was first made (to pattern UZ7) in cast iron but a new one in cast steel was sent out subsequently. In the case of No.25114, although it was described as a 6NHP, the cylinder was of 8½" bore, making it 7NHP according to the RASE calculation, and it was much stronger in the gearing than an ordinary 6NHP. Besides this, both 25113 and 25114 were pressed to 180 p.s.i., a fact that, in the case of No.25114, taken in conjunction with the larger bore and stronger gearing, made it a very powerful engine for its size. However, because the governed speed was kept down to 165 r.p.m. this was not so apparent in published tables of power output. No.25114 was also slightly different in that it had a Graham type spark arrester. All of this series of engines for Macalister were distinguished from others of the same nominal horsepower by the addition of the letter 'Z' to the prefix of the drawing and pattern numbers. Thus the 8NHP had the prefix 'UZ' whilst No.25114 had 'TZ'.

The first two engines were both erected under Tom Staulkey as chargehand, he, like the rather older chargehands, Billy Tricker and Billy Vale, having the reputation of one to whom the slightly unusual jobs could be entrusted with confidence. Apart from the conjunction of the Works numbers and the fact of their having gone to the same importer there was nothing to suggest that they were intended to work together. However, the only surviving picture of No.25113 shows it working with a mole plough, on which duties it would have needed a lighter engine for pulling back the implement, and it is suggested that initially 25114 might have performed this role using its ordinary winding drum with a lighter gauge of rope. This conjecture is given some support by the fact that on August 19, 1907, Garretts supplied a drum and boss for 25114, designed to take 300 yards of 2" circumference wire rope, which was sent at the same time together with a drive pinion to go onto the first countershaft. No.25113 had a drum large enough for 400 yards of 2¼" circumference rope so there would still have been a degree of mis-match which leaves an air of slight mystery over the matter.

Most of the other engines in the series had drums 3' 0" diameter overall on the rear axle, intended for 300 yards of 2" circumference rope. All had 180 p.s.i. boiler pressure, compared with the 140 p.s.i. of other singles of the era and had wider and stronger gears. No.28753, an 8NHP, and 29773, a 7NHP, each had 300 yards of rope and were given Royal Show finish, and both were sent on September 30, 1911. Nos. 31127 and 31128, a 7 and a 5NHP respectively, were despatched in reversed date order, i.e. 31128 left on November 19,1912, whilst the former did not go until January 24 the following year. The smaller engine had a drum for 200 yards of 2" circumference rope and a four pinion differential. For a reason not now apparent it was ordered with gear guards flanged up out of $^3/_{16}$" plate. It had a belly tank cut down one side, a feature that was also specified on its 7NHP companion, No.31127. Both were ordered with no draw-bar, suggesting that their sole function was as winders. The design of the cast steel rope drums fitted to this series of engines was noteworthy in that in order to achieve the required rope capacity without increasing the overall width of the engine the drum was recessed on the wheel side so that it overlapped the nave of the wheel. A steel boss was placed on the axle on which was mounted a bronze bush and it was on this that the drum revolved.

The next following engine (No.31129), the lone compound example, was a rather more elaborate machine in many respects. Firstly, it was sprung on both axles and, secondly, it was a three speed engine with a disc flywheel. As the purchaser wanted a rim not less than 7" wide the usual narrow disc flywheel could not be used and a dished flywheel was fitted instead. The boiler was of Colonial type and the pressure was increased to 200 p.s.i. Other non-standard features included the fitting of a 120 gallon belly tank, planished steel lagging, a four pinion differential, and double rim brake. Incidentally, the maximum speed was 7 m.p.h. at an engine speed of 250 r.p.m. The drum on this engine carried only 125 yards of 2" circumference rope. This engine was one of the few for New Zealand against which the Garrett books noted the ultimate purchaser's name, in this case W.C. Benbow of Temuka.

Earlier engines for Macalister used belt-driven Mollerup lubricators though latterly this was not specially ordered. All had injectors. The road wheels seem to have been supplied 2" wider than standard. In all examples the specification and finish were very high. Clearly the engines were intended for heavy pulling on the wire rope, but the purpose that this capability was meant to serve is nowhere recorded. It has been suggested that they might have been used for mole drainage as was the quasi ploughing engine No.25113, whilst there has also been a question of whether or not they might have served in the exploitation of the New Zealand forests from which large quantities of Kauri pine and other commercially important timbers were extracted in the first two decades of this century. At the time of writing this question has not been answered. Of the engines supplied to Macalister only one - a 7NHP, No.29773- survives, sent on September 30, 1911. This is preserved in working order at Waimati, South Island.

It is an unfortunate fact that none of the traction engines built for direct traction ploughing seem to have survived into preservation. These were supplied, inter alia, to Australia, South America, Italy, France, North Africa and the Near East, all as compounds. Probably the first was 6NHP No.27111, despatched on July 23, 1908, to Clark & Fauset in Queensland, complete with a special cast iron nameplate on the smokebox door bearing their name. The engine had a colonial firebox but had a number of special requirements. Unusually it was arranged for right-hand steering and had angle rings on the front wheels, which were 12" wide, to assist steering on soft going. The rear wheels were 20" wide. The gears on it were specified to be machine cut and were arranged for two speeds, whilst the reversing gear was designed to work at 75% cut-off. Not altogether surprisingly it had a rack round the tender to enable it to carry wood fuel. No.27382, generally similar, followed on August 19, 1910. Working these two engines must have revealed some weaknesses for the next one ordered (No.29788 - December 12, 1911) was requested to have a wood rack 'as large as possible' and a double draw-bar standing out each end to the outer edge of the wheels. Furthermore, wider and heavier gearing in cast steel throughout, in the same style as the New Zealand tractions, was called for. A wire spark grate was fitted in the smokebox in addition to the wire cage on top of the chimney.

The first engine sent to South America for direct ploughing was No.29780 (December 8, 1911) sold through Mattos in Buenos Aires. This was in the period of superheating experiments, and Mattos made it clear that he wanted neither superheater nor piston valves. The colonial firebox, however, was required to be suitable for either oil or wood firing. Garretts did not supply the oil firing equipment which, at that time, would have been on Holden's system, as used on the Great Eastern Railway, obtained from Taite & Carlton whose office was at 63 Queen Victoria Street, London EC. The wheels were very wide - 12" on the front and 22" at the rear - though no angle rings were asked for. Unusually the front axle was sprung. To accommodate both ordinary trailer wagons and the land-working implements it had a double draw-bar, and, further, it was fitted with an awning.

A 6NHP (No.31454, April 16, 1913) for Pilter's Tunis branch had the same stronger gearing as No.29788 (which had been supplied to Clark & Fauset) plus a nickel steel rear axle, awning, belly tank, and springs to both axles. Besides having the same wide wheels and angle steering rings it also had 6" wide extension pieces for the rear wheels.

As mentioned in Chapter 3, in May and July, 1911, Grimaldi's Milan office had three 8NHP compounds (Nos. 28771, 28772, and 28773) for direct ploughing. In them the rear wheels were 24" wide with detachable extensions to bolt on by angle rings so increasing the tread width by a further 6". With speeds of 1.5 and 3.5 m.p.h. at 165 r.p.m., 4 pinion differentials, 6¼" nickel steel rear axles and wider and stronger gearing they were formidable engines. Grimaldi's Turin office also bought engines for direct ploughing with the usual double draw-bar, though in this case they were 7NHP compounds intended for both road haulage and ploughing. For this reason the steering angles on the front wheels were detachable. They were ordered with speeds of 2.2 k.p.h. (1.37 m.p.h.) and 5.8 k.p.h. (3.6 m.p.h.) so that even when on road haulage they were not expected to be fliers. The first of them (28376) was sent on June 20, 1910, followed by 30410 on September 13, 1912, the last 7NHP compound to be made.

Another interesting 8NHP compound engine for direct traction ploughing was No.28766, shipped to Fremantle, Australia, through the agency of John W. Harker & Co., Billiter Street, London EC. This had 24" wide rear wheels, fitted with detachable 6" wide extension rings, and front wheels 12" wide. Geared down to 1.06 mph for ploughing it had a four pinion differential with a specially strong driving spur ring and pinion, a 6¼" nickel steel main axle as compared with the standard 5½" mild steel, and a cast steel winding drum carrying 300 yards of 2¼" circumference wire rope of 22 tons breaking strain. In addition two pulley blocks were sent with it comprising a double sheaf block and a three sheaf block both with 11" pulleys. Land clearance and breaking of virgin ground must have been its intended vocation.

Perhaps the most impressive of the direct traction ploughers were Nos.32208 and 32300, the design of which resulted from an enquiry from Dr. A.E. Parr, the Deputy Director of Agriculture at Aligarh, United Provinces, India. This enquiry does not survive but seems to have been received in the Spring or early summer of 1913. What Dr. Parr was seeking was an engine of 50BHP of up-to-date design to be used for direct ploughing at a speed of about 2 m.p.h. but with a faster speed for travelling. Calculations and an estimate of cost were submitted to Dr. Parr in this country on August 27, 1913, and resulted in an order dated September 4, i.e. virtually by return. The financial arrangements were interesting and not altogether creditable to Parr as a public servant. Garretts arrived at a costing of £691.11.6 from which they offered him a discount of £35.0.0 as a 'special concession for first introductory order', Parr having intimated that the order was likely to be the first of a series. However Parr countered this estimate and offer with the request that instead of the whole of this discount being disclosed to his principals £30.0.0 of it should be paid to him personally in two instalments, a douceur that would have been worth not less than £3000 of 1996 money. Thus the invoice eventually rendered to his employers was in the sum of £686.11.6 which was duly paid by them, £30 of the money being paid over, in turn, to Parr. By mid January drawings were ready for issue to the Works and were scheduled in Drawing List No.150 dated February 3.

By that time the steam engine section of the drawing office had been reinforced by the appointment of several new draughtsmen, one of whom, W.G. Turner, was the team leader on this project. The design of compound traction engine that resulted was probably the most modern built at Leiston Works to that date, incorporating a nickel steel rear axle, piston valves, superheater, a working pressure of 225 p.s.i. and an engine speed of 230 r.p.m. With an eye to keeping the peripheral speed of the flywheel within bounds this was reduced to 3' 7" in diameter and 5" wide. The cylinders were 5" and 8½" in diameter by only 10" stroke, the power output being kept up by the higher engine revs and increased boiler pressure. To ensure a plentiful supply of steam the heating surfaces of the boiler totalled 129.8 sq. ft. and the grate area was an unprecedented, for the size of the engine, 7.18 sq. ft. intended to make the engine capable, if required, of burning Indian coal, with its high ash content, although the intention was to fire it with oil for which purpose it was equipped with Kermode oil burning apparatus and, uniquely for Leiston Works, a firebrick arch. Two bunkers were fitted, one of which housed the fuel tank. The engine was a three shafter, with the differential on the intermediate shaft and separate drive to each rear wheel. Other distinguishing features were right-hand steerage and, consequently, a left-hand reverser. Also it was fitted with a Victor double feed oil pump. For an engine of rather under 5NHP it was a very compact and powerful machine, and an interesting job to those involved in it - to Turner and his fellow draughtsmen, and to Tom Oakley, the chargehand erector given the task of building it up. When it left the Works on

May 25, 1914, in the chocolate brown livery used for some of the steam tractors, it must have looked a smart outfit. Moreover it must have enjoyed at least some years of successful working as spares were supplied for it on October 10, 1930.

On the critical matter of its being the first of a line, however, it failed completely. No further orders emanated from India and steam cultivation made no headway there. On the other hand the firm were able to secure the order for No.32300 from Wadhams Engineering Co. Ltd. for shipment to Smyrna. Except in a few details such as a hopper firedoor as used on the straw-burners and the omission of the oil-burning equipment it followed the same design as No.32208 though the cost, without the oil equipment, was much lower at £674 less 15% and 2½% i.e. £558. 11. 7. The order was dated February 28, 1914, and work began on April 4, but the outbreak of war in August prevented its being shipped. The components lay about the Works in an incomplete state and in the 1916 Stock Book it was written down to a mere £115. At the end of the war it was decided to finish it and to use it as the test bed for Scarab oil burning apparatus which was also tried (as related in *Garrett Wagons - Part 1*) on a 5-ton overtype wagon. Work on completing the engine began in 1919, with Sid Poynter as the chargehand erector. All the loose and scattered parts of the engine were eventually located, albeit with difficulty in some cases, with one exception. Despite searches all round the Works the angle iron steering rings for the front wheels were never found. It was completed on June 1, 1920, and exhibited at the Royal Show that year as No.33781. Though no buyer came forward at the Show itself Teddy Ballam was fortunate enough to sell it after the Show to W.E. Cooper & Son of nearby Parham for £1000. By the time it left for Parham on November 1, 1920, it had had a number of modifications. The double spring balance safety valves with which it had originally been fitted were replaced by Ramsbottom type. The hopper on the firehole had gone, of course, when the engine was fitted for oil burning but now the Scarab apparatus was stripped out as, in economic terms, the current price of oil had made it far dearer to use oil than coal for steaming.

W.E. Cooper's son Alec recalled the engine to me as a very handy tool which he and his father used for threshing, the only tiresome feature being the irritating gear driven pump. They ran it for several years until it was involved in a fire which burned off the lagging and did other damage. Rather than bother with its reinstatement they sold it to Malcolm Bloomfield of Debenham who carried out the necessary repairs, after which it was sold to the Earl of Cadogan for use on his Culford Hall Estate at Bury St. Edmunds. In 1936 it went from there to B.W. Death of Lavenham, Suffolk, who had a stable of Garrett traction engines, with whom it stayed until it was scrapped in 1948, probably the last Garrett direct ploughing engine to survive.

Fig.57. No.25113, the first 'New Zealand' traction working with a mole plough. Effectively it was a ploughing engine.

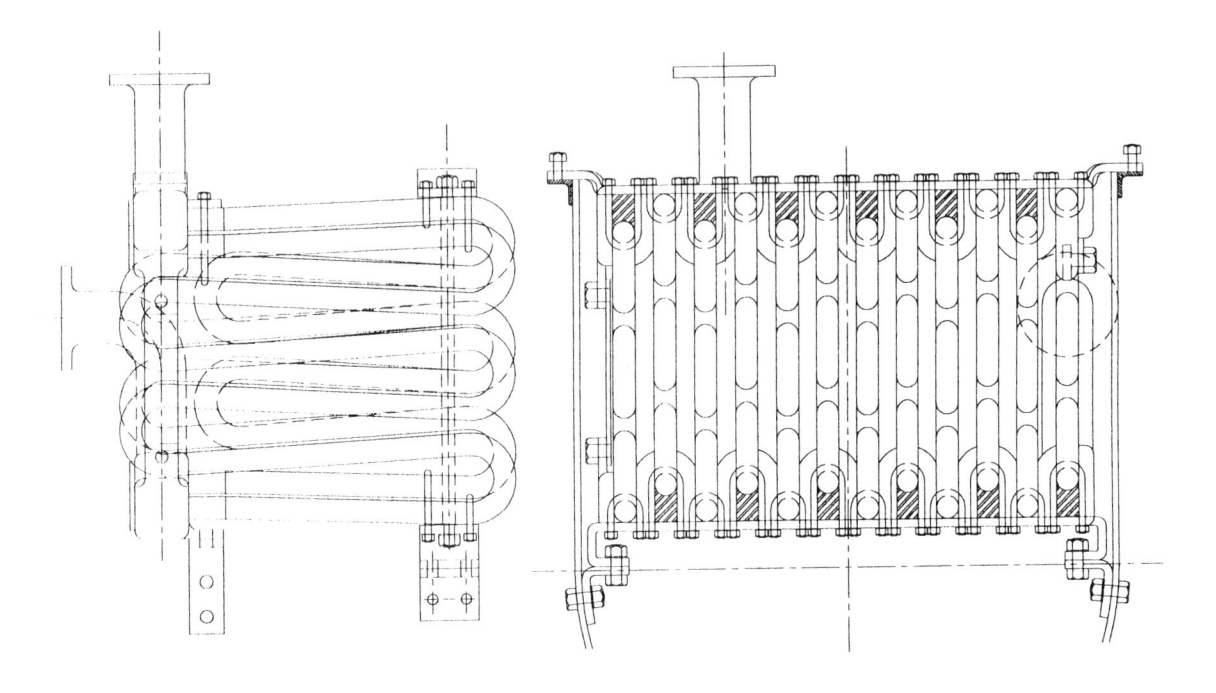

Fig. 58. *Design of superheater used in 6 and 7NHP engines.* (Drawing by M.J.Walters)

Fig. 59. *Gear side elevation of a 6NHP New Zealand traction engine.*

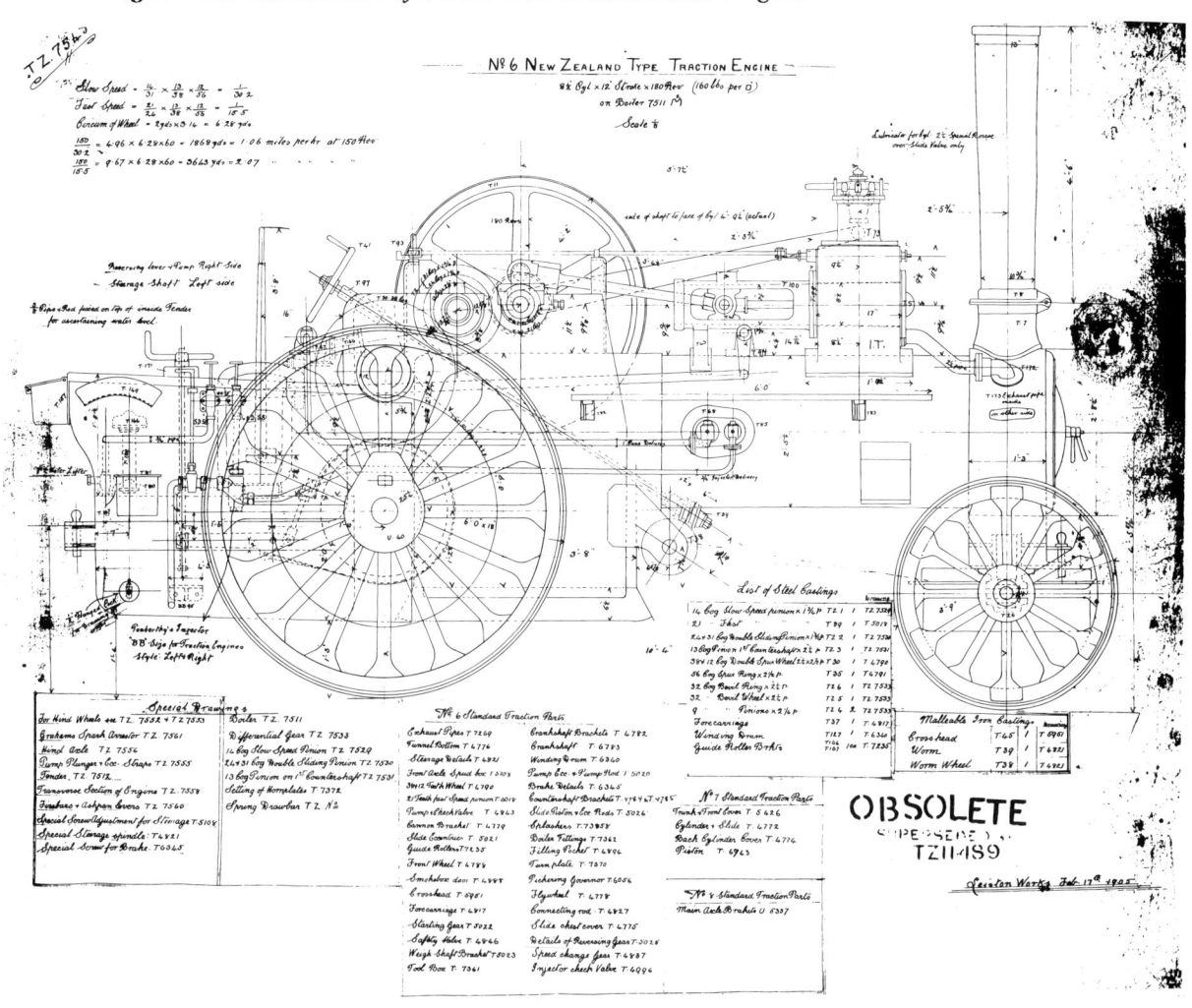

Fig.60. *A threshing scene, c.1911, on South Island, New Zealand, in which a Garrett 7NHP single fitted with Colonial firebox- almost certainly No.28752- is shown driving a Garrett Mammoth thresher.*

Fig.61. The first 50BHP plougher, No.32208, before completion and painting, on land near Valley Road, Leiston.

Fig.62. The second 50BHP plougher, originally No.32300, as completed, with the new number 33781, for the 1920 Royal Show, and fitted with a Scarab oil burner as Fig.63 (inset below).

72

Fig.64. Rear end view of No.33781, illustrating inter alia *the awkward combination of right-hand steering with a right-hand reversing lever.*

Fig.65. No.28771, one of the trio of 8NHP direct traction ploughers delivered to Grimaldi's Milan depot in 1911.

Fig.66. A working picture, unfortunately retouched, of two of these engines.

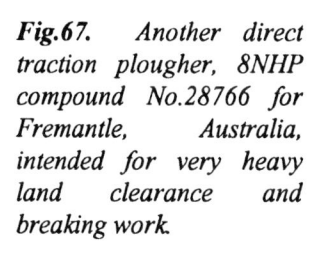

Fig.67. Another direct traction plougher, 8NHP compound No.28766 for Fremantle, Australia, intended for very heavy land clearance and breaking work.

Fig. 68. *No. 24369, the 8NHP road locomotive for Mauritius.*

Fig. 69. *Probably 24551, one of the 8NHP Johannesburg trio, in Waterloo Avenue, Leiston.*
Fig. 70. *The same, or a sister, engine on location in Johannesburg.*

Fig.71. 8NHP road loco No.25814 was supplied to Swales & Henry Forrest in 1907. Here it is seen in Cann Hall Road, Forest Gate, London, with Henry Forrest in the steersman's position and Jim Somerville, the driver, just visible behind him. The front three loads were the Razzle Dazzle and the last the 'bike' truck. The lettering is merely dubbed on.

Fig.72. This offside view shows the Moore's steam pump on the tank top. The pump was fitted because the third road speed left no room on the crankshaft for a pump eccentric.

Fig.73. Lalonde's 6NHP road loco No.26695 with three of their vans. The lettering on the cab was dubbed onto the photo for advertising purposes.

Fig. 74. Though one cannot be certain, this is believed to be a picture of No.26695 after axle failure in August, 1909. The exhaust pipe has been altered but the van behind it seems to be one of Lalondes. The two men by the smokebox are Jack Newstead (with chain) and Tom Staulkey. The plump man second from left was a labourer named Cook.

Fig. 75. No.27946, which should have been Lalonde's second engine, was sold to John Harkness of Belfast, and is seen at Pollock Dock, Belfast, in 1947, with the driver, Jim Hyndman (rt.) and second man, Alec McClements (left).
[R.G. Pratt]

Fig. 76. No.27946 (Vera) in Belfast Docks with a forged steel drum by Clarke Chapman (Newcastle-upon-Tyne) for Belfast power station.

Fig. 77. *The circumstances of this picture are not known. It is believed to be No.27763 when owned by H.L.Harding of Hungerford.*

Figs. 78 and 79. *Nearside and offside view of 6NHP No.26968, bought in 1908 by J.Purchase of Hounslow.*

77

Chapter 6

Road Locomotives and Showmen's Engines

Within eight years of the recommencement of traction engine building the firm was able to offer 6, 7, and 8NHP traction engines, road rollers, ploughing engines, and strawburners. No attempt had been made, however, to embark upon the building of road locomotives, largely the preserve thereto of Aveling & Porter Ltd. and John Fowler & Co., with Charles Burrell & Sons Ltd. and J.& H. McLaren following up. Other firms had made what they termed road locomotives which, in reality, were superior general purpose engines. How Richard Garrett & Sons Ltd. came to be a further contender is not clear, because all of the people involved were dead before my time and Victor Garrett, my source of information on most such matters, was still at boarding school when it happened.

In 1902 an enquiry was received for a compound 8NHP road locomotive for use in Mauritius by the Mauritius Estates & Assets Co.Ltd., a London based company, who required their locomotive for use in connection with their extensive estates which produced mainly sugar cane. The invitation to tender was in great detail and was received via the client's buying agent, Mr. J. Paterson. One might conclude that the enquiry having been received and the order secured the Leiston works thereupon set about producing the locomotive. However, it seems that it did not happen exactly like that for two virtually identical road locos were built, supposedly simultaneously, and eventually left within seven weeks of each other in July and August, 1903. The second one was ordered by Keep Bros. of Birmingham for shipment to Nees & Son of Wellington, New Zealand. These two facts seem to indicate that building the two engines could have been the result of a policy decision by the board of directors. and that the two orders came from an effort to sell them after that decision had been made. Were this so, Frank Garrett the younger, at that time the director overseeing sales, might have had some part in the selling. According to his brother Victor, admittedly speaking of a period three or four years later, Frank had found it relatively easy to become accepted in the London buying and confirming houses. Well educated, personable, travelled, and the heir to a considerable business, he soon realised that he had a rapport with them that the representatives of the other firms often did not have. Whereas, perhaps, they had to deal with subordinate officials frequently he was invited into a partner's office to discuss business over a cigar. The two orders for road locomotives may well have come the firm's way from conversations such as these.

The draughtsman to whom Schmach entrusted the lead role in this project was H.G. Florey. Wisely, in view of how much more onerous the life of a road loco was compared with an ordinary traction engine, no attempt was made, with trifling exceptions, to adapt anything that had gone before to serve in the new design. A few items of the basic 6NHP traction engine such as the pump and injector check valves, the filling pocket, and the Pickering governors were used together with a selection of parts from the 8NHP ploughers, notably the steering, the cannon bracket, the chimney and smokestand, the starting gear, and the smokebox. These components apart, all was fresh, the drawings receiving the prefix HU to distinguish them from any preceding eights.

The basic parameters were that the engines were four shaft compounds, with a working pressure of 180 p.s.i. (20 p.s.i. higher than their general purpose contemporaries), with the valve chests on the outer faces of the cylinders, and having Stephenson link motion reversing gear. The steering was placed on the left, the reversing lever on the right of the manstand. The Mauritius Estates' engine was a two speeder, but that for Nees Brothers had three speeds. In the former the low speed was on the offside, outside the hornplates and the fast speed inside the hornplate on the flywheel side. On the three speed engine the third and highest speed was introduced between the low pressure crank and the low pressure eccentrics on the crankshaft, displacing the pump eccentric and, hence, the pump, which was replaced by a Moore's steam pump mounted upon the offside belly tank - Garrett documents used the terms 'front', 'fore', and 'belly' tank quite indiscriminately and interchangeably. Beside the pump the engines had a No.4 Holden & Brooke injector. Rim brakes were fitted to each rear wheel, actuated by a vertical shaft and handle on the nearside.

All the gearing was of cast steel but only the gears on the crankshaft and first countershaft and the mating gear on the second countershaft were machine cut. By a curious economy only three bevels were fitted in the differential which was on the axle. The crankshaft was webbed, machined out of a single forging and balanced. Somewhat unexpectedly the firm opted for bored trunks as crosshead guides where one might have expected double slide bars. The engines were provided with awnings over the driving position. The boiler, designed by Florey in the opening phases of the move to higher boiler pressures, had represented a step up from what the Leiston drawing office and boiler shop had been used to. As originally drawn, on HU6869, the boiler barrel had a lapped and double rivetted seam, but the boiler shop copy has an amendment upon it by Arthur Girling, dated May 5, 1903, changing this to a butt joint with double 3/8" butt straps and double rivetting - very much more in line with best class practice of the time and perhaps the suggestion of the boiler insurance company.

Under Walter Rogers as chargehand, work on assembling the engine for Mauritius was completed in June, 1903, and it was despatched on July 7, 1903, as No.24369. A 330 gallon water cart and three 6 ton four wheeled wagons 'suitable for sugar cane', i.e. with staked sides, were ordered with it. Garretts sub-let the making of the wagons to Taskers of Andover, and of the water cart to Bakers of Compton. The second road locomotive, No.24429, for shipment to Nees & Son, was actually commenced on May 4, 1903, again by Walter Rogers, and was sent off on August 20. Three more generally similar road locos were begun about the time these first two left the Works. All were destined for service in Johannesburg and were of identical design though the first of them was ordered through the agency of Henry Pynegar, of London, for the Technical & Commercial Corporation Ltd. of Johannesburg, while the second two were bought by Johannesburg Municipality via Chester & Co. of London who, by the time of shipment, had been succeeded as agents by Fraser & Chalmers Ltd. It seems very probable that the first of the trio was also for the Johannesburg Municipality as an order for replacement gears both for it and for the other two came via the same source, E.W. Carling & Co. of London, on the same date in 1904. Why replacement gears were needed so early in their working lives is not explained, but nothing in the surviving Garrett records suggests that it was the result of defects in the originals.

Like Nees' engine, all three were ordered with a third speed so that the pump eccentric was again omitted to leave a space for the intermediate gear. As before, a Moore's steam pump was provided, mounted upon the offside fore tank top, to make up for the loss of the eccentric driven pump. In these three a Colonial boiler was fitted, designed specifically for them. The length of the firebox internally was increased by 6" from 3' 2" to 3' 8", though the width remained at 2' 3 3/8", an increase of just on 16% in the grate area. This larger firebox was equipped with a drop grate presumably to allow the engines to burn a high ash content coal. Also two sliding doors replaced the hinged firedoor used on the two previous engines. Spring balance safety valves were substituted for the Ramsbottom type previously used, in order to comply with the Transvaal boiler regulations. The belly tank was made deeper and a sheet steel casing was provided over the engine parts whilst the steering worm and worm wheel were also enclosed in a protective sheet iron boxing against the notorious dust of Johannesburg. The main road wheels were increased to 24" across the tyre and the fronts from 9" to 12", whilst a brake was fitted on the winding drum which, as on the earlier two, carried 75 yards of wire rope.

No.24551 was finished in late Autumn, 1903, and sent off from Leiston to the Technical & Commercial Corporation Ltd. on December 22. The gross weight, filled with coal and water when under test, was only 16 lb. under 20 tons, and the nett weight was 17 tons 19cwt. 25lb. Notwithstanding these somewhat dismaying figures a cast plate was fixed to the back of the tender giving the weight as 14½ tons. The second and third locos, Nos.24552 and 24595, left on January 20, 1904, presumably with equally untruthful weight plates.

The Mauritius engine, No.24369, had a new crankshaft ordered for it in May, 1905, and all the gears were ordered afresh, in two instalments, in May and December, 1906, together with a new steering worm and worm wheel in the first instalment. As already noted new gears had been supplied for all three of the Johannesburg engines in 1904. Whilst the new sets of gears might have been a precautionary measure the crankshaft replacement, by any standards, would seem to indicate a failure. Other than these orders for parts nothing more was heard of any of these road locos, and in the case of No.24429 for Nees & Sons no spares were ever ordered.

The seventh, and last, of these 8NHP road locomotives had the most interesting and complicated life of any of them. Originally commissioned in early 1904, it was erected by Walter Rogers' gang with Royal Show finish, painted in dark red, and was sent to the Royal Show, held that year at Park Royal, London. The engine was completed in late June and appeared in the Stock List of July 1, 1904, numbered 24893.

Despite a certain amount of favourable comment in the technical press it attracted no buyers at the asking price of £820, and remained in stock until the following Spring when the Western Counties Agricultural Cooperative Association Ltd. managed to sell it to J. Stanbury & Sons of Ashburton, Devon for the more modest sum of £770. To meet their requirements it was altered to a two speeder, the second speed being a special slow speed. After these alterations it was renumbered 25363 and shown at the Devon County Show, Exeter, from May 17 to 19, from whence it was delivered to the new owners under a hire purchase sale agreement, with an inconspicuous plate on it lettered *Richard Garrett & Sons Ltd., Owners and Lessors*. This arrangement did not work out as intended and the engine came back into the hands of the firm on October 10, 1905.

It remained on hand until March 26, 1906, when it was repainted in dark green and sent as No.25814 to G.F. Townsend of Exning, near Newmarket, who later that year took delivery of No.25858, a sprung 8NHP single with a belly tank and motion covers. It was, however, back in the Leiston fold by the time of the April Stock List, produced on May 1, 1906, and remained there for some months more before Ballam sold it finally to the showmen, Henry & Swales Forrest of Forest Gate, London, for whom it once again became a three-speeder. Other changes included the fitting of a Moore's steam pump, a protected gauge glass on the belly tank, a dynamo bracket, an extended awning with twisted brasses and an extension chimney. The engine retained its dark green livery but the colour of the wheels which had been painted in a light green for Townsend was changed to red. The road loco was put onto rail at Leiston on March 26, 1907, consigned to its new owners at Devonshire Street Station, Great Eastern Railway, not far from the Mile End Road where Swales Forrest had a fit-up Bioscope show. Although there is a picture of it (Fig.71) with Henry Forrest in the steersman's position, he was not, according to his niece Violet Reynolds [neé Forrest], able to drive it, and the regular driver about that time was Jim Somerville. Vi remarked to me once 'My Dad and Sidney Bernstein's dad had fit-ups a stone's throw apart in the Mile End Road. Dad gave it up because he could see no future in it. Now look where Sidney Bernstein's got and see where we've got!'.

In the then current wave of admiration for Japan, after its trouncing of Russia in the Russo-Japanese war, the engine was named *Empress of Japan*, carried in gold leaf lettering on each motion plate. Unfortunately there is no authentic record of how the fascias were lettered, the lettering in Fig.71 being merely dubbed on for use in a catalogue. In defiance of veracity a weight plate '12 tons' was put on it. As originally delivered to the Stanburys it had topped 18 tons, and a good deal of weight (extended awning, dynamo bracket, and the dynamo itself) had been added since those days. It was used for a while with the Razzle Dazzle loads, and later in life with the Gallopers. Early in 1912 it went back to Leiston Works for general repairs, invoiced on March 27 at £115.16.3. plus a further £1.10.0. for 50 cwt. of coal for the journey back to London on its own wheels. Sundry spares were sent from time to time, and the engine went on until 1930 when it was exchanged with Matt Lynch of Strood, Kent, for a Fowler road engine. At this juncture it was probably scrapped. No unusual trouble is known to have been experienced with the gearing, and it seems probable, therefore, that the apparent gear problems with the same engines in Mauritius and South Africa may have been the result of dust invasion. That aside, on the whole, the Garrett was not the equal of a comparable Burrell or Fowler but, on the other hand, the Forrests obviously liked it well enough as they bought further Garretts. For their part Garrett people, particularly Ballam, liked and respected Swales Forrest, and on an occasion when they had had to repossess an engine from another showman it was to Swales Forrest that they entrusted it for safe custody.

The next development in road locomotives came about in a slightly curious fashion. The furniture removing firm of Lalonde Brothers & Parham of Weston-super-Mare had been dealing with John Fowler & Co for the supply of road locomotives. In the opening decade of this century Fowlers were flushed with orders and had developed a rather cavalier attitude to customers' preferences, particularly as regards boiler design, taking the somewhat lofty line that they knew rather better than the client how much boiler capacity was needed by a given design of engine. Lalondes wished to commission a road loco incorporating some ideas of their own but Fowlers expressed no interest in such a proposal, though whether they refused summarily or merely priced themselves out of the market is not related. By a train of events of which I have no details but owing something to E.W. Rudd, the London haulage contractor who was a friend of Frank Garrett Senior, they were put in touch with Leiston Works.

The Garretts not only welcomed Lalondes' involvement in the design of the new engine, for which they tendered a price of £604, but further undertook to make an allowance of £54 off the price in consideration for the help they had thus received in setting up the parameters. The deal was clinched on March 6, 1907, when Garretts were given an order for two spring mounted 6NHP road locomotives, the first for delivery in March, 1908, and the second in January, 1909. By a combined effort in the drawing office finished drawings were beginning to appear by mid-April, 1907.

During the time of our researches into Garrett engines, conducted in the sixties and early seventies, a stack containing the cartridge paper originals from which the linen transparencies were later traced existed in the drawing office store. Those of the 6NHP road engine were among them. Apart from the intrinsic appeal of having one of the actual sheets on which the designer had worked, complete with doodling on the margins and peripheral calculations, they were of intense interest in respect of the 6NHP road locos because the drawings, mainly by Tom Jones, though other draughtsmen including Gordon Thomson and Arthur Girling were also involved, bore Schmach's comments upon what had been proposed, often in very sarcastic terms which suggest he cannot have been an easy man to have worked for. In one particular instance Jones had drawn a 6" diameter rear axle which Schmach derided 'What are you designing? A battleship?' As a consequence the diameter was reduced to 5½", a reduction of just on 16% in cross sectional area. Schmach, of course, was worried about weights. We have seen already the disparity between weighbridge weights and 'painters' weights' in the case of the 8NHPs but the reduction in the rear axle was proved by events to have been too sweeping and broken axles plagued the engines of this design throughout their lives. Sad to say the cartridge paper originals were not amongst the material sent to the Suffolk Records Office but were disposed of as waste paper.

Apart from a few trifling items such as the water pocket and the ever recurring steering wheel to pattern T41 practically everything in the engines was designed anew, the prefix HT being applied to all drawings and patterns. For publicity purposes the design was called *Express* though known on the Works as 'Lalondes' engine', this even appearing in brackets as part of the title on the drawing list. Since it was designed to supplant a Fowler loco of similar characteristics it is no great surprise that a good many features of it replicated what might have been found on a corresponding two speed Fowler such as the arrangement of the change speed gears on the crankshaft and first countershaft, though the gears moved upon a squared section of the shaft rather than upon a splined shaft as on the Fowler. The spring system, too, was much inferior to that on a Fowler, being Garretts' own as described in Chapter 3. Lalondes' hand was visible in a number of points of detail: a 9" gong instead of a whistle; sliding doors to the firehole, normally used only on 8NHP Garrett engines; asbestos packed fittings; and reflex gauge glasses. The first of the engines, which became No.26695, was commenced in the erecting shop on October 17, 1907, under Walter Rogers as chargehand, and was finished during November, 1907, appearing in the stock list of December 1. It was not despatched, however, until March 14, 1908, probably because it was put through a series of road tests, but no details of these survive.

Under the agreement Lalondes had £550 to pay, after deducting their discount, and this debt was discharged in two equal instalments on May 21 and June 29, 1909. The payments came within the brief honeymoon period when the engine appeared to be performing well and when Lalondes wrote a (doubtless inspired) letter to Garretts praising its performance and looking forward to the delivery of the second example - an epistle that duly figured in sales literature. This period of bliss was shortly to be dispelled never to return. The engine had, however, not been free of problems even in the early days as in November, 1908, a 'temporary rear axle' had been sent, suggesting the breakage of the axle on the road. A permanent axle was sent on October 26, 1909, in which the specification was changed to nickel steel. This again had a short life as a fourth axle had to be despatched on February 5, 1910, the material for which was a nickel steel alloy referred to in the drawing office as 'torpedo steel'. This appears to have stopped the rot for the time being as no more replacement axles appeared in the books, but crankshaft problems began to erupt, necessitating a new crankshaft being sent on December 31, 1910. The unreliability of the engine had led to increasingly fractious exchanges between Lalondes and Garretts. Doubtless there was some private recrimination in the Leiston drawing office, too, after the inadequacy of the reduced diameter of axle became apparent.

Discussions between the two parties deteriorated to the point at which neither would communicate with the other except through solicitors. Lalondes were incensed by the problems they had encountered but the treatment to which the engine had been subjected must have had some bearing upon the matter. The late Tom Newell, who drove for Lalondes at the time, recalled that the drivers were required to flog the engines along without mercy. Eventually the two firms of solicitors arrived at an agreement whereby

Garretts agreed to pay the sum of £77.16.4 to Lalondes in final settlement of their claim for compensation. The order for the second engine (No.27946) had already been cancelled, and it remained in its makers' hands after completion. It was given Royal Show finish and placed upon the Garrett stand at the Royal Smithfield Show of 1909, having been sold to John Harkness & Co. of Belfast to whom it was despatched on December 29, 1909. Sundry alterations had been made for Harkness, the most important of which was the substitution of 18" wide wheels for the 16" wheels originally fitted. It also received a fixed winding drum to carry 100 yards of ⅝" rope, a Schäffer & Budenburg injector, a Mollerup oil pump, and a special steerage spindle with a flanged coupling. With Harkness it survived to be probably the last working road locomotive in Britain, but axle breakages plagued it all through its life. It has been known throughout its working life and in preservation as *Vera*. Even as this is written it is about to receive a complete refit, including a new firebox.

The first of the pair, however, does not survive. A crankshaft to a new design was prepared for it in 1917, and was sent in October, 1917. Less than a year later, on July 3, 1918, it was sold to Norman E. Box, the celebrated Manchester heavy haulier. Admittedly the shortage of engines brought on by the 1914-18 war was then at its peak but Box was the most hard-headed of hard-headed men and not one to buy or tolerate rubbish. It remained with him until at least 1926, during which time it was registered NC 2026, so it must have had merits not acknowledged by its initial owners. Subsequent owners were John Kellett of Plas Newydd, and E. Maxwell of Bedford, but there is no definite date known when it was scrapped.

The third engine of this batch, No.27763, was sold to Alfred Dawson of Rushmere, Ipswich, a near neighbour of Teddy Ballam, the Garrett sales manager, leaving the Works on November 2, 1909. For reasons not now clear, the height of the firebox was increased by 4" (i.e. from 2' 9⅜" to 3' 1⅜") with an extra row of horizontal stay bolts, but the engine seems not to have pleased Dawson as it was back at the Works permanently by the time the stock list of October 1, 1910, was prepared. It was soon re-sold to H.L. Harding of Hungerford, having first undergone some alterations to satisfy his requirements. Once again 18" wide wheels were asked for as also was a 4' 2" diameter flywheel as against the 3' 7" wheel originally provided. The left-hand waterlifter was removed and blanked off, and a belt roller was fitted to the belly tank. Similarly the toolbox was moved from the tank top to the rear of the tender to be out of the way of the belt. Obviously Harding intended it for threshing as he requested a Pickering governor. Less obvious is why he asked for a semi-circular spud rack in front of the steering ring. Garretts charged him £500 for the engine thus altered, of which £450 was credited to Dawson. Either in the course of this work or soon after, it received a new nickel steel axle. By the Summer of 1924 the engine belonged to W. Brumby, the North of England showman, but 1929 was the last year in which it was licensed, and it was later scrapped by Longstaffs of Hull.

The last of the quartet was No.27854 which was sold to E. Hill of Kingsmill Brickworks, Swindon. Hill's preoccupation seems to have been with boiler feed water. He not only insisted upon a Schäffer & Budenburg injector but he also required the engine to be fitted with a specially designed feed pump with a rocking link enabling the stroke to be adjusted. Further he asked for two especially large water lifters, obviously intent on enabling his driver to snatch a fill of water rapidly when occasion demanded. Hill paid relatively dearly for his engine compared with the £604 paid by Lalondes. He was charged £920 less 10% discount (i.e. £828 nett), receiving an allowance of £175 for his old Aveling & Porter engine, No.3365, thereby reducing his debt to a nett total of £653 which was covered by a hire purchase agreement. As the old Aveling was virtually worthless this savours of putting a bit on to knock a bit off. Hill did not have as much trouble as some other owners but was sent a new 5⅝" nickel steel main axle gratis at the end of April, 1910. In 1912 he failed on his hire purchase payments and the engine was re-possessed though it was soon sold to R.J. Colcomb of Sellack, Herefordshire, who already had 6NHP superheated traction No.29764. No.27854 was repainted dark green with red wheels, the wheel strakes were renewed, a Pickering governor was put on, and a Victor oil pump fitted. Another alteration was that the injector overflow was rearranged to discharge onto the ground instead of into the tender tank. Colcomb also required a flywheel brake to be fitted, a belt roller to be put onto the nearside belly tank top, and the awning to have side and rear curtains. A name plate *Man of Ross* was made in cast brass and thus accoutred it left Leiston again on May 22, 1912. It would be nice to record that it lived happily ever after, but in fact it had at least six subsequent owners, the last of whom, Fred Duckwith of Pocklington in the East Riding of Yorkshire, appears to have sold it for scrap.

The inadvertent shortcomings such as the failures of the rear axle noted above were, for obvious reasons, very annoying to the owners of the engines. However, the feature which most disqualified the group as road locomotives was the use of the Garrett springing system to the rear axle with which the amount of spring movement was so limited as not to be consistent with their intended duties. This aside their dimensions and arrangements were compatible with the general requirements of a road locomotive. As in the 8NHPs a webbed right angle crankshaft was used, forged out of a single billet, and this was, as would have been expected, balanced. The crankshaft was 4" diameter in the bearings and 3½" diameter between the webs. The first countershaft was 4¼" diameter, squared to 3⅝" where the gears moved upon it. The bearing dimensions were reasonable, if not generous. The crankshaft brasses were 6" wide; those on the first countershaft were 7" on the offside and 6" on the nearside where, perhaps, 7" would have been better. The original injector used was a Schäffer, an unusual choice for Garretts, but in later years a Penberthy BB3 was substituted. Although in the extent of the machine cut gears the No.6 road locomotive was well abreast of the field, on the width of the teeth things were cut perhaps a little too fine. Thus the low speed crankshaft pinion and the mating pinion were only 2" wide though the high speed were 2¼", a width used on most of the other gears except the road spur on the axle and the countershaft pinion mating with it, both of which were 3¼" wide, on the slender side for a road locomotive.

Three further similar engines were built for showmen. The reference in the Garrett order book to the first of them (No.26968) originally described it as a '6NHP general purpose three speed traction engine' but this was changed to 'road locomotive'. All subsequent entries called the class 'road locomotives'. In this trio of engines the modifications were limited generally to such as were required to enable them to fulfil the requirements of a fairground locomotive. The driving wheels were 18" wide by 6' 6" diameter, and a 10' 0" extension chimney was supplied. The dynamo bracket was rolled in one with the smokebox and the rails were bolted down to it with five ¾" diameter bolts each side, all somewhat light for the work. A full length awning was fitted, in the design of which Tom Jones had obviously taken more than a fleeting glance at a Fowler. The first engine of the new class to be actually completed and despatched bore the higher Works number of 26999. This was sent off on May 27, 1908, to Robert Body at Meopham, near Gravesend, Kent. The one bearing the earlier number, 26968, did not leave until August 25, 1908, and was consigned to J. Purchase at Hounslow. Whether or not it was bought on his own behalf or for the partnership of Purchase & Rose is not clear as the Purchase & Rose name was used on many subsequent transactions, coupled to the address of The Fairground, Tower Bridge Road, London, SE1. This engine bore the name *Surprise*, though to what this rather whimsical soubriquet referred no one now seems to know. The dynamo was put on at Leiston and was supplied by R.H. Hayne & Co. Ltd., but the name of the maker is not recorded. Because of this Purchase paid £775 for the engine, compared with the £740 which Robert Body paid for his without a dynamo. Both were sold on hire purchase for a down payment of £100 and the balance in twenty quarterly instalments. Body's engine was painted in light green, with red wheels, and was heavily decorated with scroll-work in gold leaf, which called for special mention on the order. Other special requirements were double pin drive on the nearside and the duplication of both the injector and the waterlifter. This latter feature would undoubtedly have saved time at pick-up points.

Neither engine had a happy career with its first owner and it is interesting to consider some of the problems encountered, beginning with those of No.26968. It appears that Purchase had no driver available when he took delivery because from then until October 2, 1908, it was driven by one of the Works drivers, J. Smith. Repairs were carried out in October, 1909, and cost, with the new parts supplied, £20.15.0. In April the following year the axle broke. By the end of the 1910 travelling season Purchase had declined to continue to pay the instalments. At this juncture the engine seems to have been out of repair again as two men, Spital and Raynes, were sent from Leiston to get it going and it was then seized for default, £37.6.7 being added to Purchase's indebtedness to cover the repairs and the seizure. In December 1910, the engine was sold to Samuel Jones, then at 64 High Street, Hounslow, for £750, made up of a down payment of £30 and the rest at £30 a quarter. Thus it had depreciated by only £25 over a period of twenty-eight months. Jones honoured the bargain despite the fact that he did not escape problems. The following is a list of the charges made by the firm for repairs and renewals during his first five years as owner.

Jan. 14, 1911	Hoses, brasses etc.	£19. 16. 0
April 24, 1913	New crankshaft	£20. 8. 0
June 24, 1913	Repairs	£13. 11. 7
July 11, 1914	Fitters time	£15. 0. 0
Oct. 30, 1914	Main axle	£20. 0. 0

Jan. 4, 1915	Driving pinion	£ 6. 0. 0
Feb. 8, 1915	Main spur ring	£17. 10. 0
Mar.5, 1915	Front spring, brasses etc.	£20. 4. 0
April 18, 1915	Fitters time, etc.	£10. 18. 10
Sept. 1, 1915	Brass bush	£ 6. 15. 0
Sept. 25, 1915	Fitter Fowles expenses	£ 4. 12. 10
Oct. 7, 1915	Cannon bracket	£ 3. 6. 0
October 25, 1915	Front spring	£ 8. 6. 6

Whilst, without doubt, a number of these charges related to routine renewals the new crankshaft appears to have rankled, and after consideration Garretts issued a credit in full for the cost of it.

In the case of Body's engine, No.26999, I have not kept such an extensive note of the repairs but it is worth recording that it had a new crankshaft and crank bracket cap fitted at Ightham, Kent, in September, 1911, suggesting a breakdown whilst at work. Relations between Garretts and Robert Body deteriorated and at one point discussions were conducted via solicitors. Finally Body seems to have refused to make further payments for an engine he found unsatisfactory and it came back into the firm's hands, being lodged for safe keeping with Swales Forrest to whom Ballam was able to sell it for £450 in April, 1915, a sufficient sum to leave Body free of debt. With the Forrests its career was much less chequered though I have a note that a new firebox for it, costing £40.15.2 was sent to Frederick Clark & Co. Ltd. at Elwick Iron Works, Ashford, Kent, in November, 1922. They still had it in 1932, but out of use, and it was subsequently cut up. Incidentally No.26968 was reboxed by Gowers of Bedford in April, 1923.

The third No.6 road loco to be supplied to a showman was No.27343, sold to James Manders, The Showground, Lillie Road, Fulham, London, which was sent off on March 27, 1909, with the name *Frances* carried on a brass plate at the foot of the cylinder. Manders had his own name and address engraved upon brass name plates which were mounted on the steam chest covers. He also had a grossly deceptive weight plate '10 tons' displayed on the engine which weighed more like 14½ tons. As the books are silent concerning the livery it was probably painted dark red.

After this no 6NHP engines were sold to showmen but two 7NHP spring mounted traction engines were made with fittings to showmen's requirements. They were ordered in 1908 by R.H. Hayne & Co. of Gloucester Mansions, Cambridge Circus, London W.C.2. These were Nos. 27359 and 27360 built to identical specifications during the Winter of 1908/09. Essentially they were two speed general purpose traction engines with a number of refinements which included motion covers, rim brakes on the rear wheels, full length awning, extended smokebox and dynamo rails as on the No.6 engines, renewable bushes in the rear wheels, a spoked flywheel with a bolted on steel disc, Empire oil pump, 20" wide rear wheels, coal rails to the tenders, 125 gallon belly tanks, 10' extension chimneys, and double pins to the near side driving wheel. Haynes supplied the dynamos but Garretts provided the waterproof covers for them and also fitted the engines with extra long waterproof curtains ordered as reaching down to the ground. No.27360 was erected by Barnard but No.27359 was assembled by Tom Staulkey who was also involved in the testing of finished engines in the brake house, a function then loosely under the control of the erecting shop foreman but soon to be shaken up and reorganised by Frank Walker. Tom's star waxed under the revised system and ultimately he became the company's first travelling service inspector as related in *Garrett Wagons - Part 2*. Tom Barnard was a veteran erector and fitter who had worked on traction engines since the early 1870s, in those days having been one of the band of fitters sent to attend to customers' engines 'in the field'.

A few parts were in common with the preceding 6NHP showmen's locos, such as the piston rods and glands, the cylinder cocks and the starting slide, but the pressure was only 160 p.s.i. compared with the 180 p.s.i. used in the road locos. Inevitably this made them a little less efficient thermally but more docile to handle. The engines were sold for a gross price of £717.17.0 each, payable as to £410 with the order and the balance over three years in equal quarterly instalments. For their part as agents Haynes were allowed commission amounting to £246.3.7 for the two engines. The first of them, No.27359, left Leiston on March 18, 1909, destined for Ardwick. Manchester, Goods Station on the Great Central Railway. For whom it worked in its initial few months is not known, but by July, 1909, it was owned by Swales and Henry Forrest. From quite early days the crankshaft was found to be not quite man enough for the job. In May, 1910, stiffening blocks and new crankshaft brasses were supplied and this remedial work answered for some years but eventually a new crankshaft of stiffer pattern to drawing T10216 was manufactured and sent in October, 1918. By contrast No.27360 which went on March 29, 1909, to William Mitchell & Sons at Preston seems to have avoided this problem or, if it did occur, it was dealt with locally. By 1911 the engine had passed to James Dewhurst, then at Moorbrook Street, Preston, but later in Green Bank Street, off Brook Street, Preston, by whom it was used until the closing days of steam on fairgrounds, being last licensed in 1949.

It is, perhaps, appropriate to mention here three other engines which, though not built for fairground use, nevertheless spent many years in the business. The oldest of them was 8NHP single No.25858, supplied to G.F. Townsend of Exning, Newmarket, on July 19, 1906, and mentioned earlier in the chapter. Although a single this was turned out with regular road haulage obviously in mind, sprung on both axles, fitted with a belly tank, having rear wheels 6' 6" in diameter by 20" on the rims, and provided with a balanced crankshaft. Various other amendments to the standard specification marked it out as a favourite engine. All the pipework, for instance, was in copper; it had motion covers, a Hopkins patent water gauge, a cast iron chimney, two toolboxes, and a spud rail instead of the then customary spud pan. A number of parts were plated, including all four wheelcaps, the flywheel key cap, the starting lever, reversing lever and reach rod, the cylinder tap rod, the top bar of the safety valve, the governor and its pulley, the gear change lever, and the smokebox door handles. Before 1924 it had been sold to Joseph Castle of Chichester by whom it was named *Greyhound*, and about 1926 passed to G. Baker of Southampton.

The second of these three engines was No.27160, a 6NHP spring mounted general purpose engine supplied new to Alfred Dawson at Rushmere on June 26, 1908, and painted in Dawson's usual livery of dark green with red wheels. Obviously he had in mind a life for it involving a considerable amount of road work - probably haulage of road stone, as he was also a steam rolling and road-making contractor. Although the spoked flywheel was retained he had renewable bushes as well as rim brakes fitted to the rear wheels, and twin Klinger gauge glasses. In the Autumn of 1909, as narrated earlier in the chapter, he bought No.27763, aimed more seriously at haulage, and No.27160 went back to Leiston, most probably because Ballam had agreed to help sell it for him. The customer he found was William E. Swallow of Lower Guiting, Cheltenham, for whom it was fitted with an awning, a coal rack, and a belly tank with a belt roller on top. Swallow called the engine *Cotswold Queen*, and it was sent off to him on May 18, 1910. The engine received a new crankshaft in December, 1911, and six weeks later a new nickel steel main axle was sent to Notgrove Station. By 1921 it was owned by T. Walker & Sons Ltd. of Tewkesbury. Walkers rebuilt it as a showman's engine named *British Hero*, though for whom I do not know. Subsequently it became the property of Tom Sheppard, then of Wellingborough, Northants, who used it with his Tidman three-abreast set of gallopers. About 1935 it left the fairground life when it was sold to the late John Rundle at New Bolingbroke, and in 1956 entered preservation with R.L. Orth at Maldon, Essex.

The third engine was a spring mounted 7NHP compound (No.27333 of December, 1908) originally sold to A. Kelly of Writtle near Chelmsford, Essex; again with some customised features including 18" wide rear wheels with rim brakes, double driving pins and a coal rack. It returned to the hands of its builders on July 31, 1910, where it was rebuilt to showman's specification for Swales Bolesworth, then based in Mile End Road, East London. In the course of this rebuilding it was given new gears, a belly tank with a larger water lifter, a new injector, a Manzell oil pump, a solid flywheel (in place of the original spoked flywheel), a dynamo plate, a full length awning on six brass encased columns, motion covers with brass stars in brass circles, similar stars and rings on each end of the belly tank, a brass steering wheel, a 10' 0" extension chimney, brass false covers to the cylinders, a brass brake wheel, and a brass name plate *King George V*. The extension chimney, described by Garretts as a 'thin funnel', was made from 22 BWG ($^1/_{32}$") galvanized steel sheet, tapered to fit into the top of the main chimney to a depth of 12", an 1½"angle ring, $^1/_8$" thick, being rivetted on to stop it being jammed in further. How this worked in practice must be at least questionable. The livery was crimson with red wheels, the spokes lined in gold. The steam chest covers had brass plates bearing its owner's name and address. Bolesworth paid £650 for it, divided as to £100 down and the balance in twenty quarterly payments. He ran it until the Autumn of 1915 when it was taken back by Garretts for £350. The next year it was sold to J.E. Corfield, the threshing, haulage and rolling contractor of Newtown, Monmouthshire, for whom the dynamo bracket and extension chimney were removed, and the awning shortened. Its last recorded owner was the Cothercote Mining Co. Ltd. in Shropshire.

How the Garrett road locomotives were looked upon on the fairgrounds is not now readily ascertainable. Those who used the three most popular makes of engine - Burrell, Foster, and Fowler - were, on the whole, scathing about the Garretts. The only Garrett-owning family with whom I had any extended contact were the Forrests, mainly the late Dougal Reynolds and his wife, Vi (neé Forrest). Dougal's considered opinion was that with care it was possible to get useful work out of them but he conceded that the old Fowler which succeeded *Empress of Japan* was a handier engine to work with. On the whole I believe that the designs did not cover the firm with glory and that by a very limited increase in the manufacturing cost they might have been made to deliver a much superior performance. Probably the best feature was their steam raising capacity which, in all cases, was ample. It has been suggested that in undertaking the supply of road locomotives Garretts were venturing into a field of which they had no experience, little understanding and, consequently, little hope of success. Superficially this is a theory that may be considered to explain the observed facts but when one considers the history of their No.4 compound steam tractor, designed just as much from scratch in a line of manufacture they had never practised before, it is possible to see that it is not really tenable.

Fig.80. *No.27160, the 6NHP that began life as a general purpose engine with Alfred Dawson at Rushmere, Ipswich, in 1908, moved to William Swallow in the Cotswolds where it became* Cotswold Queen. *By 1921 it was owned by T.Walker & Sons of Tewkesbury and had become a showman's engine* British Hero. *Later it belonged to Tom Sheppard of Wellingborough who by the time that this photo was taken at Bicester Fair c.1938 had moved to Olney, Bucks, and the engine's name had changed yet again to* Crimson Lady.   [A.J. Martin collection]

Fig.81. 8NHP single speed three shaft Continental type traction engine No.25323 at work in Turkish Asia Minor, exported via George Chisnell of Constantinople. The roof is a late local addition.

Fig.82. Rear end view of a 6NHP Continental type, likely to have been No.25428, built for stock in 1905 and eventually sold in 1907, after modification to suit English requirements, to Horace Bennett of Stoke Ash, Suffolk, being the only three shaft Garrett traction engine of 6NHP and over to be used in the U.K.

Fig.83. Remains of Garrett 6NHP portable, converted to a chain-drive self-mover, now at Lahemaa National Park, Estonia.
[Lahemaa National Park]

Fig.84. Continental type No.29786, a 5NHP two speeder, built in 1911 for H.Jungclaussen of Ahrensbök, near Kiel. Holes were drilled for an awning to be added on arrival in Germany.

Fig.85. The two speed version of the 5NHP single traction with piston valve. This is No.31551, supplied to Henninger of Darmstadt in October, 1913. Two further engines for him (Nos.32030 and 32273) were similar but had exhaust steam water heaters. This picture appeared in the German language catalogue as a 'Grosse No.5' (Large No.5) by contrast to the standard Continental type.

Fig.86. The oil burning 5NHP type No.28730 sold via Burn & Co.,Calcutta, in 1910 for direct ploughing. It had Kermode oil-burning equipment.

88

Fig.87. Pilter's Dieppe office had No.28755 at Christmas, 1910. Despite its thoroughly Continental appearance it was, more or less, the same as an English pattern 5NHP. Finished crimson lake and lined in gold it must have been a smart engine.

Fig.88. When the Bordeaux office of the same firm had two speeder No.28987 the next spring, it followed the Continental design.

Fig.89. The three shafters Nos.28387 and 28388, sent to Clark & Fauset in Queensland in 1910 for direct ploughing owed as much to the 5NHP English traction engine as to the Continental design. They had a firebox 3' 6" long for wood fuel.

Fig.90. One of the 5NHP singles (probably No.28389) built for Zehder. John Creasey, the paintshop foreman, is posed as driver.
[SRO]

Chapter 7

Continental Traction Engines

As we saw earlier, when discussing strawburners, steam threshing on the continent of Europe was dominated by the portable engine for some fifty years, and Garretts gained only a limited foothold in the market for straw-burning traction engines. Although the manufacture of these was begun with eastern Europe in view it turned into a trade mainly with South America. The Austro-Hungarian empire, which then embraced the South Tirol (now in Italy), Slovenia, Croatia and Bosnia, all of the present Czech and Slovak republics, and territories now in Poland, Russia, and Roumania, had long been a target for the selling of Garrett portables but as the nineteenth century drew to a close it had become increasingly protectionist, thereby forestalling any useful attempts to market traction engines there. Even Clayton & Shuttleworth, who had established a daughter works in Floridsdorf, on the northern outskirts of Vienna, found it convenient to allow it to pass into Austrian hands as Hofherr & Schrantz, in what would now be called a management buy-out.

Such success as was gained in Austria-Hungary by traction engines as a class was achieved by the type emanating from Hofherr & Schrantz, i.e. stripped of every refinement and left with only the barest essentials. Because the economics of Richard Garrett & Sons Ltd. were so tied to trade with Europe the emergence there of a simplified variety of traction engine aroused an interest in the production of such engines at Leiston Works. As the Continental trade was largely the domain of Remy it is probable that his influence was behind both the initiation and the marketing of these engines, though, as in other similar instances, it would be hard to say whether designs preceded enquiries or vice versa. Designs for a lighter type of three shaft 6 and 8NHP single cylinder engine were produced, more or less in parallel, during the Summer and Autumn of 1902 with H.G. Florey as the leading draughtsman. The drawings of the 8NHP were completed first, probably because the design involved the least new work. The forecarriage jaw was borrowed from the 6HP standard traction paired up with the axle and wheels of the 8HP strawburner. The cylinder and piston, most of the reversing gear, starting gear, connecting rod, crosshead and trunks were from the 8HP standard engine, together with details such as the crankshaft brackets and weighshaft brackets and smokebox door. The tender also came from this source. The 8HP strawburner design, being also three shaft, yielded virtually all of the remainder. The boiler, however, was entirely new as was the pump body, though the rod and plunger came from the strawburner. The 6NHP version was not derivative to the same degree since, although it was able to use the engine work from the standard 6HP single and such things as the flywheel, differential gear, winding drum and parts of the gearing and brackets from the 8HP strawburner, a larger number of parts had to be designed afresh, starting, of course, with the boiler but including the wheels, axles and steerage, crankshaft and brackets.

These engines had three shafts and were equipped with only a single road speed. As to the cylinder, piston, valve and valve gear, they utilised standard parts. The wheels were conventional in design though of lighter than standard construction. Although the tender followed standard practice the draw-bar was rivetted directly to it there being no straps forward to the driving axle. In contrast to the extensive protection around the train of gears which was standard for the home market the gear casing on these engines was reduced to a light plate between the manstand and the large intermediate gear with a return at the top to cover the teeth of the gear on the upper third of its circumference. By these means an appreciable saving in weight resulted together with some economy of manufacturing costs, but neither factor was carried to a degree that enabled the design to capture the attention of the potential market. No.25428, built for stock in the Summer of 1905, remained on the Works unsold for over two years, probably used during that time as a yard engine. Towards the end of 1907 Ballam was able to interest Horace Bennett of Stoke Ash, Suffolk, in the engine. Bennett had the reputation of buying anything useful provided the price was right. From time to time he took various second-hand engines off the firm's hands but on this occasion he asked for the engine to be given a thorough overhaul and to be turned out in 'as new' condition. The changes made involved the fitting of standard safety valves in place of spring balances and probably the provision of improved gear guards. It left on January 15, 1908, believed to be the only 6NHP three shaft Garrett traction engine to have worked in the United Kingdom.

Through these engines and the strawburners described in Chapter 4 the company demonstrated its willingness to build three shaft engines where it deemed that a market existed for them, but the reactions of the purchasing public seemed to indicate a preference for traction engines in which the change speed gears were, as at least one owner termed it, 'indoors' i.e. between the hornplates. Thus, notwithstanding the loss of mechanical efficiency by reason of the use of four shafts instead of three, to potential purchasers it appeared to impart enhanced mechanical stability for which they were prepared to pay. This body of buyers may be termed 'the traditionalists', not because there really was a very extended tradition of using four shafts but because those who preferred them often seemed to act as if defending a long established custom against innovation. In any event few buyers can have based their attitudes on scientific knowledge if only for the reason that not many of them had had the kind of training that would have implanted it. One suspects that most were guided by their own appreciation of how a particular maker's engines had served them or their acquaintances in the past. The advent of steam tractors for one man operation, made legal in 1896, changed the numerical balance between the three and four shaft fraternities markedly. It may be significant that one of the first firms to appreciate the potential of steam tractors was Wallis & Steevens, firmly in the three shaft camp, but on the other hand the weight restrictions upon tractors were so severe as virtually to inhibit the use of four shafts on grounds of weight alone.

By comparison with Wallis & Steevens, Garretts were a little on the late side in beginning to build steam tractors. Their first 3-tonner did not emerge onto the market until mid-1905, probably profiting by noting how the Basingstoke firm had fared with theirs. All makers who essayed a 3-ton tractor reached the conclusion that it was too small to attract useful sales. The revision of the weight limit to 5 tons, which became effective in 1905, permitted a very useful size of machine to be built that could still be legally managed by one man. At Leiston the first 5 ton tractor (No.25646) was a single, despatched in 1906, followed by the first compound in May, 1907. Though the history of these steam tractors is intended to be dealt with in a subsequent volume they are mentioned here because they led to a design of light three shaft traction engine that attracted a reasonable number of Continental and Colonial sales. It may be objected, and with truth, that in reality any steam tractor is merely a small traction engine, but the term, rightly or wrongly, has acquired a connotation which distinguishes it from that of a traction engine and it is submitted that it is not simply sophistry that leads me to classify some of the Garrett output of 4NHP engines as tractions while reserving others to be treated later as steam tractors.

It has already been related in Chapter 3 how an enquiry from Ed. Zehder in Riga for a light and inexpensive 5NHP traction engine sparked off a revived interest in building engines of that horsepower for the home market. Zehder had a very flourishing import agency, dealing mainly with portable engines. Until 1898 Richard Garrett & Sons had had a warehouse in Riga under their direct control, but in March that year they transferred the business to a concern entitled Rigaer Eisengiesserei und Maschinenfabrik (the Riga Iron Foundry & Machine Works) which had formerly traded as Felser & Co. In December, 1900 it again changed ownership, this time to Zehder. The scale of trading with Garretts was already considerable, but Zehder developed it still further with large orders for portables, mainly of 6NHP or smaller, and threshers to accompany them.

Since about 1990 a number of self-moving engines, based on Garrett portables, have been reported in the Baltic States. One of these stands in Lahemaa National Park in Estonia. Essentially it is a 6NHP single cylinder portable modified to make it reversible, and fitted with a live rear axle, light pattern traction engine wheels with angle strakes, a steel driving platform with tub bunkers, and steering arrangements to the front axle. A gear on the nearside end of the crankshaft slides on a key and can be put into and out of drive with a gear on a stub shaft, to which a chain sprocket is fixed. A chain ran to a double sprocket bracketed to the outer throat plate of the firebox and a secondary chain drove from there to the rear axle below the firehole. The driving chain is in the grass beside it. No engines in this form were supplied from Leiston Works, and the inescapable conclusion appears to be that they were ingenious and well executed local reconstructions. In the absence of evidence in any other direction one is tempted to conjecture that this conversion was done by Zehder. It is equally tempting, and just as unsupported by tangible evidence, to imagine that the same thinking that inspired the reconstruction of the engine now at Lahemaa led Zehder or one of his clients on to order the first purpose built Continental type 5NHP engine.

This initial engine (No.27855), created by boring out the cylinder of a 4NHP single cylinder tractor ½" larger and mounting it upon a No.4 tractor boiler with a colonial firebox, was unsprung and had only one travelling speed. It was followed by four others of essentially the same design (Nos.28390, 28394, 28407, and 28754) - the last of which left on October 14, 1910 - and by one engine (No.28389) generally the same but with a second road speed. Three other engines (28759, 28765, and 28987), all described as 'Continental' traction engines went to Grimaldi (Italy), Henninger (Germany), and Pilter (France) respectively.

The success of these engines led to the development of a heavier 5NHP Continental type with a rather larger boiler, in which the barrel was increased in length from 3' 10³/₁₆" to 6' 1¼" and the diameter from 1'10½" to 2' 4½". In turn this modification made it possible to increase the tube diameter to 2¼", whilst still keeping the number at 28. Taken in conjunction with a rather larger firebox, giving a grate area of 6.5 square feet, these changes produced a total heating surface of 139 square feet with a working pressure of 180 p.s.i. and a governed speed of 230 r.p.m. The maximum brake horse power generated was 30 when on test at the Works burning Llangenneck or similar good steam coal of about 14000 BTU per pound. Probably at their intended places of work they were meant to run either on wood or on brown coal briquettes. Not much road work can have been contemplated as the gear ratio of 1:22.2 produced a maximum travelling speed of 2 m.p.h. Like the strawburners and the earlier 6NHP Continentals they were black engines with only working or fitting surfaces being machined. Almost invariably they were supplied with a wire spark arrester in the chimney top. The rear wheels, of conventional pattern but lighter in construction than those for home use, were 5' 6" in diameter and 16" across the tread.

The first of these newer and stronger 5NHP Continental tractions was No.28989, completed and taken into stock at the end of February, 1911, and sent to Zehder on June 1. Between then and the outbreak of war in August, 1914, fifteen further 5NHP single cylinder tractions were shipped to Europe. Of these, eight were for Zehder, the remaining seven being divided between Grimaldi, (four), Pilter, Jungclaussen, and Haasemann. Only No.29786 of 1911 for Jungclaussen, and No.30969 of 1912 for Haasemann were two speeders, all the others being single speed. Despite the useful performance characteristics of these 5NHP engines they were, in fact, substantially bigger and heavier than No.27855, the engine first sent to Zehder, so that the question arose of building an engine with the cylinder of the 4NHP single tractor on a 4NHP Colonial boiler without springs or second road speed, but with the broader wheels and simplified finish which characterised the 5NHPs. How this debate was conducted between Zehder and Remy cannot now be determined, though the suggestion seems to have emanated from Zehder.

The first of the design which resulted from these talks was No.28992, despatched on April 15, 1911, followed by five more (Nos.28993 to 28997 inclusive) sent in July, August, and September. All were single speed, all identical, and all to Zehder. He had another five, Nos.29789, 30288, 30991, 31058, and 31081, in 1912, followed by three more, (Nos.32343, 32444, and 32474) in 1914. At that point the trade was ended by the outbreak of war. Garretts found themselves with large debts from Russia which were detained there under a moratorium declared by the Czarist government and eventually disclaimed altogether by the Communists after the October, 1917, revolution. As with most engines supplied to Continental agents little is known about the ultimate purchasers. Only in the case of No.28996 (4NHP) do we have any subsequent history. Spares for that were ordered by Woldemar Major of Riga in April, 1939. When the war began three 4NHPs (Nos.32510, 32557, and 32560) together with a 5NHP (No.32576) were left in progress at Leiston, and were eventually requisitioned by the Army impressing officer, going in November, 1916, and January, 1917, to the Area Director of Works in Salonika.

Both 4 and 5NHP engines were fitted with geared pumps and a Moore's steam pump. The majority had open tenders with coal boxes each side, the feed water being carried in a belly tank. Additionally Zehder's standard specification for both sizes stipulated a single speed, winding drum, rope guide roller, a Graham (later Munktels) spark arrester in the base of the chimney, a spark grate in the smokebox, a band brake on the rear axle, Pickering governors, spring balance safety valves, an Empire mechanical lubricator, gauge cocks on the belly tank, and an ashpan with two doors. Grimaldi, the Italian agent with depots in Milan and Turin, had the Empire oil pump on his earlier purchases but latterly went over to Italian pumps made in Milan by Ghiringhelli Giovanni, whose office was in Via Ippolito Rosellini 18. He also preferred wired tops to the chimneys rather than the Graham arresters favoured by Zehder. On No.29001 he specified splash lubrication to the connecting rod big end, a messy and wasteful expedient even when arranged with a deflector to direct surplus oil back into the dip pot. This engine had no winding drum. By contrast, the two speeder No.28731 supplied to Haasemann in Germany had a Manzell oil pump. It also had an awning over the manstand and an exhaust steam feedwater heater. The left-hand coal box was rearranged as a tool box. There was also a steersman's step fitted on the left-hand side, and the steering wheel was a little lower. Unlike most other Continentals it was painted in brown rather than the standard green.

One Continental type 5NHP was sold to Burn & Co. Ltd. in Calcutta for direct traction ploughing. This was No.28730, sent off on November 22, 1910, in Royal Show finish, intended for showing at the Allahabad Exhibition. For ploughing it had removable extension pieces to the wheels. The ploughing speed, at 230 r.p.m., was 1.16 m.p.h., and the travelling speed was 3.36 m.p.h. Additionally it was equipped for oil burning on Kermode's system, one bunker holding the oil tank and the other coal for lighting up.

No.28765, the only 5NHP Continental type supplied to Henninger, had no winding drum or wire rope but otherwise conformed to standard design. No.29786, the Continental supplied to Jungclaussen, another German agent, was generally conformist except that it was two speed and made to comply with the new and more stringent German boiler regulations introduced in 1910. Pilter, the French agent, had his first 5NHP traction (No.28755) to the English pattern - two speed, sprung, fitted with a slotted and balanced crankshaft, provided with an awning, having rim brakes to the rear wheels, and an English type tender. It had a geared pump but not the Moore's steam pump used on the subsequent Continentals. Somewhat unusually it was painted in crimson lake and lined in gold. Whereas this engine went to the Dieppe depot, the next 5NHP (No.28987) was supplied to the firm at Bordeaux and was a straightforward Continental type, albeit with two speeds, but Pilter ordered the wired top to the chimney rather than the Graham-type arrester used on the Zehder engines.

One of this group, No.28755, is in a private collection at Laas in France along with a Garrett No.4 compound tractor and a number of Garrett portables. What survives in the Baltic States is not known for certain but a number of Garretts are undoubtedly there.

Fig.91. Gas Hill, Leiston, early in 1914 after a test on 6NHP compound No.32125 (leading). The record of this test is lost but in a similar one in July, 1913, 6NHP No.31611 successfully hauled up the hill a load of 56.8 tons made up of 4NHP traction No.31639; Colonial tractor No.31647 ; a CSIV boiler on a trolley; an OBC engine; and 5 ton wagon No.31353, loaded with pig iron. The original, from the ruins of the test house, was much defaced, but shows a line-up essentially the same as in the 1913 test.

Fig.92. 7NHP sprung single No.33442 (Aug. 1919) sold to H.Baylis, Hatford, Berks, via the agency of T.Baker & Sons of Compton who often had supplied Garretts with water carts. In the picture it was owned by Wilcox & Frost, the Witney hay merchants, and had probably been baling. It is preserved.
[A.J. Martin collection]

Fig.93. Leslie Cooper's 5NHP piston valved single No.34045, used as a yard engine until he had it, after overhaul, in Sept. 1922, seen here on July 29, 1936, at Pear Tree Farm, Knodishall.
[R.G. Pratt]

Fig.94. No.34727, a 6NHP compound rigid traction (May 23, 1925) for Dublin C.C. with motion guards and, curiously, spring balance safety valves.

Fig.95. Roscommon C.C.'s 6NHP No.34125 of 1923. The all-over roof looks ungainly but was very useful in the soft climate of Ireland.
[A.J. Martin collection]

Figs. 96, 97, and 98. *Three views of the 80 BHP plougher No.34937 at Station Works, Leiston, prior to shipment to W.H. Cullington in Buenos Aires in September, 1926. They illustrate, inter alia, the care taken in designing the wet bottomed ashpan, and also the firehole door position which would appear to inhibit the use of coal as a fuel.*

Fig.99. The last 7NHP single cylinder engine made at Leiston, No.35140 (1929) at Clarencefield, Dumfries, Sept.12, 1938.
[A.J. Martin collection]

Fig.100. The last Garrett traction, 6NHP No.35461 new to Geo. Ewen Ltd., Petersfield, Hants, in Chris Lambert's yard at Horsmonden not long after his death. [J.Love]

Fig.101. Showman's engine 7NHP No.27360 at Chorley, April 9, 1936, when owned by James Dewhurst of Preston.
[A.J. Martin collection]

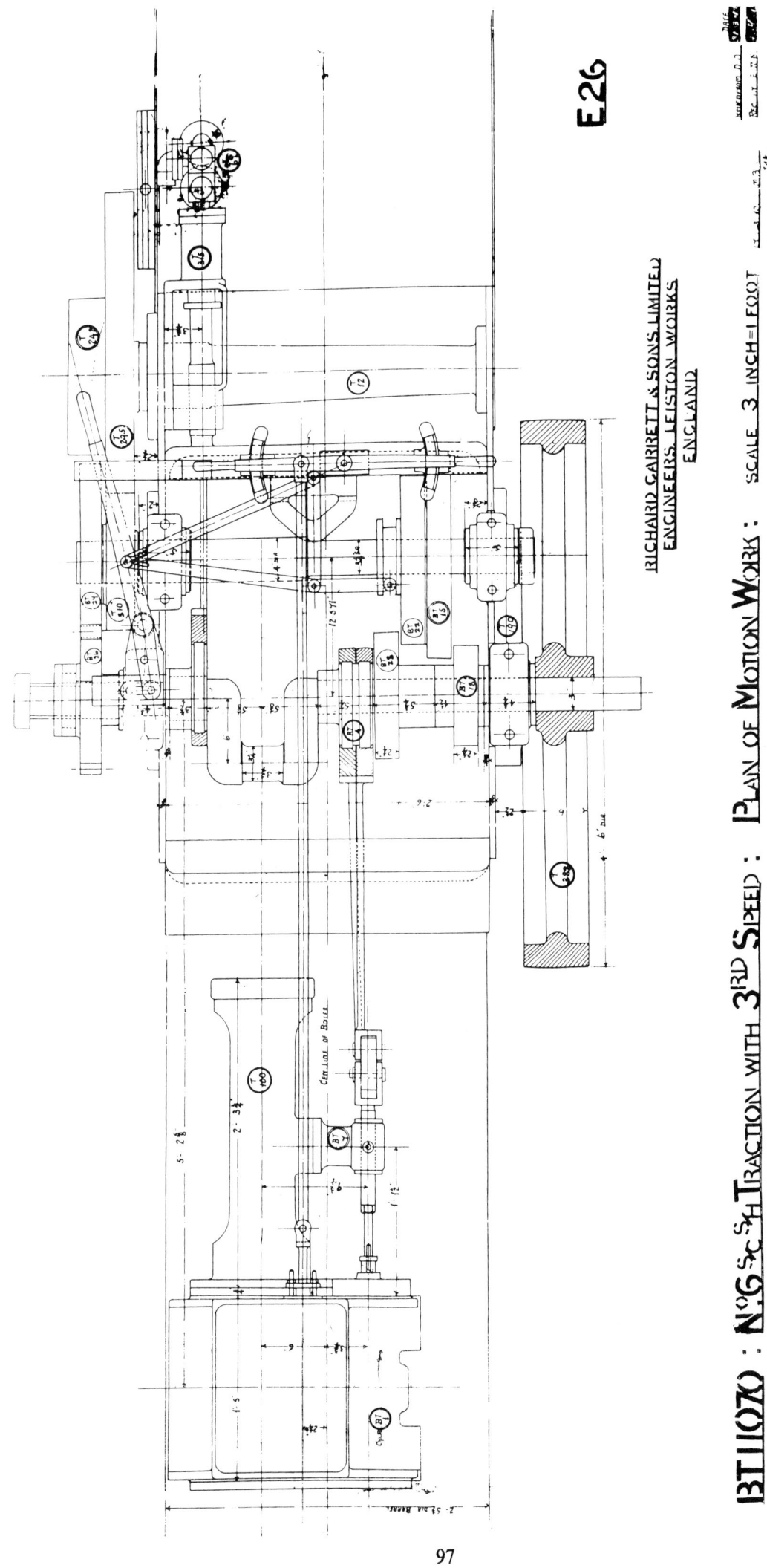

Fig.102. Tom Jones's design of the engine work of a 6NHP single cylinder traction arranged for a third speed outside the hornplates. This shows the interlocking mechanism used.

Chapter 8

Final Days

As I have related in earlier books Garretts emerged from the 1914-18 war with their overseas trade, upon which their prosperity had so long depended, shattered, in part because of the physical and political devastation in Germany and the former Austro-Hungarian empire, in part because American firms had moved into their Antipodean and South American markets left unsupplied whilst Leiston concentrated upon its war effort and in part, again, because it had proved impossible to extricate the monies due to them from Russia. Refuge from these and other problems was sought by the firm becoming part of the Agricultural & General Engineers combine (AGE) in the Summer of 1919. One of the planks of the platform from which the idea of AGE was canvassed was that it would enable the member firms to co-ordinate their output, thus reducing duplication of facilities and cutting costs. Like many schemes of its type devised, broad brush, in the heady atmosphere of amalgamation it proved less than easy to accomplish and very disappointing in its financial outcome.

The decision by the central administration of AGE to base the whole selling effort of the new combine upon the London head office brought problems in its wake for William Marshall who had been a member of the pre-amalgamation Garrett board since 1916 and had provided the main thrust in developing and selling the CCS and other power plants, his particular client being the Borneo Company Ltd., through which numerous sets had been sold in South East Asia. The new management equated the skills required to sell such machinery with those needed to sell bananas in a street market - a glib tongue and persistence - and regarded salesmen as menials. Marshall, a chartered mechanical engineer, who had spent more than a decade establishing amongst the London purchasing engineers his reputation for reliability and good sense, thus found that the new system had no place for him and quietly withdrew in February, 1920, taking up a managerial position with the Scarab Oil Burning Co. Ltd in their office at 28 Charles Street, off Haymarket in the West End of London. As in so many other things the AGE management soon found itself mistaken in its belief in central selling which was disbanded and its functions redistributed to the constituent companies. The assessment of W.J. Marshall as an elegant boardroom ornament was discovered to have been equally erroneous, and after an absence of some two years he was invited back onto the Leiston board in June, 1922, and accepted the recantation with his usual good grace.

During his period at Scarab he retained his contacts both with the technical staff of Richard Garrett & Sons Ltd. and with the Garretts themselves. As a result, during his two years away from the company he was able to bring about a series of experiments to test the practical and financial consequences of applying oil firing to steam wagons (described in *Garrett Wagons - Part 1*) and traction engines. Oil firing had already been used on various Garrett engines, mostly portables or locomobiles, using either the Holden or the Kermode system. The former was the invention of James Holden whilst chief mechanical engineer of the Great Eastern Railway and arose initially from the need to dispose economically of the unwanted residual oils left from the manufacture at Stratford Works, London, of gas for lighting railway carriages. At first the company had discharged the oily waste into a watercourse that ran by the works, but having been told to cease this pernicious practice it instructed Holden to find better means of getting rid of it. His oil burning system, first applied to the 2-4-0 locomotive *Petrolea*, was the outcome and enjoyed some success. It did, however, require a small fire of coal to be maintained. In the general commercial market it was sold by Taite & Carlton of Queen Victoria Street in the City of London.

The Kermode system, used by Garretts on the 50BHP plougher No.32208 for India, was developed by Kermode's Ltd., Dale Street, Liverpool, for marine use and was a satisfactory method except that, like Holden's system, it required a firebrick lining to part of the firebox and also a brick arch to force the flames to circulate.

The Scarab system worked by allowing the oil to emerge from an outlet into the path of a jet of steam or compressed air by which it was atomised. For this reason it was not prone to blockage unless, by mischance, totally gross impurities were admitted to the feed pipe. On the other hand their proposed lighting up method, involving hand pumping air and the use of an auxiliary steam coil as a kind of flash generator was both extremely laborious and ineffective. An experiment in April and May, 1920, using a twin burner installation on 5 ton wagon No.33750 was described in *Garrett Wagons - Part 1*. Except for the cumbersome procedure for lighting up the trial was a practical success, though the cost of firing by oil exceeded that of coal by a substantial margin.

In early June, 1920, it was decided to put a single larger Scarab burner on to the 50BHP plougher No.33781 as a follow up to this experiment. No attempt was made to use the Scarab system to light up, or any modification of it, but instead a fire of wood and coal was used until steam pressure was high enough to work the atomising system. This perpetuated Holden's method of twenty years before. The larger single burner answered well but, once again, the economics of oil were against it so long as supplies of sound steam coal could be obtained. Industrial unrest in the mines, however, was causing interruption of supplies, and it was this circumstance that had been one of the prompts for the experiment, but the conclusion was that with regular coal supplies available the oil firing would have been ruled out by price.

The wagon experiments were begun under H.D. Lobley who was dismissed before its completion in the aftermath of what later would have been called 'industrial espionage' and continued under Jack Simpson, whom I had the good fortune to know. The change of experimental officer had no bearing upon the conclusions, upon which the two men were agreed, namely, [i] that, aside from lighting up, the Scarab burning system was the most effective that had been tried at Leiston, and [ii] that it had the great advantage of requiring no structural changes to the engine in the form of brick arches or burner apertures through the firebox water legs since the Scarab burner was mounted in a rather deeper pan lined with firebrick which replaced the ashpan. However, the experiments would have needed to have been of much longer duration, years rather than days, to have determined the effect of oil firing upon the life expectancy of the boiler, and no conclusions were asked for or attempted on this matter. At the finish of the experiment the results were reported to Scarab and the apparatus was returned to them. It is believed from word of mouth accounts that Scarab supplied the parts without charge whilst Garretts financed the installation and operation, but documentation on this is lacking.

Three firms that went into the AGE combine had serious claims to be manufacturers of traction engines. The most prominent of these was Charles Burrell & Sons Ltd. of Thetford, followed by Garretts and, finally, by Aveling & Porter. The same three firms also made steam rollers, steam tractors and steam wagons. Another member company, Davey Paxman, who had begun to build traction engines in a small way in the decade before the war, had had so little sales success that they were considered to have no claim. After much bargaining traction engine making was declared to the province of Burrells, and in return Garretts were given a free hand with steam wagons, a part share in steam tractors - the balance going to Aveling & Porter - and all compound portables, singles being relinquished to Davey Paxman. Aveling & Porter were meant to make all the group steam rollers. These arrangements were subject to the proviso that the constituent firms were to be allowed to use up stocks of parts or to honour customer preference.

During the twelve month period when this policy was being worked out and put into what was hoped to be a workable form the Works delivered nine 6 and 7 NHP single traction engines for users in the British Isles plus the 50 BHP direct plougher converted to an ordinary agricultural engine (as noted in Chapter 5). Thereafter traction engine sales ceased abruptly, only one 6 NHP single, No.34016, being sold in 1921. Engines of 7 NHP continued to be sold intermittently, two in 1922, one in 1924, a fourth in 1927, and the final example in 1929, and a 7 NHP with a colonial firebox (No.34918) was sold in June, 1926. Four 6NHP engines were sold up to 1925, and thereafter there was a gap until No.35461, the very last Garrett traction engine of all, left on June 13, 1931, for George Ewens of Petersfield, Sussex.

In 1912 work had been started in the drawing office, mostly under Gordon Thomson, on a new design of 5NHP engine for sale in Britain. This was to use piston valves and a higher boiler pressure than hitherto employed in single cylindered tractions, but not a superheater, which feature had been found to have no customer appeal. A prototype was built and tried but not sold. During the 1914-18 war it was used on the Works for internal transport, and so continued after the war ended. It had been hoped that engines of both 5 and 6NHP of this revised design would enable the firm to make a substantial inroad into the home traction engine market. In this they suffered a grievous disappointment. No matter how much the piston valve appealed to manufacturers because of the ease of manufacture - being mostly machine work compared with the lengthy hand labour involved in scraping in port face and valve - the purchasing public remained aloof, only a handful buying piston valved engines. In what was probably the most sustained effort to popularise the piston valve, Aveling & Porter used it for virtually their whole steam engine output through most of the twenties but, in the end, had to revert to the slide valve, their persistence in the use of the piston valve having, in the interim, contributed to a pronounced down-turn in their share of the market. None of this proves that the piston valve, of itself, was a bad idea, merely that to succeed, a manufacturer must offer his market what it wants and not what he believes it ought to want.

In its German language catalogue the firm described the 1912 piston valved design as the 'grosse No.5' (large No.5) compared with the 'leicht' (light) No.5 of the type being supplied to Zehder and others. In 1922 the prototype was given the number 34045 on the occasion of its sale to Leslie J.S. Cooper of Leiston. Although a scion of a local family Leslie had led an adventurous life up to that time, mostly abroad and much of it in the Argentine where his activities had included the breeding and breaking in of horses. He was on good terms with the younger Garretts and up to the time of his death he maintained a correspondence with Victor. Indeed it was as a result of Victor's introduction that we went to see Leslie a few months before he died. A discussion on the merits of the engine, which he considered the equal of most 6NHPs, was followed by colourful and amusing reminiscences of his youthful adventures. The meeting led to correspondence between us, in the course of which he affirmed his belief that the piston valved 5NHP was an excellent design that had deserved a much greater acceptance than it received. In fact only two others were made, No.34039 which went to W. Logan of Coleraine on September 6, 1922, and No.34046 which was despatched a week later to H. Hawes of Stradbroke, near Eye, Suffolk. This latter engine had a thirty year working life.

In these engines, known as PV1s, the cylinder diameter was increased to 8", the stroke being 10", but the boiler pressure was only 160 p.s.i. compared with 180 p.s.i. used in the No.5 light Continental tractions supplied to Zehder. This apparently retrograde step would have made them more amenable, no doubt, in the restricted spaces of many English stackyards. On test No.34039 earned itself a name for being a little awkward for a quite different reason, namely of failing to stop when the reversing lever was centred. Various suggestions were made as to how to alter this, and J.K. Peecock of the Testing Department was deputed to conduct an investigation into the effect of reducing the length between the steam edges of the valve body from 6¼" to 6", the overall length of the valve remaining at 9³/₈". No.34039 was fitted with a piston valve of this modified pattern and tested on the brake on March 3, 1921. On this test the engine could be stopped by centring the lever. The results of the test, which bear out Leslie Cooper's contention that the type performed well, are quoted below:

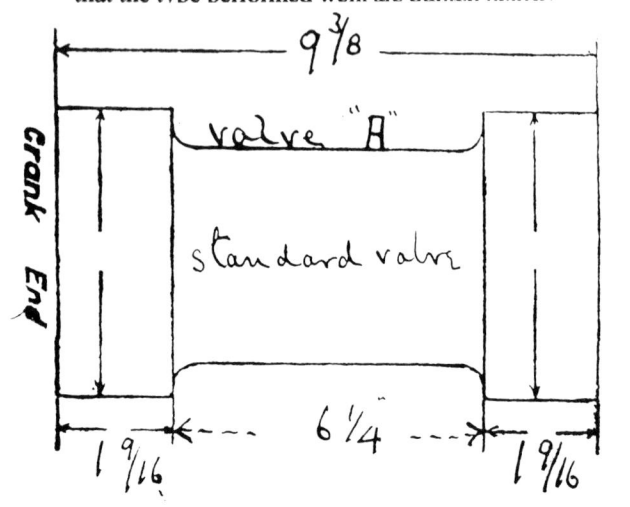

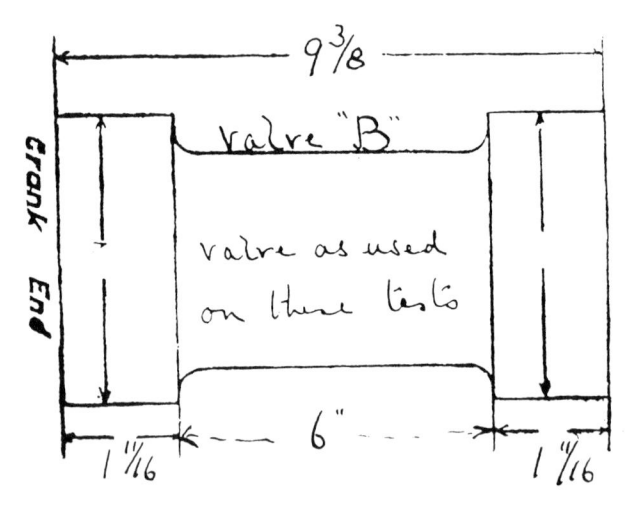

With the standard valve 'A' the engine would not stop with the reversing lever in mid position.
With the modified valve 'B'; this was accomplished.

	Max. Spec. BHP	Max. BHP	I.H.P.	Mech. Eff.	R.P.M.	Blr. Press	Admission Press
With governors	30	46.4	52.2	89.2	228	160	125
Without governors	30	59.0	64.0	90	230	160	149

Type of brake used: wood blocks on water cooled brake wheel.
Type of indicators used: Crosby Spring 1

100

A road run of March 29, for which the engine had had the standard piston valve, with 6¼" between the steam edges, put back, showed how well it could perform.

> On this run the roads were in a very heavy condition - probably the heaviest condition, i.e. thick mud and soft road and no rain for the previous 24 hours.
>
> The load hauled was a 6HP traction with water in the tank and boiler, but no coal in bunker, and gearing in motion. Behind this was coupled the standard tractor test load, i.e. 8.2 tons of pig iron on a trailer. Assuming the weight of the 6HP traction to be 10 tons and the known weight of the trailer was 8.2 tons, total weight hauled = 18.2 tons on 4 axles.
>
> The engine was driven in the full forward notch the whole way (this of course was unnecessary). She climbed all hills on top gear with ease, and would have climbed the test hill had it not been necessary to draw aside into soft ground and stop for a restive horse. It was found impossible to start on top gear.
>
> During this run the engine primed once. I suggest relief valves be fitted. On arriving at the top of the test hill 3¼ miles from Leiston, the tank was found to be empty. The same was observed on the return journey, after filling at the top of the hill. The capacity of the tank is 1050 lbs. of water, therefore the amount of water used per ton mile =
>
> $$\frac{1050}{3.25 \times 18.2} = 17.7 \text{ lbs.}$$
>
> I was particularly struck by the following:
> a] The amount of water used, and the capacity of the tank.
> b] The size and quantity of burning pieces of coal thrown out of the chimney.
> c] The fact that when either the water lifter or injector was used, the water in the gauge glasses was drawn up so that they showed a full glass.
> d] That the engine would not stop in mid gear.
>
> As regards:
> a] This was due partly to the overload hauled, which was close on 100%, and partly to the fact that the engine was not notched up when running easily. At the same time, I think a belly tank would be a great advantage.
> b] This was most marked, and had it been hauling a threshing set would quite likely have set fire to it. This again is partly due to the overload, but some simple form of spark arrestor would be an improvement.
> c] This, I think, must be due to the hole in the boiler below the casting which supplied steam to the water gauges, injector and waterlifter not being large enough. If it were enlarged I think this difficulty would be overcome.
> d] When running forward, and the reversing lever is pulled into mid position, the engine continues to run forward. If running backwards continues to run backwards. This is due to the fact that when in mid gear the valve travel is 1 $^{13}/_{16}$ and the ports open $^5/_{32}$. The lead is $^1/_{16}$. If therefore the valve be lengthened ¼ on the steam edges, there will be no lead - in fact, there will be negative lead, and therefore the angle of retardation should be <u>decreased.</u>

A month later, on April 27, over roads in much better condition, he tried it with 6" between the steam edges. The test load of 10 tons was more appropriate to the size of engine and because it was not pulling so hard and was not constantly in full forward notch the coal throwing was much diminished though, judging by the report (below), nothing had been done about the drawing of the water in the gauge glasses.

> | | |
> |---|---|
> | Distance | 6½ miles. |
> | Load | 10 tons. |
> | Speed | 4.6 M.P.H. |
> | Coal per mile | 26.5 |
> | Water per mile | 163 |
> | Coal per ton mile | 2.65 |
> | Water per ton mile | 16.3 |
> | Evaporation | 6.15 |
> | Class of fuel | Hard steam coal |
> | Conditions of roads | Good. |
>
> REMARKS:
> On the outward journey, when a crank bearing ran hot and gave trouble, the reversing lever was in various positions, i.e. in the 1st, 2nd and third notches. On the return journey the reversing lever was in the 3rd notch the whole way, including hills.
> Some difficulty was experienced in starting on hills.
> The engine did not throw much coal out of the funnel, neither did she prime. She would not stop running with the reversing lever in mid gear.
> The remarks in the previous report on this engine apply equally in this case.
> The engine pulls and steams well, and is easy to handle.

It is not known for certain whether No.34039 went to her purchaser with 6¼" or 6" between the steam edges of the piston valve, nor what was done with No.34046 but as they had long lives the nett outcome must have been satisfactory. The tender remained virtually as in the No.5 English slide valve tractions which had a coal capacity of 9 cubic feet, although for some now obscure reason this was stated in PV1 sales literature at the much lower figure of 6¾ cubic feet. The boiler barrel was the same, albeit 5' 1¾" compared with 5' 1³/₁₆" in the No.5 English, but the firebox was much smaller, giving a grate area of 4.03 square feet against 5.27 square feet in the earlier design.

The market appeal of the PV1 tractions was never put to the test because of the merger into AGE and the cessation of traction engine building at Leiston, but experiences elsewhere in the group and in the industry as a whole suggest that their potential was not as high as had been hoped. Apart from the fact that by the time they appeared the day of the traction engine was already well spent it is to be feared that the piston valve would have condemned them to a mediocre share of what market remained.

However, two further new products did seem to offer better hopes of a good market. The first of these was the reopening of the trade in light traction engines at the eastern end of the Baltic Sea where Latvia, Lithuania, and Estonia had emerged as sovereign states from the wreckage of the Russian Empire. In Riga, capital of Latvia, Ed. Zehder had somehow survived the political and commercial turmoil, and had begun again to operate his importing business. His re-emergence led to hope of the revival of Garretts' continental trade. A fresh enquiry from him during 1922 gave rise to enough expectation to cause the firm to reappraise and update the designs of both the 4 and 5NHP single cylinder engines that had been supplied to him pre-1914. Many of the changes were relatively minor - the rear wheels, while remaining 5' 6" in diameter, were increased from 16" to 20" on the tread whilst the fore wheels were 10" in lieu of 8". In the drive arrangements, however, they were considerably amended, a fourth shaft carrying a 45 tooth idler pinion being introduced. This meant doing afresh the general and boiler front arrangement drawings and the relevant details of the drive train but leaving unchanged the cylinder, reversing gear, motion work, clutch steerage, and boiler drawings. The engines still had the open tenders and Munktels spark arresters as used earlier.

The first of the new series to be completed was No.34176, a 5NHP despatched on November 25, 1922. This was given 'local show finish' and was obviously intended to be Zehder's showroom and exhibition engine. One particular feature requested by Zehder was the fitting of a Manzell lubricator with the discharge pipe directly onto the slide valve. Notwithstanding the efforts to sell the piston valved No.5, Zehder obviously would not entertain it, doubtless for the very relevant reason that, having been already beset by the problems of a backward but slowly emerging agricultural system in a newly independent country with fiscal and economic problems, coping with the uncertainties of finding buyers for piston valved engines was one worry he could well do without. It would be good to be able to record that the arrival of this show engine unleashed a flood of orders. In reality the outcome was a trickle of orders through 1923 and 1924, followed by orders for single 5NHP engines (Nos.34964 and 35064) in 1926 and 1927. These brought the total to six 4NHPs and ten 5NHPs. The trade ceased not so much because there was no demand for the engines as because Zehder's trading position appears to have become progressively more difficult. National borders now split up what was once his undivided territory. In order to trade in Estonia he used the firm of W. Schneider & Co. of Reval as sub-agents. Zehder himself was receiving his goods 'on consignment' i.e. he held them, until sold, as agent for Garretts rather than as a principal. This, in turn, led to a dispute over payment for the items sold via Schneider - whether they should pay him and he pay Garretts, or whether privity of contract existed between Schneider and Garretts. The last machines were sold at a reduced price, and the relationship ended with more than a hint of acrimony.

With the petering out of the long standing connection with Zehder hopes of a revival of the export trade in traction engines ebbed with it but there was one last flash of promise. In the mid-twenties Col. Garrett was the director on the AGE main board with the oversight of sales. Early in 1926 he was requested by Rowland, the chairman, to undertake a tour of South America in an endeavour to retrieve some of the trade lost to the United States during the 1914-18 war. It was widely believed at Leiston Works then and for years afterwards that Rowland's true purpose in sending Col. Garrett out of the country for an extended period was to enable Leiston Works to be closed during his absence, a step which he would assuredly have resisted most stubbornly if he had been present. If this was the case it would have been a cynical trick even by Rowland's standard of behaviour as Col. Garrett had been a consistent and loyal backer of his actions thereto. Whether or not the intention was there can never now be established. If it was, it did not succeed, and contrary to expectations a number of useful enquiries resulted from the visit, amongst which can be noted those for the Lima trolleybuses (see *Garrett Wagons - Part 3*), a number of portable engines, an American style all-steel threshing machine and large strawburning traction engines.

Col. Garrett had noted that the withdrawal of Clayton & Shuttleworth from the Argentinian scene had created an opening for this latter type of machine in a market previously served by the Lincolnshire firm.

The outcome of the latter was the compound 80 brake horse power strawburner, given the prefix letters 'SU', the same classification as had been used previously for the 10NHP strawburners designed for Mattos. The basis of the engine was what the firm described as an 'oversize colonial boiler', with the customary deep firebox for straw firing, and designed for a working pressure of 160 p.s.i. This was the same as the boiler designed for the Mattos strawburners (to drawing SU 8219) but with a firebox 10" longer. The other features, such as the gusset plate stays, remained the same, together with twelve 2½" stay tubes and thirty-two 2½" ordinary tubes, all 7' 3" long. The cylinders were 7¾" and 12" bore by 12" stroke (making it a 10NHP on the outdated RASE system), fitted with slide valves actuated by Stephenson link motion reversing gear. The gears were arranged on the four shaft principle on the right-hand side of the engine, to give a single road speed, set into and out of motion by a friction clutch in the flywheel which, of course, was also on the right-hand side as was the steering as well. The first engine to be delivered, No.34937, which left Leiston on September 29, 1926, had an eccentric driven pump but this was replaced by a gear driven pump (to drawing SU23375) sent out in 1927, and all subsequent examples were fitted with this type. The governor speed could be varied from the manstand by a long adjusting rod. The cylinders had a double feed oil pump with a displacement lubricator as a standby. Unusually, for an engine designed for cheapness, a balanced crankshaft was used. The rear wheels were 6' 6" in diameter and no less than 2' 9" across the treads, with three angle rings and triple spokes but they were otherwise built on the conventional principle. The front wheels were 4' 6" in diameter by 10" wide and were provided with steerage rings.

As on earlier strawburners the manstand was on two levels, the higher position for the driver and the lower for the fireman. In addition a hinged platform dropped down on chains behind the drawbar. Though the driver had the benefit of a short awning the fireman was left to fend for himself against the sun. Although no winding drum was fitted a 75 yards length of ¾" diameter wire rope was shipped with each engine. A specially deep ashpan was fitted with both front and rear doors, the pan being extended and deepened at the doors to form water troughs, whilst the chimney was capped with a spark arrester. The engine was consigned to W.H. Cullington in Buenos Aires but the name of the ultimate purchaser is not known. It was charged out from Leiston at £830 but the price paid by the Argentinian client was determined, of course, by the ramifications of the AGE export department. Three more, Nos.35067, 35068, and 35069, followed, all of which left Leiston in August, 1927, but thereafter the orders dried up, and another promising outlet came to nothing.

It seems clear that when on the move the engines must have worked with a tender, carrying fuel and water and probably a roof over the fireman, yet it was said that they were used, inter alia, for direct ploughing. With a tender inserted behind the engine this task would seem to have been not without problems though, supposedly, with the long distances between turns which would have occurred in the Argentinian wheatlands this might conceivably have been a workable arrangement.

After No.35069 only two Garrett traction engines were made at Leiston. The earlier of these was the sprung 7NHP single No.35140 sent to R. Robinson & Son of Annan on September 7, 1929. This was turned out in show finish, the wheels red and the remainder in standard green. Robinsons asked for a Ferodo lined band brake on the main axle, a chimney - in their words - '1/16" thicker than usual', a 6" high plain extension to the bunker, and an extended awning with cross stays in the middle and back posts and a covering of sheet iron coated with tar. This engine was made with a balanced crankshaft.

Finally came No.35461, a rigid 6NHP single again turned out in show finish, the purchaser of which was George Ewens of Petersfield. He asked for few changes or embellishments but he did, however, require the steering to be on the left-hand side. Besides this he had a copper top to the chimney and a brass false cover, complete with a brass star, to the back end cylinder cover. When delivered it was named *Pride of Petersfield* but in recent years it has been renamed *Rob Roy*. Its last commercial owner was the late Chris Lambert of Horsmonden. Chris, never a man to bestow compliments lightly, rated it as 'not a bad engine'. Thus traction engine building to Leiston designs expired.

One further twist of the story remains to be unfolded. The life of Charles Burrell & Sons Ltd. at Thetford was not happy under AGE control. In the partial rationalisation after the 1919 amalgamation traction engine building had been allocated to Thetford Works. Unfortunately the demand for traction engines sank to a very low level so that, despite an attempt to launch an improved overtype wagon, contrary to group policy, and the successful designing and building of the series of showmen's engines usually loosely referred to as 'the Scenics' the works found itself with virtually nothing to do. This resulted in its closure from June 4, 1928, and the transfer of the remaining functions, along with drawings, records, partially completed work, stocks of parts, and a few key staff to Leiston. Engines completed or built after the transfer were 4087, 4088, and 4090 to 4094 inclusive. In the Garrett books engines were referred to as merely 'completed' when the boiler was one brought from Thetford and 'built' when the boiler was a Leiston product. Three of these engines fortunately survive (Nos.4088, 4093 and 4094). Of those built at Leiston probably the most celebrated was No.4092, the 8NHP showman's road locomotive *Simplicity*, delivered to Mrs. A. Deakin of Brynmawr.

Of the handful of Thetford men moved to Leiston one of the best known was Billy Greenwood who had charge of the Burrell parts store. The building set aside for the Burrell parts became known as No.9 Parts Store, and was situated alongside Haylings Road, commencing a little to the North of Cross Street and extending to the Gas Hill tally house. Earlier it had been used for the assembly of undertype wagons, and earlier still as the paint shop, presided over by that redoubtable Yorkshireman, John Creasey, of the powerful voice and opinionated outlook on cricket. Billy Greenwood arrived there with the loads of Burrell parts in early Summer, 1928. Sadly, his reign was short. As the doomed AGE combine settled lower and lower into the waters of economic problems frantic efforts were made to keep up the buoyancy of Leiston Works by slashing expenditure in every department, as was narrated in the story of *Garrett Wagons*. On February 6, 1931, following the appointment of a new foreman named Liddemore (at a salary of £3. 10. 0 per week) to take charge of all the stores, Burrell's included, P.A. Leggett, the acting Works manager, wrote a memo to Alan Thurston, the company secretary, in which he noted the new appointment, adding a further paragraph:

> I have accordingly given Greenwood (Burrell's Dept.) a fortnight's notice and his employment is to terminate on 21st February, 1931.

Thus ended a lifetime of service with Burrells and an unrivalled knowledge of the components that made up their engines. Time had its revenge, however, for a year later Leggett himself was to share Greenwood's predicament.

Fig.103. *A post-script to two distinguished firms, both by then insolvent, as Burrell 8NHP No.4094 is seen on a well wagon at Leiston Station on June 11, 1932. It was built at Leiston Works.*

Figs.104 and 105. The nearside and offside views of Burrell 8NHP showman's engine No.4092, Simplicity, built at Leiston Works in 1930 for Mrs. A. Deakin & Sons of Brynmawr. Thirty years later Jimmy Drane and others who worked on the engine recalled with pride having done so.

Fig.106. 6NHP compound No.29788 supplied to Clark & Fauset in 1911 for Normanby Shire Council, seen here outside their office in Harrisville, c.1920, hauling its stone crusher, skip elevator and two wagons. It had heavier main gearing of NZ type, including a stronger differential. [Queensland Museum]

Fig.107. In the golden decade of shows the firm went to the Worcester Show with this 6NHP sprung compound engine No.28393 which had already been to the Royal. It was sold via J.L.Larkworthy to J.Davis of Redmarley.

Fig.108. Wm. Rawlings of Collingbourne Ducis loved show engines. Sprung 7NHP No.33560 was sold from the 1919 Royal to F.Swanton of Overton, Marlborough, but came to Rawlings after the end of the 1939/45 war. It is seen in sad terminal decline in his yard in April, 1956.
[A.J. Martin collection]

Fig.109. 7NHP single No.26618 (1907) new to Henry Upton of Clophill, Beds, in use by an Army baling team in the first war. Afterwards it belonged to Bomford Bros. of Pitchill.

Fig.110. George Thurlow of Stowmarket was an active agent. His firm sold No.23641 originally to A. Kelly of Writtle, Essex, in 1902. Seventeen years later they had it back and resold it to T. Harrison of Stamford Bridge, East Riding.
[the late Jack Peirson]

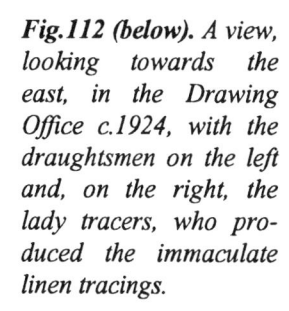

Fig.111. 7NHP single No.27901 at Mark Loader & Sons' Five Way Works, Winton, June 20, 1942.
[A.C. Durrant]

Fig.112 (below). A view, looking towards the east, in the Drawing Office c.1924, with the draughtsmen on the left and, on the right, the lady tracers, who produced the immaculate linen tracings.

Chapter 9

Agents and Buyers

By the time that the Garretts embarked upon the building of traction engines they had already long outgrown the concept of the local firm catering for the needs of its immediate surroundings and had established international agencies and connections. Of these one of the longest standing and most enduring was that with the French firm of Th. Pilter, founded in 1864, whose head office was at 24, Rue Alibert, Paris, but which also added branch offices in Bordeaux, Toulouse, and Marseille, and, later, in various parts of French North Africa. This association continued until Leiston Works closed in 1932. Other early links were formed in Germany and Russia, mainly for the sale of threshers and portables, though self-mover No.2167 was sold through O. Kohan of Odessa in 1868.

In home sales the partners' uncle, Balls Garrett, found customers for at least nine traction engines and self-movers through his implement business in Maidstone. It is known that 8NHP self-mover No.9644 passed through one further set of hands before reaching the ultimate customer. Balls Garrett sold it on to Hammond & Hussey of Croydon - primarily ironmongers and tool dealers - who in their turn delivered it to their customer, a Mr. Brown of Oxted, Surrey. This engine had an unfortunate history after its delivery on October 21, 1876. In February, 1877, when it was little more than three months old, Robert Farrell, one of the Works' senior fitters, spent 87¼ hours working on it at Hammond & Hussey's depot at Croydon. This clearly was no minor adjustment. Things did not stop there, however, for from March 15 to 20 he spent a further 61¼ hours on the engine followed by 120¾ hours at Brown's own premises at Oxted from April 23 to May 4. This must have proved too much for its owner as on June 14 and 15, 1878, we find Farrell in London giving evidence at the arbitration of Balls Garrett v Hammond & Hussey. Since, by the nature of the process, the results of arbitration cases are not made public we do not know the outcome of this case, but however it was adjusted between the two parties little credit was reflected on the way the engine had been made in the first place.

Aside from the engines sold through Balls Garrett at least three others went through agents. The Aveling type engine numbered 12 (Aveling Royalty No.261) was sold, possibly with further unidentified examples, through J. Shaw & Son of Wolverhampton, who traded with South America, whilst the later type 8NHP traction engine No.9884 of 1877 went through the hands of Johns Brothers of Swindon, who had also sold portables. No.2017, an 8NHP self-mover for Charles Doubleday of Outwell, was sold through the agency of J. Davey.

Besides sales to foreign and distant users the firm found a number of early customers in Suffolk and the adjacent counties. The successive partners had kept a high profile in local and national affairs. Richard III had been a guarantor of the Great Exhibition of 1851 whilst nearer home he had campaigned ceaselessly to get the East Suffolk Railway built and had had a decisive part in raising the funds that built and endowed Framlingham College. In quite a different sphere, his son Richard IV was celebrated for his membership of the Suffolk Horse Society and his having saved the champion Suffolk stallion Cupbearer from being sold to overseas buyers. Again, both father and son were respected as powerful lobbyists for the brewing of pure beer and as castigators of the adulterated and impure concoctions passed off onto the public by some unprincipled brewers. These activities may have had some effect in attracting East Anglian customers, such as William Hunt of Culpho, near Ipswich, who had 8NHP self-mover No.8696, or Binney of the then rural town of Ilford, Essex, a farmer and contractor who twenty years later was to be a well-known roller owner in that area. One wonders whether they were disappointed with what they got. For example, in September, 1877, when Hunt's engine was two years old, Charles Rodwell, from the erecting shop, spent 52 hours on repair work to the engine and another 9 hours in the following March. The erectors seem to have taken such outwork by turns. As we have seen, Rodwell and Farrell took leading roles, together with Tom Barnard, another erector, and a fourth man, James Crane. The practice of providing a driver to set an engine to work and to instruct the new owner's driver was already in place in the 1870s and seems to have been shared between Charles Woods and a man named Clow who must have been a fitter also as from time to time he appears in the *Journeyman's Ledger No.2* as executing repairs. Allowances were paid to such outworkers over and above their hourly rate. Thus for every day of 10¼ hours when they were away overnight or on a Sunday they received 3 shillings (15p) but if home at night only one shilling and sixpence. Apprentices received two thirds of these rates.

Just as the selling system that evolved in Europe, later to be nurtured and expanded by Carl Remy, was founded upon portable engines, with some of the agents subsequently selling traction engines and/or rollers, so the presence of the Garrett marque in the Antipodes owed its beginnings to portables. Probably the oldest Garrett portable engine extant in Australia is No.3908, which left Leiston on August 26, 1870, for T. McPherson, an agent in Melbourne, at a time when there was only limited settlement of Western Australia where it now resides. However, few of the Australian agents who sold Garrett portables went on to become importers of traction engines. Two who did so, albeit on a limited scale, were the firms of T.M. Goodall & Co. of Sydney, New South Wales, who had 8NHP single No.24062 in December, 1903, and Dehle Bennison & Co. of Hobart, Tasmania, who imported 6NHP No.24424 in July of the same year, and No.24938 the following year. The only one of the importers of portables to go on to handle larger numbers of traction engines was Clark & Fauset of Brisbane, who sold eleven. Although the first two supplied (Nos.23510 and 24320) were 6NHP singles Clark & Fauset turned to compounds when they became available. Their next 6NHP, No.25070, was a compound followed, in October, 1905, by No.25331, an 8NHP compound. After a gap of rather more than three years Nos.27115 and 27204, both 8NHP compounds, were imported together with 6NHP compound, No.27111, all of them on colonial boilers to make them better suited for burning wood. Two years later, in 1910, they had a further 6NHP compound (No.27382) and, interestingly, were able to sell two of the 5NHP singles, Nos.28387 and 28388, similar to the engines which had caused the difference of opinion between Garretts and the Agricultural Engineers' Association when offered in the home market. This pair sent to Queensland, however, had the rather larger colonial firebox. These were almost the end of Clark & Fauset's orders for traction engines, the final one being No.29788, a further 6NHP compound sent off from Leiston in December, 1911. Other Australian agents had low scores in selling Garrett tractions. Horrocks Roxburgh in Melbourne sold No.32582, a 6NHP compound, to the Shire of Benalla Council in November, 1914, and in 1924, Frank Perrott of Perth arranged the sale of No.34417, the last 8NHP compound traction made, to the Western Australian Government.

While the sales of engines in the Southern hemisphere were not to be despised they were exceeded many times over by the extent of the European market for Garrett products. It was the degree of dependence upon selling to Europe that roused unease in Frank (Junior) and Alfred Garrett or, perhaps, foreboding, seeing the rapidity with which the manufacture of traction engines, ploughing engines, and rollers had become established in Germany. Whether or not they had taken in the full significance of this latter development they had certainly reached the conclusion that an entry into the home market was needed as a counterbalance to a potential diminution of their share of European sales. It was this that prompted the appointment of E.J.C. Ballam to give practical form to the intention. To a considerable extent he modelled the organisation he set up upon what Remy had done abroad, namely to use agents recruited from among firms or individuals who had already established reputations as suppliers or operators in the trade. In doing so, however, he came up against the problem that many whom he would have liked to have used had already made arrangements with rival manufacturers. The most successful of those he was able to recruit was George Thurlow & Sons of Stowmarket who in a period of twenty years (1902-1922) sold some forty engines as well as threshers and portables. Thurlows were a firm held in the greatest respect by engine owners not only throughout East Anglia but further afield, acting as engineers and repairers, and holding stocks of the requisites needed to keep engines running - tools, lamps, gauge glasses, workshop equipment, belts, gland packings, jointing materials. There was not much, in fact, that an engine owner or contractor might need that the firm could not arrange for him, but it was not only this versatility but the high standards of service and integrity which accounted most for the esteem which surrounded Thurlows.

In Scotland Watson Brothers of Banff, who also enjoyed a good name, held Garrett spares for some thirty years but had only one flash of success in selling traction engines. In October, 1909, three engines - all 7NHP singles - were sent to customers introduced by them. No.27907, which left on October 21, 1909, and Nos.27908 and 27910 which preceded it, leaving on October 2 and October 10 respectively, all went to customers not far from Banff - W. McKay at Abercheder, G. Morrison at Fisherie, and S.G. Addison at Keith. The following year they sold No.28737 to Alex Gray of Huntly. Mr. Gray became somewhat of a devotee of Garretts, in later years owning overtype wagons.

As to trade in Ireland where, in early days, several sales were transacted via William O'Neill of Athy, Ballam struck up a useful accord with the Irish Agricultural Wholesale Society who not only had a successful run with traction engines but also sold a number of steam tractors. Nearer home, the efforts of the Eastern Counties Farmers' Cooperative Society did not achieve quite the same degree of success, perhaps being overshadowed in that area by the impressive reputation and irreproachable experience of George Thurlow.

Aside from sales introduced by these sources a substantial number arose from Ballam's own efforts as head salesman, either from personal contacts made on the company's stand at agricultural shows or from leads passed on to him by his many friends and well-wishers in the trade or by firms such as J.L. Larkworthy & Co. of Worcester who had dealt in Garrett machines for many years. Relationships with agents and informants were complicated by the rule of the Agricultural Engineers Association, to which some reference has already been made in Chapter 3, that required the names of all agents to be registered with the Association together with the products in which they were authorised to deal. Notwithstanding these stipulations, however, Ballam had trade contacts up and down the country and where these relationships were cordial, as most were, rules still could not prevent useful leads being passed on to Ballam. When a sale resulted doubtless the informant was rewarded discreetly.

Assiduous attendance at agricultural shows was used as a method of securing direct contact with potential clients, albeit one requiring a discerning eye in the personnel of the stand, able to distinguish the visitor with a real transaction in mind from the mere Hooray Henry intent only upon taking a dram of whiskey at Garretts' expense. In the decade preceding the first world war all the major shows would have had a stand as a matter of course. The Royal, the Bath & West, the Suffolk, and the Royal Smithfield Shows were visited annually, without exception, but provincial shows not so regularly. In the nineteen show seasons from 1896 to 1914, the firm had a stand at the Royal Counties - covering the South and South-West - on eleven occasions (1901-1910 and 1912), the Essex Show on ten, the Norfolk on nine, and the Devon on seven. Other visits were really occasional events; the Dublin Show, the Highland Show, and the Yorkshire each four times, the Peterborough thrice, Cornwall and Wiltshire twice, but Cambridge, Lincolnshire, Stowmarket, Ulster (Belfast) and Worcester only once each. The Stowmarket attendance in 1908 was mainly as a compliment to George Thurlow who was prominent in organising it.

The year 1910 may be taken as typical of these prosperous years. The itinerary began with the Royal Dublin at Balls Bridge on April 19 to 22, and took in twelve shows in all ending with the Royal Smithfield at Agricultural Hall, Islington, from December 5 to 9. The Worcester Show was attended on the firm's behalf by J.L. Larkworthy & Co., its agents in that city, but otherwise the shows were manned and run from Leiston, often with family members in attendance. The exhibits at Balls Bridge included No.6 s/c traction 28256, No.5 s/c colonial traction 28257, 48" ordinary thresher 12875, and 48" light thresher 12898. The stand at the Devon County at Exmouth from May13 to 16 had one traction engine, No.6 s/c 28392, together with No.4 c/d tractor 28258 and 48" thresher 12940. The next show was the Royal Ulster in Belfast from May 25 to 27, and this was attended by No.4 c/d tractor 28386, 5 ton wagon 28381, No.5 traction 28257, and 48" light thresher 12898 (the two latter items had been to the Dublin Show). The Suffolk Show at Saxmundham on June 2 and 3 offered No.7 s/c traction 28385, No.4 c/d 28391, SSIII superheated portable 28559, WSI s/c portable 28580, a 54" thresher and a 54" light thresher. The display at the Royal Counties at Winchester consisted of 5 ton wagon 28381 (back from Belfast), No.7 s/c 28396, No.4 c/d tractor 28397, and a 54" thresher, but only No.6 c/d traction 28393 was present at Worcester on June 5 and 6. The Essex Show at Witham followed closely on June 8 and 9, and this time the exhibits were No.7 s/c traction 28385 and No.4 c/d tractor 28391, both of which had been at Saxmundham, plus a 54" thresher. These exhibits then appeared a week later at the Norfolk Show in Kings Lynn (June 15 and 16). The 5 ton wagon, the No.7 traction, and the No.4 c/d tractor that had been shown at Winchester were assembled for the Royal at Liverpool from June 21 to 25, together with the SSIII portable and WSI portable from the Suffolk Show, the No.6 c/d traction from Worcester, and 10 ton superheated roller 28049. The No.4 c/d tractor and the WSI portable also went to Peterborough (July 5 to 7) in addition to No.7 s/c traction 28406 and a 54" thresher. Two weeks later (July 19-20) 28406 and 28391 were at the Highland Show at Dumfries where 28375, a No.6 s/c traction with 3 speeds, springs to the hind wheels and a full length awning, for A. Meikle, was on view, as well as a 54" thresher. The final show of the year was Smithfield from December 5 to 9, and here the engines were No.7 s/c 28744, No.4 c/d tractor 28745, CCSIII c/d superheated semi-portable 28671, No.5 s/c 28756, a light 3-shaft English type engine with 2 speeds, plus a 54" thresher.

The exhibits themselves were given the treatment referred to on the Works and in Works documents as 'Royal Show finish'. This comprised not only a superfine quality of painting and varnishing but also the extensive use of polished copper for pipework, brass boiler bands, and a mirror finish to bright work such as connecting rods and motion, together with a good deal of what the Army expressively terms 'b------t' in the form of a burnished finish to items like cab standards and fairlead rollers. For 'local show finish' the effect was the same but not so strained to perfection and with some of the excess polishing and burnishing toned down.

There was a belief among purchasers, not altogether belied by fact, that if one bought a show engine one received a slightly better made machine than one produced in the ordinary course of business. This could, however, mean deferred delivery if the show engine had a full round of summer attendances to fulfil. The brothers Jack and George Newstead, already introduced in *Garrett Wagons*, were often involved in setting up the exhibits at major shows, Jack, on the whole, playing the leading part. Both had been agricultural labourers before going onto the Works but had acquired names as skilled and resourceful drivers of all types of machines, engaged mainly in preparing and steaming engines in the test house and driving on road trials when not on the show circuit.

A satisfied and loyal customer for show exhibits was William Rawlings of Collingbourne Ducis, Wiltshire. Rawlings was an established threshing contractor who had observed the potential of roller hire as an adjunct to the trade. His initial purchases from Leiston, in which Thurlow figured as the introducing agent, were three 10 ton single cylinder rollers, No.23377 (June 10,1901), No.23501 (March 29, 1902), and No.23745 (June 30,1902), but thereafter he took to purchasing the firm's exhibit at the Royal Smithfield show. From the 1902 show he had the 6NHP single No.23981, together with a 54" threshing drum. The next December this was followed by No.24601, again a 6NHP and once more with a thresher. After a three year pause he had the 7NHP single No.26062 in December, 1906. I understood from Victor Garrett that William Rawlings was one of the trusted customers whose preferences led the Garretts into building the 7NHP engines. Victor himself was not involved with Works affairs in 1906 but twenty years later, when managing director of the Eddison Steam Rolling Co. Ltd., he got to know William Rawlings much better. Although Rawlings had thus become an important client, and realised it, the rules of the AEA barred Garretts from recognising this by allowing him better than standard terms. The dilemma was solved by a device that satisfied both parties. He was appointed an agent in his own right, thus securing a 5% commission on his own purchases and giving him the chance to earn more by convincing others that they needed Garrett engines and machines. He was in the best possible position to do this since by being the obviously satisfied owner and operator of a fleet of Garrett engines he was able to demonstrate the confidence he had in them. In the two years 1911 and 1912, for example, he drew his commission for selling the second-hand No.6 road locomotive No.27763 to H.L. Harding of Hungerford, the No.4 tractor No.28076 to L.P. Stokes, and the No.7 traction engine No.28744 to W. Mortimer of Bourton. In addition he had sold three threshing machines, a further, unidentified traction engine and traction wagons. In the meantime he had added to his own fleet. On January 14, 1908, he had another 7NHP (No.26721) which had attended the 1907 Smithfield show, and on Christmas Eve, 1908, took delivery of No.27341, his third and last new 7NHP, each of which had been accompanied by a 54" drum. These successive purchases made him the possessor of a very well equipped business. Subsequently he was also to own five second-hand Garretts (Nos.28406, 28412, 29031, 33560, and 33738). Later still he almost became the purchaser of one of the 5NHP *Suffolk Punch* tractors (No.33179) but it seems the shrewdness that had served him so well led him to opt out of the transaction. There was a certain amount of 'cloak and dagger' about this agency arrangement, for letters or payments relating to commission were never sent to his office at Collingbourne Ducis but to his private address at Trenches Farm, Andover.

A similar arrangement was come to with R. Dingle & Sons of Stoke Climsland, another firm making use of Garrett equipment. They, too, were granted agent status in their dealings, arranging the sales of useful numbers of engines and machines not only to other branches of the family but also to outside purchasers.

When an engine was bought at a local show delivery to the purchaser often involved no more than a few miles of steaming over local roads, driven by one or both of the Newsteads. Similarly delivery to customers local to Leiston was done in much the same way. More distant deliveries, however, were carried out by rail. At Leiston Station there was a dock with an overhead gantry primarily for loading Garrett shipments onto rail wagons. On the Aldeburgh branch, Leiston was the first station out of Saxmundham, the junction with the main line. When the Works was in its heyday the loading siding was cleared each afternoon. Instances were not unknown of a painter travelling with an engine or machine as far as Saxmundham to put final touches to some part of the paintwork deemed to have been found wanting after a rush to finish it for shipment.

For home sales Ballam, or his clerk, made a set of notes of what was to be provided as standard. These were:

<u>Traction Engines</u>
Steam Pressure: To specification stamped on makers name plate.
Pressure Gauge: Graduated in lbs per sq.in. red line at working press.
Makers Nameplate: To have stamped on Engine No. and steam pressure.
Boiler Fittings: To Drgs.
Safety Valve: Ramsbottom.
Starting Gear Guard:] Reading
Clean out Plate:] in
Working Position Plate:] English.
Lubricators: For S/C Tractions: Two displacement lubricators to SD244, 1 on starting and 1 on slide chest;
    For C/D Tractions: Three displacement lubricators.
    When oil pump is specially ordered it is to be connected to starting slide chest in place of displacement lubricator.
Painting:
Lagging: Wood frame filled with asbestos wadding close lagged with wood and ordinary lagging sheets.
Brass Bands:
Weight Plates:

No.4 S/C = 6 Tons	No.7 S/C = 9½ Tons
No.5 S/C = 7 Tons	No.7 C/D = 10½ Tons
No.6 S/C = 9 Tons	No.8 S/C = 10¼ Tons
No.6 C/D = 9½ Tons	No.8 C/D = 11 Tons
No.6 S/C S/H = Tons	No.7 S/C S/H = 9½ Tons
No.8 S/C S/H = Tons	

Outfit: 1 set frost pegs, 1 set of spuds with bolts + cotters, 4 spare firebars, 1 coal shovel, 1 clinker do, 1 rake, 1 tube-brush, 1 filling funnel, 1 tommey, 6 double spanners for all sizes of nuts, 1 spanner for waterlifter union, 1 screw spanner, 1 hammer, 1 caulking tool, 1 chisel, 1 pt. size spring oil feeder, 1 qt. oil bottle, 6 governor springs, 2 lamps with shutters for smokebox, 1 red tail lamp, 1 water-gauge lamp, 26 ft. waterlifter hose with union, 6 spare gauge glasses and grummets, governor strap, waterproof cover, toolbox with padlock, 1 box spanner for plug in smokebox, spanner for adjusting spring gear to be sent with spring engines only.

All the weight plates understated, by a substantial amount, the actual weights of the engines. One wonders what inhibited the writer of the notes from allocating fictitious weights to the 6 and 8NHP superheated engines. It was probably worth noting that painting was included in the standard home price as many export engines were priced to be left either in grey primer or, as with the Argentinian strawburners, in a sparse two-coat painting job. The Sack ploughers, one of the groups of engines sold in grey primer, were fitted with planished steel boiler lagging which must have imparted a handsome appearance.

With orders from abroad things were far from standard, and the notebook abounds with special requirements. For instance, with a strawburning engine a tube scraper was invariably supplied instead of a flue brush because of the tacky nature of the deposit left from straw. Safety valves were a more complex issue. Orders for German and Italian agents and some (but not all) for South America required two spring balances with ferrules. Pilter, supplying France and French North Africa, also asked for double spring balances but of a type special to him. Orders for Spain, India, Burma, and Straits Settlement (Malaysia) needed one spring balance and one lock-up dome. This also applied to customers of the Russian agents. New Zealand, mercifully, accepted the Ramsbottom type. Holland, whilst accepting double spring balances, insisted that they should be of a special 'lock-up' type.

Not altogether surprisingly instruction plates were normally required to be in the language of the customer country, but Dutch law went further by stipulating a standardised rectangular nameplate 140mm by 80mm high fixed by four copper studs screwed into tapped holes in the boiler and peened over flush into countersunk holes in the plate. These plates had to have the maker's name in the top row of lettering and address on the bottom row. In between was a row containing, on the left, the Works number and, on the right, the year of building, both of these put on with letter stamps, whilst between them the boiler pressure was cast on. It was also a Dutch requirement that when the water disappeared below the bottom nut of the glass there was still to be 2" (5 cm) above the top of the firebox.

German boiler laws, revised and intensified in 1910, insisted that the maker's plate had to be fixed to the actual boiler, the preferred place being the offside of the firebox, about the level of the top two rows of stays and at the barrel end. These regulations were very onerous when they dealt with boiler and firebox plates. The detail notebook summarised the requirements thus:

> To be applicable to all German agents.
>
> All plates to have a tensile strength of 31-41 kilos per mm², with a maximum elongation of 28% and 25% respectively in a length of 200mm.
>
> All plates to be stamped F1 in a position to be easily recognised. To facilitate finding this stamp it is to be surrounded with a ring of white paint.
>
> Certificates of tests of boiler plates to be supplied by makers.
>
> For firebox plates the actual results of each plate is to be given separately.
>
> For other plates only charge test is required.

Other provisions of the 1910 German regulations were that the handles on the plugs of gauge and try cocks had to be able to be turned through 360° with brass distance pieces between them and the boiler to permit this. These distance pieces were drawn on Standard Detail 269. The holes through the plugs of cocks had to be elongated toward the greater end of the taper to ensure that the clearway was not reduced by successive grindings in of the plugs. As with the Dutch regulations there was a provision of a minimum water cover over the firebox when the water left the bottom of the glass but the German law fixed this at 30mm (1³/₁₆"). The boiler front was required to have a chisel line on it 1¼" long and 100mm above the level of the firebox crown, with the letter 'N' stamped into the plate at the left end and 'W' at the right, both ½" high. Glass guards were stipulated to gauge glasses and a brass water level plate, corresponding to the level on the incised line, had to be fixed behind the gauge glass indicating 'Niedrigsten wasserstand' (minimum water level). The lagging had to consist of a wood skeleton frame fixed in with asbestos flexible mats, readily removable.

Not all countries had such detailed and, to the manufacturers at least, tiresome regulations as Germany, but they all became burdensome because they were so diverse. Foreign orders, too, produced complications in packing. Engines sent away in a fully built-up state, whether for home or foreign sales near to home, had the tube brushes and filling funnel in the smokebox, the governor, lamps, spuds, spare firebars, frost pegs, waterlifting hose, firing tools, and oil bottle in the tender, and all other tools and oddments in the toolbox. All bright parts were covered with what the notebook called 'anti-rust composition', the exact formula for which seems not to have been recorded. Further, the end of the crankshaft was to be protected by 'oil paper properly tied on'. The lagging was protected by brown paper. Once on the railway wagon the engine was protected by a waterproof cover of Birkmyre or Willesdon cloth securely tied.

With engines close packed and facing long voyages the treatment was more radical. All covers were removed after the final test and the internal surfaces of the cylinder block were dried and greased before the covers were replaced. The rear wheels were removed and sent unpacked, but the remainder of the engine was enclosed in a heavily built packing case with a floor of sufficient strength to take the weight when lifted by crane. The axle was withdrawn together with the main spurwheel, winding drum and related items. Within the main case a separate smaller box was provided to contain such easily damaged items as gauge glasses, the pressure gauge (still in the small wooden box in which it would have arrived from its makers), the throttle valve - complete with instructions on how to re-fix it, the governor and such small items as cylinder drains. A further larger box contained tube brushes or scrapers, tools, shovels, fire-irons, and the spring balances (if fitted) of the safety valve. Often the flywheel was taken off, in which case the key would have been in this box. The art of close packing was to ensure that nothing broke loose in loading or unloading, or in rough seas during the voyage. Reducing the size of the box to a minimum was important as it saved shipping costs. Items easily supplied at the destination were not shipped. Engines, for instance, sent to Clark & Fauset in Queensland had only the ironwork of cabs sent but not the woodwork, and the bulky iron lattice extensions to tenders, enabling wood to be carried, were assembled with bolts and nuts so that they could be taken apart for shipment, thus reducing the space needed. When the export business was at its zenith in, say, the first decade of this century, a staff of woodworkers at Leiston did little else but packing for export. Because of the high weight of the contents and the amount of handling each of the cases had to undergo they were built of good materials. In the austere period in the opening years of the twenties when Leiston Works was so short of work the possibility was investigated of tendering for the supply of joinery to the new housing estates being developed by the then London County Council at Dagenham since there was a well equipped joiners' shop at Station Works much under used at that time. The report that came back was not encouraging, inter alia remarking, wryly, that the timber being used for joinery at Dagenham was inferior to that being used on the Works for export cases, a reflection, perhaps, of the importance attached to sound packing.

The completion of the railway to Leiston in 1859 made it much easier for the firm to conduct its export business, hitherto cramped by the need to ship in small vessels from Slaughden Quay at Aldeburgh. Whilst such vessels could make the voyage across the North Sea to Rotterdam or Hamburg, or to the French and Belgian Channel ports, shipments involving ocean crossings meant a tiresome transshipment at perhaps London or Hull to a larger ship. With the new freedom from such restraints the burgeoning trade with Russia and the Baltic was often, though not invariably, routed via Hull making use of the steam ships of Thomas Wilson & Co. Ltd., but shipments to Zehder and his predecessors in Riga were sent out at times via the Millwall Docks in London. Paul Kotzo in Hungary generally received his goods via Rotterdam and the railways. After the extensive development of Parkeston Quay by the Great Eastern Railway this formed a convenient port in this country. Cargoes for Pilter in Metropolitan France were sent either through the General Steam Navigation Co. at Irongate and St. Katherines Wharf in London or, later, were sometimes consigned to the London Brighton & South Coast Railway's stationmaster at Newhaven, Sussex, from which port Pilter made his own arrangements. Pilter's orders for North Africa and all orders for the Americas were served mostly from Liverpool or, later on, from Manchester. In the case of the Americas this was varied from time to time by shipments via London, usually at the Victoria Docks. In the latter part of the last century Liverpool was at the summit of its prosperity with as much traffic as it could handle, developing, in consequence, a bad name for delays, congestion, and a 'take it or leave it' attitude which increasingly led Garretts to prefer London or the newly opened Manchester Docks. The Antipodes were mostly served via London's South West India Docks.

What the various overseas agents received for their services is difficult to state succinctly, not only because the information in many cases is simply not available, but also for the reason that terms were subject to renegotiation from time to time. For example, take the case of Th. Pilter. When he sold traction engine No.23652 in May, 1902, it was invoiced at £413.0.0 less a trade discount of 15%, amounting to £61.17.6, yet two years later when he sold Nos.24845 and 24864 he was charged £375.0.0 and £468.0.0 respectively less, in each case, a trade discount of only 10%.The same year A.P. & W. Muscate in Danzig had No.24755 at £495.0.0 less 15%. In Italy Whitmore & Grimaldi, and later Filippo Grimaldi, trading alone after Whitmore's death, had received a discount of 10% for some forty years. However, in 1904 there seems to have been a rebellion on the part of the agent since from October 4, 1904, there was an increase in the trade discount from 10% to 15%. On the other hand Ed. Zehder in Riga seems to have been invoiced at nett prices leaving him to quote his own clients a retail price that would cover his own services. Notwithstanding this he seems still to have haggled for further small discounts. Thus in 1910 he was charged £324.5.0 for a 5NHP Continental type traction engine. By the next year the price had been dropped to £320.0.0 with the stipulation that this reduction was final and that henceforth prices were 'absolutely nett'.

Nor is it possible to detail with precision the terms upon which importers held the goods they handled. Whilst some undoubtedly purchased as principals the majority held the goods as agents on behalf of Garretts until such times as they were sold. Thus when trading with Zehder recommenced in 1922 it was agreed that nothing was due until the engine or machine was sold by him, at which time he was to remit one third of the invoiced cost followed by a further third at the end of the year of sale and the final third, plus interest on it at the rate of 6%, at a further interval of one year. The terms granted to other agents might not have been identical but were certainly similar, and meant that at any one time there was a considerable sum tied up in these agency transactions. Not all overseas agencies turned out well. That of Auschnitt in Galatz ended by his default, the firm seizing any items of his that they could get their hands upon in satisfaction of his debts.

Interest is sometimes expressed as to how actual payment was effected between distant overseas agents and the firm at Leiston. None, to my knowledge, involved the physical movement of gold coins or bullion since, by the second half of the last century, when the Garrett overseas sales had become a significant proportion of the turnover, the major banking houses of Europe and the world had established an international clearing system making use, on the one hand, of the much improved postal services made available by the growth of railways and use of steam ships and on the other, by the development of the intercontinental telegraph which, by reason of undersea cables, had enabled Australia and the Americas to be linked to Europe. The actual instrument used for payment was customarily the *bill of exchange,* a device of which the modern cheque is one specialised form. In essence a bill of exchange was drawn up by one person (the *drawer*) calling upon a second (the *drawee*) to pay a third (the *payee*) a given sum of money either at a specified date or upon demand. The bill became live, so to speak, when accepted by the drawee in writing, usually by his signature being placed upon it. Thus Paul Kotzo in Budapest might have paid his monies into, say, the Credit Anstalt who, through the clearing house system, would arrange for his bills of exchange to be honoured by a London banker, such as Rothschild, Hoare, or Child. Kotzo would proceed to draw a bill of exchange instructing the London agent to pay to the Garretts the sum due to them. If due at once it would be 'on demand' but if, as we have seen might have been the case, it was not due to be paid for three months or six months then the due date would be written into it. When, perhaps a week or so later, the bill of exchange reached Leiston it would be presented to the drawee for acceptance. An 'on demand' bill would then be paid, as would a modern cheque, but if some months distant it might either be left to 'mature' at the due date or be passed on to a bill discounting house who would pay the amount specified having first deducted from it a percentage commission. There were many facets to the system but this is not the place to explore them nor am I the person to elucidate them. For Antipodean or American transactions the system needed a little modification in that the distant agent or customer probably had a London representative or confirming house - as we have seen, Mattos in Buenos Aires was represented by Torromé in London - who would have drawn the cheque or bill of exchange on his behalf. At the outer end of the transaction the ultimate customer made payment to the agent in whatever way had been agreed between them. Thus it may have been that Mattos was sometimes paid for a straw-burner by barter involving truckloads of maize or a herd of fat cattle, but there is no evidence that Leiston was paid so exotically.

Generally with home buyers payment came in smaller sums and on less complicated terms. A cheque was customary but from time to time a few customers paid in coin of the realm. Extended terms, or hire purchase, was a common method of payment. When Swales Bolesworth bought the 7NHP compound No.27333, converted to showman's style, he paid £650.0.0 of which £100.0.0 was paid on delivery, with the balance of twenty equal quarterly instalments incurring interest at 5% per annum, a typical arrangement. On the other hand, when Swales and Henry Forrest had the No.6 road locomotive No.26999, repossessed from Robert Body, they paid £450.0.0 in cash for it, reputedly in notes and coin.

Fig.113. A view in the boiler shop, Leiston Works.

Fig.114. The Leiston Works pattern store, c.1923. On the right is shop foreman George Vale. This amazing collection of patterns, going back 130 years, was intact until 1964.

Fig.115. A view down the main casting bay of the iron foundry in the early 1960s.
[B.J. Finch]

Fig.116. A view eastwards through the main turnery, Town Works. The arched opening (far end) is into the Long Shop. The man in the white coat is George Greenacre, at that time assistant foreman.

Chapter 10

An Evaluation

The drift of opinion tends to place the scale of Garretts' traction engine building firmly in the minor league. To some extent this may be because not very many examples have survived into preservation making them rare on rally fields, but with a traction engine output of over 500 the firm occupied too large a niche to deserve the cavalier banishment to the ranks of 'also-rans' which has commonly been its lot. Of the total some sixty, of various types, were built before traction engine building was temporarily abandoned in the eighteen-eighties, admittedly a small number and much outweighed by a prodigious output of portables and semi-portable engines, but the balance of 440 plus, built between 1895 and 1930, is far from negligible. When Herman Marshall set down in his diaries a league table of engines built up to 1892, Garretts stood third with an estimated total of 18729, surpassed only by Clayton & Shuttleworth, and by Marshalls themselves. This places them firmly above the status of the struggling country firm.

Nor were they backward in tackling development. Their corrugated firebox crown introduced in 1877 was one of the best of the stayless types and coincided, more or less, with the introduction of steel and machine flanging to their boiler-making. Soon afterwards came compounding. Generally speaking the standards of workmanship were high, notwithstanding the occasional lapses that have been recounted in the preceding chapters. Boiler-making at Leiston began in the 'modern' era and thus never used punched holes or angle iron joints, thereby avoiding what Wansborough described as the forcible combination of unwilling pieces of plate by the use of 'persuasive instruments known as drifts and cramps'.

The practice introduced into the initial 6NHP traction engines of the nineties, discounting the brief dalliance with the shifting eccentric valve gear in No.20485, was on the whole conformist rather than innovative, yet it made use of machine cut gears, where many firms were still dressing up from the black, and made all gears of cast steel. Iron castings were invariably Leiston made, as were bearing brasses, and clacks, though smaller non-ferrous items such as cylinder drain cocks, try cocks, pressure gauge mountings and gauge glass fittings were bought in. Steel casting was never attempted at Leiston, not so much from any softening of resolve as because the economics of scale were so against it. Early steel castings were obtained from Krupp of Essen or through August Reichwald, who had a London office but is believed to have been the agent for Krupp. Other pre-1914 suppliers were J. Ghion of 120 Moorgate, London EC1, who was the agent for Acieries Allard in Belgium, and the Medway Steel Co. The severing of connections with Germany and Belgium after August, 1914, led to the use of the National Steel Foundry at Leven, Fife; Catton & Co. Ltd. of Hunslet, Leeds; and, somewhat later, Kryn & Lahy Ltd. at Letchworth, Herts, a firm set up by refugees from Belgium. In AGE days many firms were used but traction engine parts were hardly involved.

The making of iron and non-ferrous castings at Leiston had many positive advantages. There was no time lost in inviting estimates, no sending away and, later, retrieving patterns and core boxes, and, of course, a quick response to orders. On the other hand there was a down side. The foundry foreman and his senior men, possessing, as they did, knowledge and skills not widely disseminated, tended to elitism. In turn, this made them feel slightly detached in the face of any criticism from the rest of the works and reluctant to modify or supplant existing practices. Despite his being seen as a chilly and aloof man Frank Garrett the elder was more liberal in his attitude to the opinions of his staff than many employers of the time, and gave cautious respect to firmly held technical views once he was convinced that they were not rooted in mere obstinacy. His particular interest was non-ferrous bearings. As a younger man he had devised the method used on the Works of casting bearings for threshers in cast iron chills to reduce or remove the need for machining, and had initiated research into the mixes of bronzes and brasses used there. In the first decade of this century there were five standard brass mixes in use as tabulated below:

Ingredients per melt in pounds

	BRASS No. 1	2	3	4	5
Copper	32	32	32	32	32
Tin	5	3½	4	3	2
Spelter	½	1	1½	3	2
Lead	-	-	1	1	4

There was also a very poor mixture called 5A containing 16 lbs. of copper, 12 lbs. of old white metal lined bearing scrap, 1 lb. of spelter and enough No.5 scrap to fill the pot. This was used, so far as tractions were concerned, only for minor items such as oil cups, packing pieces for the large end of connecting rod brasses, suction unions and nuts, suction roses, gauge glass guards, name-plates, and the like. No.5 mix proper was used only for 'small stuff' such as cock wheels. Going up the scale, No.4 was used for blast cocks, pump caps and similar items; No.3 was not used on tractions at all. Mixes 1 and 2, which except for the minor adulteration with spelter (commercial zinc) were virtually bronzes, were used for everything important. No.2 was for starting (throttle) slides, safety valves, pump valves, all bushes except main axle bushes, and clutch gear rings on the strawburning tractions. No.1 mix, the best, was the material for axle bushes, connecting rod brasses, gland bushes, and slide rod bushes. However, phosphor bronze was used for the connecting rod brasses of the road locomotives.

Frank Garrett's personal interest in foundry work led him to correspond with acquaintances in the business, such as R.S. Lloyd of Hayward Tyler & Co. in Luton and, in 1912, when bearing metals for the CCS power plants were under discussion, with Frederick Merrils, the consulting metallurgist whose laboratories were in Figtree Lane, Sheffield. One of the first trials conducted by F.E. Walker was in early November, 1909, when he ran a controlled series of identical runs on the brake with a 10 NHP single cylinder portable to test the merits of various brass and bronze mixes for connecting rod bearings. The phosphor bronze and Garretts' No.3 mix were tried against gun-metal, Admiralty mixture (44 of copper, 5 of tin, and 1 of zinc), a bronze consisting of 90% copper and 10% tin, and 'Dewrance's bronze'. The phosphor bronze was the clear winner, followed by the Admiralty mix. The others gave much inferior results.

A.W. James, the foundry foreman, did not take kindly to the intrusion of those he regarded as outsiders into his domain. Soon after Maurice Plane arrived in the drawing office he was asked about the brass mixes used at Davey Paxman's works in Colchester from which he had come. His chief, Schmach, passed them on to Francis Oakes, the Works Manager, who, in turn, gave them to A.W. James. The result in the latter was near apoplexy. Plane's first mix was dismissed as being 'for refrigerators, etc. Too expensive; out of date method. Can beat this 1/3 the price'. His second, for glands, brought the comment: 'Will leave you to guess what sort of stuff this is. The difference between two men. Mr. Ransome told Mr. Frank to use Admiralty for glands. The gland mixture of Mr. Plane is the same sort of stuff they make brass candlesticks of.' Maurice Plane had red hair and a temper to match, coupled with an abrasive tongue and the habit of expressing himself forcibly. His reaction to these comments must have been interesting, but James carried the day.

The work of the foundry was an intriguing combination of modern mechanical method and an intuitive pragmatism probably in an unbroken tradition from the Middle Ages. Thus in 1925 when J.W. Jackman & Co. of Manchester had just supplied a Wadsworth core-making machine they replied to a query about the required consistency of the material as follows:

A rough and ready rule for the right temper of the core mixture would appear to be to take a handful of the mixture, squeeze it in the hand and then open the hand. If, on doing, [sic] the mixture shows a decided tendency to break asunder, then the mixture is not far wrong.

Sharp sand for use in the foundry came from the firm's own pit next to Theberton Road, and soft sand from a pit at nearby Coldfair Green, but notwithstanding these local supplies as much re-use as possible was made of sand from old moulds after passing through the sifting machine. In May, 1912, at a time when experiments were going on to test the efficacy of Poulson's No.1 and No.2 sand renovator compositions the following notes were jotted down of mixes for three types of work:

For loam work: 264 lbs. black (used) sand; 4 shovelfuls manure; 7lbs. No.2 Renovator; ½ shovelful coal dust.
For cyl. cores: 264 lbs. black sand; 1½ shovelfuls manure; 66 lbs. coal dust; 7lbs. No.2.
For Greensand work: 264 lbs. black sand; 66 lbs. coal dust; 9 lbs. No.2.

Would the proper term for this be technology or alchemy?

As most Garrett products were sold in foreign countries or the colonies, where the prices were not cushioned by the price fixing agreement of the Agricultural Engineers Association, price was a constant factor in policy decisions. Notwithstanding the language used in catalogues and publicity the standards they used in traction engine building were not those of high class locomotive practice nor, may it be said, were those of most makers, if only for the reason that the demands upon a traction engine were so much less exacting than those upon an express railway locomotive. This need for economical design came out in such things as the use of trunk guides for crossheads and the squaring of the first intermediate shaft for the gears to slide upon it in preference to using a splined shaft and broached keyways in the gears. There was a market for engines with such refinements, but it was not unlimited and was considered to be catered for already by Burrell, Fowler, and, to a lesser extent, Foden. McLarens, on the other hand, also regarded - and quite rightly - as a high class firm, favoured the squared shaft. Burrells went further than most by their untiring advocacy of the three shaft arrangement and by using the freedom it conferred to increase the width of their gears to what all other makers regarded as an uneconomic extent.

However, within these design parameters that they had set themselves the Garretts endeavoured to do everything well, although there were lapses from time to time. The use of limit gauges kept hand fitting of components to a minimum, a characteristic that was liked by engine owners and their fitters when it ensured that spare parts went into place readily. Though the policy was to make everything possible at home certain items were invariably bought out. These were springs of all types, pressure gauges, gauge glass fittings, lamps, belts, injectors and mechanical lubricators. Under the pricing rules the two latter items were extras and usually chosen by the purchaser. When the choice was left to Garretts they mostly used an injector from Holden & Brooke, who made a very high class range of instruments. Their selected mechanical lubricator - at any rate in the 1895-1910 period - was the Mollerup, but other makes were fitted, probably at the instance of the purchaser. For pressure gauges the Schäffer & Budenburg was frequently fitted whilst Dewrance gauge glass fittings were favoured. Road springs customarily came from Jonas Woodhead of Sheffield; coil springs from any convenient source. Belts were supplied by George Thurlow & Sons of Stowmarket who had their own strap shop. Lamps were normally obtained from Eli Griffiths & Sons of Birmingham but others were provided on request.

One of the strengths of Garrett engines was the generating capacity of their boilers. Whilst it would be rash to say that the Works never produced a poor steamer the general reputation was good. Boilermaking, like foundry work, was, and is, an esoteric craft the actual practice of which is not so much learned from text books as passed on by the emulation of elders. The designs of boilers produced at Leiston satisfied the principal boiler insurance offices, the most senior of which, the Manchester Steam Users' Association was referred to in the specification which accompanied the tender for the supply of an engine but the lucidly set out rule book of the National Boiler Insurance Company was the one actually followed in the drawing office. Whilst the design of the boiler was thus settled in the drawing office the translation of it into practice by calculating the shapes of the constituent plates in the flat, making the necessary templates, and marking out was in the hands of the shop foreman and his chargemen. When George Hambling, the last of the line of boiler shop foremen, retired he presented me with the book in which he and his predecessors had recorded the sizes and thicknesses of the plates for boilers, noting the grade of plate (shell, firebox, or flanging) used for each component. The templates, of course, were destroyed when the old boiler shop site was cleared.

Although I had the pleasure of knowing some of the men who worked upon the erection of the last few traction engines - Jimmy Drane, Dick and Jack Feller, and Walter Hall, for example - none were left who had worked upon them in their hey-day. Nor did the activities of Tom Staulkey, whose laconic reports of the visits he made to various steam wagons during his period as a travelling service inspector gave such a vivid picture of how the wagons behaved, extend in any degree to traction engines. There is, therefore, nothing like the amount of anecdotal information relating to traction engines that there was in relation to wagons. However, a few of the later test house log sheets remain to give a little flavour of the problems dealt with before an engine left the Works. Some, like the odd trace of steam or water round a stud or stay, are found on most first steamings; others are not so readily excusable. Thus when 6NHP single No.34353 was tested on October 8, 1923, by J.K. Peecock, with George Whipps as the driver, the list of defects entered in the Testing Department log book was:

> Pump delivery pipe leaked. Pump checkvalve handle on wrong way. Pin in reversing lever too long and fouled gear guard. Driving pins would not go in. Piston leaked badly and had to have new rings fitted. Check valves repacked. Cyl. leaked through stud hole, this was plugged with copper. Pump return handle too long and fouled reversing lever when in backward position. Handle on steerage wheel had sharp point on end, this was turned down suitably. Stop valve leaked.

Whilst one can understand that erectors were often struggling against time there was not much excuse for Sid Poynter, the chargehand in this case, leaving, for instance, the pin in the reversing lever fouling the gear guard. It was he, again, who was responsible for erecting No.35064, a 5NHP Continental type for Zehder. This was tested by Cyril Plane, son of Maurice Plane, the chief designer, on August 19, 1927, and as the report (below) shows there were some silly defects in it that should never have got out of the erecting shop. In fact one wonders how the defective pump gears had managed to emerge from the turnery.

> Flywheel side main bearing heated up; The sheet iron footplate in front of tender fouls firedoor when the latter is open. The two coal bunkers had to be moved back 1" to allow clips on roadwheels to pass. Rear footstep - this had to be moved back because it was $^3/_8$" out of square. Locking plates on driving and differential pins too thick to allow proper size split pin to be used, a half round groove was filed in to remedy trouble. Two firebox side stays leaked junction of side of firebox shell and boiler barrel - leaked rather badly. The rod operating the governor valve from the platform was too short and this allowed the lever to drop down to a horizontal position.
> This engine was taken on stock ground and towed the pig iron trailer round for about 45 mins.
> Pump gears were noisy when the pump was working. It was found that one gear was slightly cut eccentric and this caused the teeth to engage too deeply in one place. $^1/_{16}$" was turned off the top of the teeth on both wheels.

When my late friend Jack Simpson began his premium apprenticeship at the Works in 1907, the Testing Department was not a separate entity but was, loosely at any rate, under the erecting shop foreman. Minor defects were remedied either in the test house, as they were with several of those on No.35064, or by having a word in the ear of the erector responsible without the formality of a log book. Only if a defect was too major, or the erector too recalcitrant, to deal with in these two ways was a formal complaint made. However, there would not have been much chance of using the 'old pals' network' to settle the first defect entered in the log sheet by J.K. Peecock when he tested No.34417, the last 8NHP engine made, on March 1, 1924. This was for the Western Australian Government.

> No provision was made for locking 2nd gear. This was afterwards altered by the D.O. Bad leak in firebox above furnace door. 1 stud on HP valve cover leaked. 2 studs on LP valve cover leaked. Tank bracket on RH side of boiler leaked. Injector steam cock leaked. Water gauge glasses would not clear cannon bracket, the latter was therefore cut away.

Whilst it would be wrong to linger overmuch on these private records of minor mishaps, for undoubtedly they happened in every firm, I am tempted to quote the test house log of No.34727, the 6NHP compound for Dublin County Council, tested by J.K. Peecock on May 18, 1925, with one of the Newstead brothers driving.

> This traction would not pull at all well when first tested, both valves were blind and the exhaust cone was too small. Finally an 1½" exhaust cone was fitted and both valves given $^1/_{16}$" full lead each end. The engine pulled well and dragged 22 tons on top gear to Middleton. 2 muddoors leaked. Double HP rod to have stay fitted. Filling pocket cap leaked. Double spring balance safety valves had to be fitted in place of the original Ramsbottom valves owing to the governor pulley fouling the rear column of the latter valve. There was a small leak in the HP steam chest which was successfully caulked. Starting brackets marked wrongly, 'open and shut' plates to be fitted. Press. gauge marked 160 lbs. sq." instead of 180 (altered in PS).

It is to be wondered how the relapse into archaic practice with the safety valves was explained to the client, just as it would be interesting to know how many of those who observed the use of spring balances launched into learned speculation as to why they were chosen when the simple, although probably never admitted, explanation was that they were fitted to correct an erector's error!

The story of Garrett's traction engine building cannot be closed without a summation of where they stood and what their footing was in that sphere. What did they achieve and what landmarks did they set up? They were early in the field with both chain and gear driven self-movers, having first tried and quickly moved away from the Boydell system. Through friendship with Thomas Aveling they were pioneer builders of the engines of his design that laid the foundations of the traction engine as a regular article of commerce. Succeeding, almost beyond their expectations, as builders of portable engines and threshers they left the traction engine alone for a decade. Upon their return to the market they launched a range of engines marked by the soundness and competence of their performance. All did well, with the possible exception of the road locomotives, and even here the few examples they made had longish lives with one of them, No.27946 *Vera*, surviving to be almost the last road locomotive in commercial use. Their 4NHP steam tractors, intended to be the subject of the next volume in this series, were outstanding.

During most of the 'modern' phase of traction engine building, from 1894 to the 1914 war, the major share holder and dominant force of the Works was Frank Garrett whose abiding interest was in portables and threshers and the markets for them in Central and Eastern Europe. The trade in traction engines, home or overseas, had little attraction for him and each new venture initiated by the burgeoning influence of his sons had to be tested against his scepticism as parent, senior director, and majority shareholder. Each case, therefore, had to be backed by convincing assessment and careful design to win his consent. The failure of the first attempt to build steam wagons was an instance in which the progressive sons had to admit defeat to their father. The 1914-18 war destroyed him. It killed Stephen, his favourite son; cost him his trusted colleague and confidant, Carl Remy; and ripped apart the network of contacts and agencies across Europe, making enemies of many of the men he had come to regard as friends through years of trading and whose sons, often, he had had as pupils on the Works. The calamity vindicated his own sons' insistence upon building up a trade in the home market but the volume of sales at home was in no way sufficient to make up for that lost abroad as a result of the war.

However, in the twenty years from 1894 - when the first of the new generation of traction engines was launched - to 1914 - when the cracks destroyed the mirror - it must have been exhilarating to experience the insistent push towards new markets and new products, with the staff increasing year after year, the Works growing and turnover going up and up, all seeming to presage a brilliant future. The optimism in the firm reflected the optimism that filled the country, the feeling of Great Britain becoming greater. Garretts did, in truth, have many things to be proud of. They had built up a range of traction engines that could equal or excel most other makes. Probably only Burrell or Fowler were ahead of them, whilst even the former was open to the charge of over-design and the latter to dragging its feet in standardisation. Fowler boilers, for example, abounded in tappings at 14 threads to the inch when the consensus of makers had gone over to 11 threads as standard. When we were discussing *A Review of Steam Tractors* the late Eric Alley once gave me his definition of a real engineer: 'One who can do for five shillings what any fool can do for a pound', a sentiment that would have appealed to Frank Garrett Senior. It is a narrow path between proper thrift and undue meanness but, with the occasional lapse, Garretts trod it with skill. The Garrett achievements and the calibre of the men they recruited in those golden two decades of traction engine building entitle them to acclaim that has not readily been accorded to them.

Fig.117. 8NHP Single No.25858, supplied on July 19, 1906, to G.F. Townsend of Exning, near Newmarket, on the road with two truckloads of the wheat being threshed in the picture on the front cover. The engine was equipped with some of the outward attributes of a road locomotive, such as a belly tank and motion covers, but remained basically an agricultural engine. Garretts tended to refer to engines with such extras as 'general purpose engines', a term never assigned any precise definition but used to infer that the engine in question possessed features that made it more versatile.

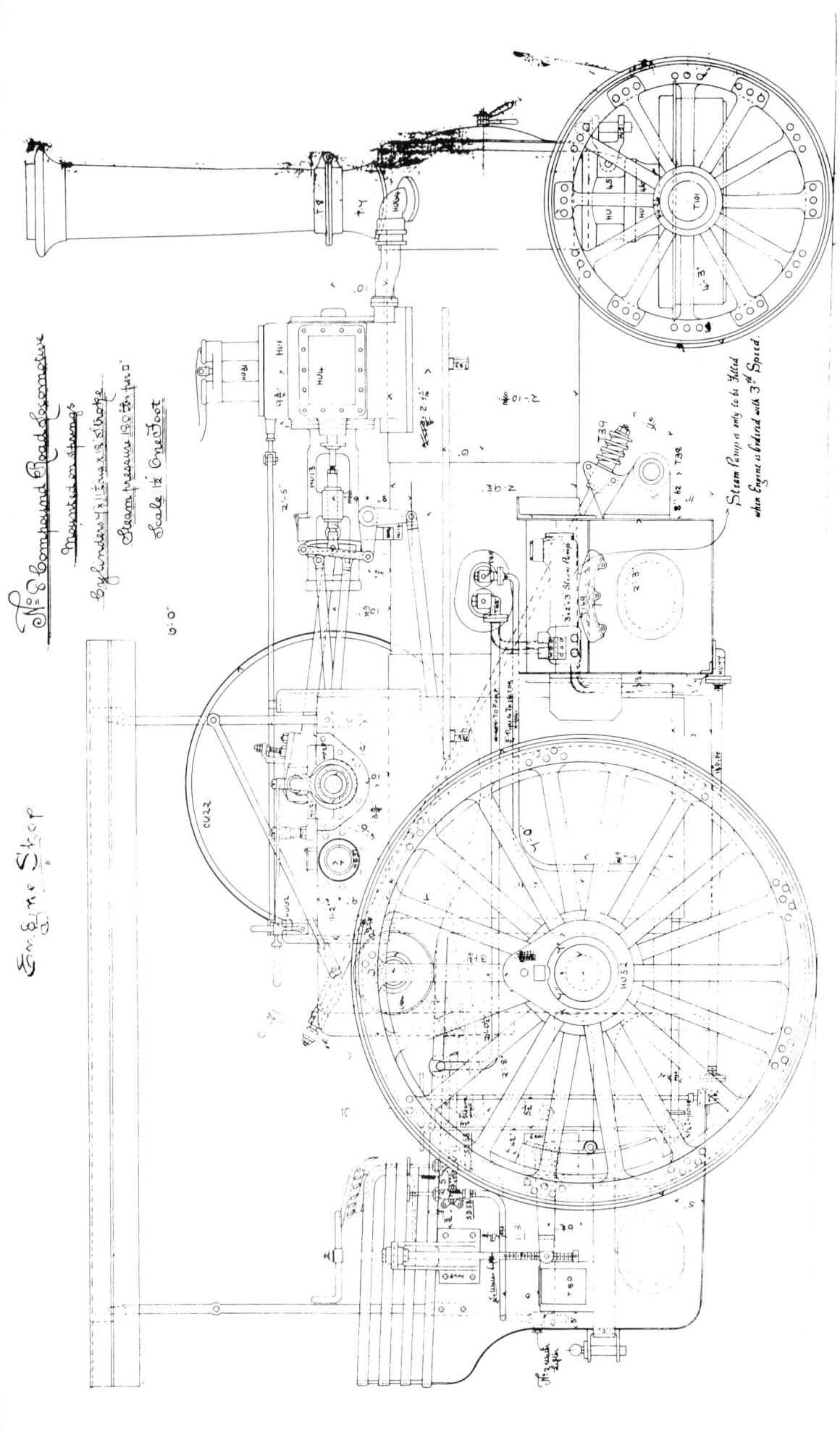

Fig.118. *The 8NHP compound road locomotive of 1903 drawn by H.G. Florey.*

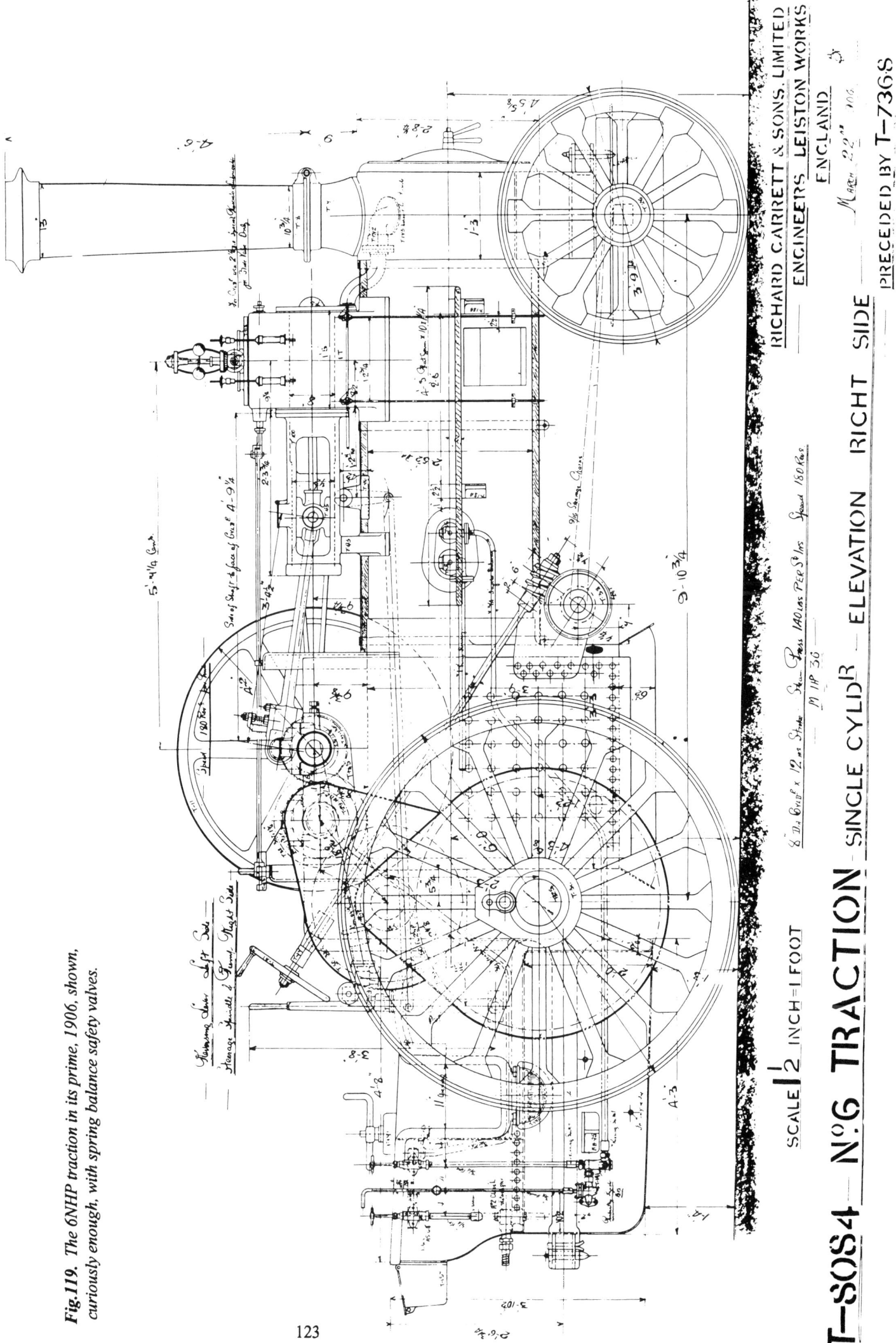

Fig.119. *The 6NHP traction in its prime, 1906, shown, curiously enough, with spring balance safety valves.*

Fig.120. The 6NHP showman's road locomotive.

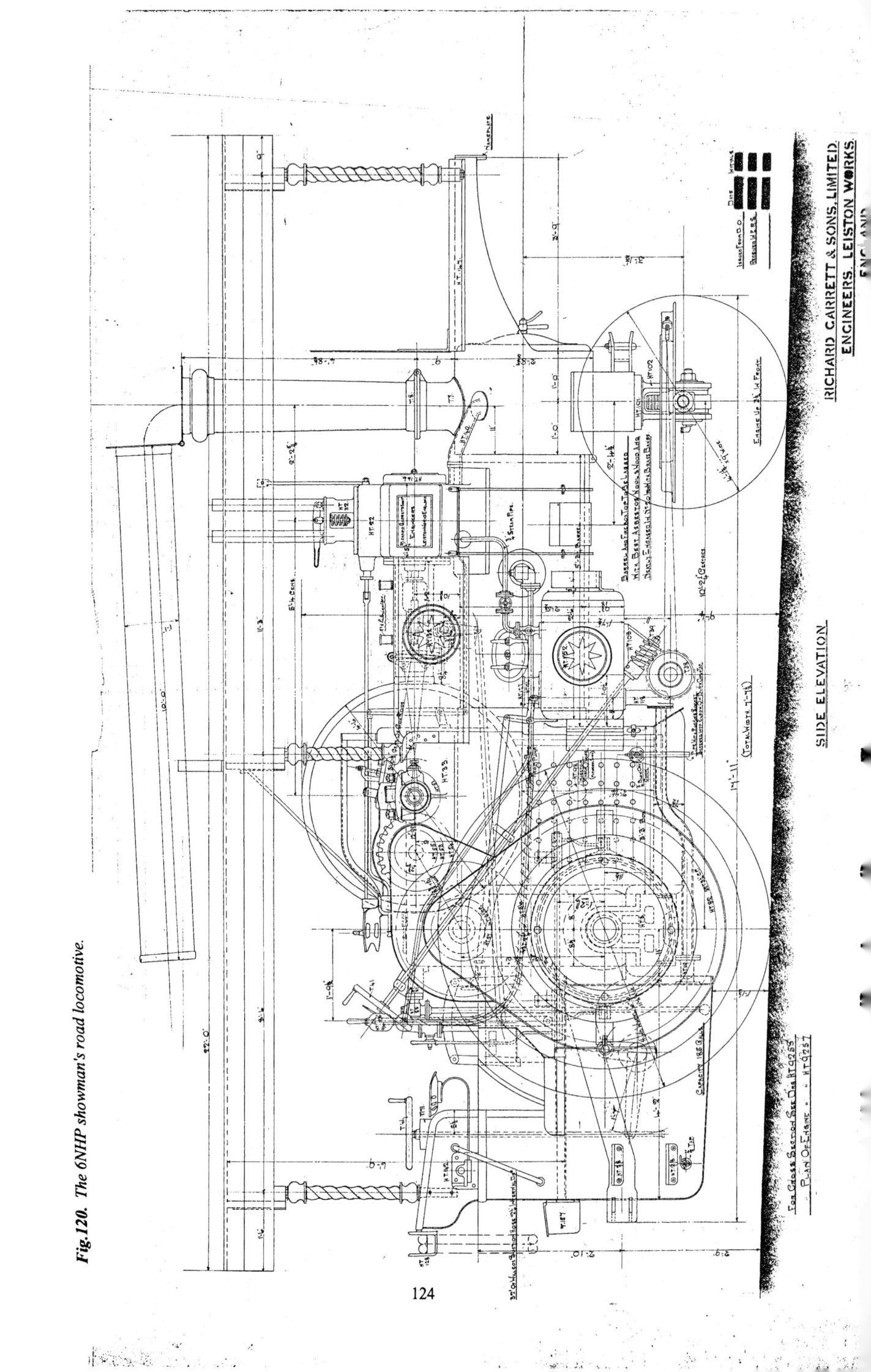

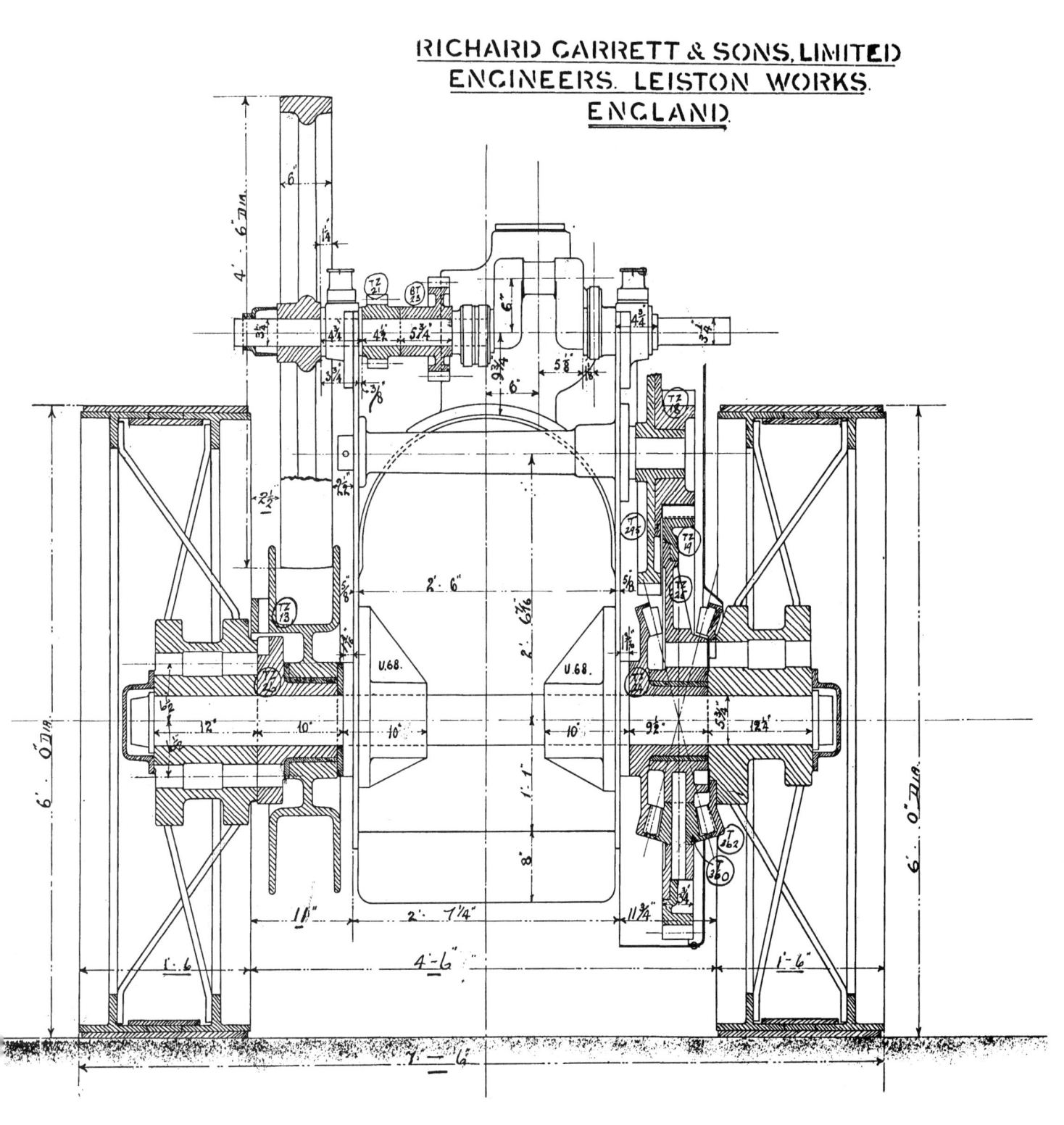

Fig.121. Cross-section through the rear axle of the 7NHP New Zealand traction engine, 1910.
(Drawing TZ11492)

Fig.122. The maintenance of traction engines was often undertaken with minimal facilities. Here 6NHP No.23403 (1901) is undergoing repair, c.1935, in the yard of R.E. Caulkett, Clare, Suffolk. It was owned by H.S. Orbell, also of Clare. [R.G.Pratt]

Fig.123. Harkness's Vera *(No.27946)* did not live in palatial surroundings between contracts. Here she is standing in their yard in Belfast in August, 1955.
[A.J.Martin collection]

Fig.124. The late Derek Stoyel photographed 7NHP single, No.27961, owned by John White of Raydon, Suffolk, at East Bergholt on 5th September, 1938.
[A.J.Martin collection]

Fig.125. Bonny Jean (6NHP superheated. single No.28375) owned by Allan Meikle, demonstrating its capabilities with a 54" thresher and a straw baler.

Fig.126. The 1950s saw many sales of steam threshing businesses, the engines paraded in steam to look their best but often the only serious bidder was the scrapman. Here the fleet of Radwinter Threshers Ltd. is lined up for sale at Hall Farm, Radwinter, Essex, on 2nd August, 1950, with 6NHP single No.28410 in the foreground.
[A.J.Martin collection]

Fig.127. Threshing in happier days. Edmund Cheney's 5NHP No.28382 at Mill Farm, Kelsale, Autumn, 1910.

NEW IMPROVED
AGRICULTURAL SELF-MOVING ENGINES.

Richard Garrett & Sons have just brought out a **self-moving** Engine upon an entirely new design, embodying all recent improvements and eminently suited to every description of agricultural work, as well as to traction and contractors' purposes.

It is provided with an ingenious arrangement for **two speeds**. The motion being transmitted to the **rims** of the travelling wheels by means of spur-gearing direct from the crank-shaft, by which arrangement a great saving in friction and wear and tear is secured.

For rounding corners an arrangement is provided for throwing the travelling wheels out of gear by means of a simple striking lever on either side, and without recourse to the most objectionable "Jack in the box" differential gearing, which has been proved so productive of unnecessary friction and consequent breakages.

The boilers are calculated for a maximum working pressure of 150lbs. on the square inch, and Richard Garrett & Sons have every confidence in recommending these Engines to their customers as the simplest and most efficient yet produced.

Reference to users of these Engines will be furnished on application.

PRICES as per List attached.

	£	s.	d.
8-Horse Power, complete			
10 ,, ,,			

Fig.128. Page 12 of Garretts' 1876 catalogue when the new 8NHP traction engines were introduced. The way the lack of a differential is presented as a virtue is amusing. In a similar vein, when I was a boy a corner shop near home offered cheap vinegar made from commercial acetic acid coloured with caramel, the label proclaiming 'Guaranteed non-brewed'.

TELEGRAMS: "GARRETT, LEISTON."
TELEPHONE: No. 16 LEISTON, G.P.O.

CODES: A.B.C. 5TH EDITION
& BENTLEY'S

FROM

RICHARD GARRETT & SONS, Ltd.

ESTABLISHED 1778.

ENGINEERS,
LEISTON WORKS, LEISTON, ENGLAND.

LEISTON, _____ 19____

To _____   Ref. _____

SPECIFICATION & ESTIMATE FOR
"GARRETT"
GENERAL PURPOSE TRACTION ENGINE.

```
                    Code Word—
CYLINDER         –   – Diameter     –   –
   ,,                  Stroke       –   –
CRANKSHAFT       –   – Diameter     –   –
MAIN AXLE        –   – Diameter     –   –
HIND DRIVING WHEELS  – Diameter     –   –
   ,,        ,,      – Width        –   –
FRONT WHEELS     –   – Diameter     –   –
   ,,                – Width        –   –
FLYWHEEL         –   – Diameter     –   –
   ,,                – Width        –   –
EXTREME WIDTH OVER HIND DRIVING WHEELS  –
GRATE AREA       –   –      –       –   –
TOTAL HEATING SURFACE       –       –   –
HYDRAULIC TEST PRESSURE (cold water) –  –
WORKING STEAM PRESSURE      –       –   –
NORMAL ENGINE SPEED    Revs. per minute
MAX. TEST LOAD OR TEMPORARY OVERLOAD – –
   (at Normal Engine Speed and Steam Pressure.)
RECOMMENDED MAX. CONTINUOUS WORKING LOAD –
   (at Normal Engine Speed and Steam Pressure.)
APPROX. HAULAGE CAPACITY    –       –   –
   (on good level Macadam Roads)  {Gross  –
                                  {Nett   –
TRAVELLING SPEEDS (at Normal Engine Speed) –
APPROX. WEIGHT EMPTY  –     –       –   –
   ,,       ,,    IN WORKING ORDER  –   –
```

Price complete as above and according to SPECIFICATION on pages 2 to 5, including the GARRETT CORRUGATED FIREBOX; Pickering Type High Speed Governor; Feedpump driven by eccentric off Crankshaft; Waterlifter with 26 feet of special wire-bound Suction Hose; and complete with Waterproof Cover and all usual tools and accessories   –   –   –   –   –

£   s.   d.

RICHARD GARRETT & SONS, Ltd., Leiston Works, ENGLAND

SPECIFICATION of the "GARRETT"
General Purpose Type Traction Engine

GENERAL DESCRIPTION. These Engines are constructed on the four-shaft principle.

Steel has been substituted for iron throughout wherever it has been found practicable to do so.

Every practical device for ensuring economy of fuel and water, without increasing the complication of wearing parts and thus adding to the cost of upkeep, has been adopted.

Special care has been given to the question of the proportion of Engine to boiler, and the Garrett Standard General Purpose Type Traction Engines are mounted on boilers (fitted with the **Garrett Corrugated Firebox**—see page 4) of such sizes as to be capable of supplying steam in the driest possible condition well in excess of the maximum requirements of the Engines mounted upon them without being unduly forced: to this must be attributed in some measure the unrivalled reputation which the Garrett General Purpose Type Traction Engines enjoy for **economy of fuel, unequalled steaming and hauling qualities, and low cost of upkeep.**

CYLINDERS. Of a special mixture of best cold-blast, close-grained cast-iron: steam jacketed and surmounted by steam dome, wherein are placed the safety valves and starting valve, ensuring the use of dry steam.

Lagged with approved non-conducting material and covered with sheet steel casing.

Provided with all necessary fittings and lubricators of the most substantial and approved design, and of first-class quality throughout.

SPECIAL NOTE.—The cylinders of the Garrett Standard Compound General Purpose Type Traction Engines are constructed with **outside valve chests, making the slide valves easily accessible**, and are provided with an auxiliary valve to admit high pressure steam into low pressure cylinder when starting Engine: this auxiliary valve is operated from the footplate and arranged to close automatically.

PISTON. Accurately fitted with rings and springs of most approved patterns. Piston rod is of best quality mild steel.

CROSSHEAD GUIDES. These are of the **trunk type**, cast in one piece with the front cylinder cover. They are bored and faced at one setting, so that perfect alignment is obtained.

CROSSHEADS. These are of finest cast steel fitted with slippers of special mixture cast-iron and of large bearing surface, being accurately machined to fit inside the trunk guide, and adjustable so that wear can be taken up.

The gudgeon, through which the small end of connecting rod is secured, is of large diameter, deeply case-hardened and ground to an exact fit, and has tapered seatings.

CONNECTING RODS. Forged out of hammered ingots of finest quality steel, machined to limit gauges and polished. The large ends of connecting rods are of exceptionally substantial design, the strap being bolted to the rod and the bearings adjusted by steel cotters.

CRANKSHAFT. The Garrett Standard Single Cylinder and Compound General Purpose Type Traction Engines have crankshafts made from solid forgings of finest steel, the webs being machined out of the solid according to the best locomotive practice.

No. 885.

RICHARD GARRETT & SONS, Ltd., Leiston Works, ENGLAND

Specification of the Garrett General Purpose Type Traction Engine.—*Continued.*

COUNTERSHAFTS AND MAIN AXLE. The two countershafts and main axle are forged from hammered ingots of finest steel and machined to limit gauges.

The first countershaft is machined "square" where the "change speed" double pinion slides, so that all loose keys are dispensed with.

GEARING. All the gearing is of the best crucible cast steel of a special mixture which long experience has proved to be the most durable.

All the fast-running gear wheels (*i.e.* for the first and second transmissions) **are "machine-cut"** by our own special machinery with the most **mathematical accuracy,** with the result that **all the vibration,** usually set up by fast-running gear wheels with the old-fashioned cast teeth or cogs **is entirely avoided, thus reducing the wear and tear throughout the whole Engine and boiler to the lowest possible point** as well as **rendering the Engine noiseless when travelling on the road.**

The gearing is arranged for two speeds, and in such a way that only one speed can be put into gear at one time. It can, moreover, be easily disconnected to enable threshers, pumps, sawbenches, mills, or any other suitable fixed machinery to be driven by a belt off the flywheel of the Engine.

The whole of the outer gearing is enclosed in stout flanged steel casing.

DIFFERENTIAL OR COMPENSATING GEAR. Consisting of **three** bevel pinions of best crucible cast steel having shrouded teeth or cogs, the shrouds being so arranged that they cannot gear too deeply.

The action of the differential gear is automatic and allows the hind driving wheels to revolve at different speeds or even in opposite directions, whereby all grinding action on the road surface with the consequent undue strain on the driving wheels, main axle, bearings and gearing, &c., is avoided, when turning even the sharpest corners.

REVERSING GEAR. Link motion reversing gear of the most approved and up-to-date locomotive type with double powerful lifting levers and made of best Yorkshire iron throughout.

The joints and wearing surfaces are extra large, deeply case-hardened and ground to an exact fit.

FLYWHEEL. Cast-iron flywheel of the spoke type. The face of the rim is turned to correct radius to take belt for driving machinery.

GOVERNOR. The engine is fitted with one of Garrett's latest improved high-speed Pickering type governors.

This type of governor has no equal for quick and sensitive action, the sensitiveness being about $1\frac{3}{4}\%$. Owing to the extreme simplicity of construction, and the absence of the usual connecting levers and pins common to most other types, it is exceptionally durable and easy to manage.

BEARINGS. All bearings and bushes are of best quality gun-metal and of exceptional width to ensure cool running: they are fitted into recesses bored in the hornplates, so that all strains are taken by the plates, which are specially stayed up to receive these strains.

STEERAGE. Of the worm and worm-wheel type.

SPECIAL CONVENIENCES FOR DRIVING. The starting and reversing levers, "change-speed" gear lever, feedpump, brake handle and steerage wheels are all placed in convenient positions round the driver's stand so as all to be within easy reach of the driver, thus enabling one man to both drive and steer.

LUBRICATION. The greatest possible care has been given to the question of providing efficient lubrication for all moving parts of the Engine, and especially for those bearings and moving parts which cannot be attended to when the Engine is moving.

BRAKE. The Garrett Standard General Purpose Type Traction Engines are fitted with a powerful friction band brake, acting on drum.

WINDING DRUM. A fast and loose type winding drum, which can be easily and quickly thrown in and out of gear, is fitted to main axle, and is provided with 50 yards of steel wire rope of special quality.

FEEDPUMP. Of ample capacity, fitted inside hornplates and driven by separate eccentric off crankshaft and provided with all necessary pipe connections, clack box, &c. A special cock is also provided between clack box and boiler by means of which the pump can be entirely disconnected from the boiler: this is most convenient should dirt or grit get under the pump valves, necessitating their being taken out and cleaned whilst the Engine is under steam.

WATER LIFTER. Powerful steam water lifter with all necessary cocks (including special gland-packed steam cock) and 26 feet of special wire-bound suction hose.

RICHARD GARRETT & SONS, Ltd., Leiston Works, ENGLAND

Specification of the Garrett General Purpose Type Traction Engine.—*Continued.*

BOILERS. The boilers are designed and constructed throughout according to the requirements of the British Board of Trade, The Manchester Steam Users' Association, and all first-class Boiler Insurance Companies, and will pass their respective tests for the working steam pressures for which they are sold, being of the same strength and workmanship as adopted in the best locomotive practice.

Siemens-Martin mild steel plates, properly annealed, are used throughout—the shell plates, internal firebox plates and round tube-plates being of the respective qualities specified by the British Board of Trade.

All plates are specially tested and certified by Lloyd's Surveyor for Richard Garrett & Sons, Ltd., before leaving the makers' works.

All edges are planed or milled and properly fullered with a broad tool after riveting.

All holes for rivets and stays where possible are drilled in position after the boiler has been plated together.

Riveting is done by the most modern hydraulic machinery available.

Flanging is done by powerful hydraulic flanging presses **at one heat.**

Outer faces of flanges to round tube-plates are machined to ensure perfect fullering.

The hornplates are of extra strong steel plates, and are strongly stayed together with two specially designed, stout, transverse stay-plates fitted in between them and securely bolted to them: these transverse stay-plates are flanged over at the top as well as round at the sides, rendering it practically impossible for them to bend and thus preventing vibration of the hornplates.

Longitudinal seams are double riveted, also the circumferential seam joining firebox shell to barrel.

Solid foundation rings are fitted to all sizes of the Garrett Standard General Purpose Type Traction Engines, and angle iron is entirely dispensed with.

A number of specially stout stay-tubes threaded at both ends are securely screwed into both tube-plates, these being in accordance with the British Board of Trade's highest class regulations and greatly increasing the strength of the boiler.

The other tubes, which are expanded into both tube-plates according to the best practice, are of finest seamless steel, solid drawn.

The boiler barrel is of extra large diameter, giving an unusually large steam space and consequently ensuring the use of dry steam.

BOILER CLEANING FACILITIES. A large manhole is placed in the side of the boiler barrel within easy reach of the firebox, giving every facility for internal examination and cleaning.

Mudholes are provided at all four corners of the firebox just above the foundation ring, making the water spaces on all four sides easy to clean out: these mudholes are so placed that the bridges and covers can be easily removed for cleaning and replaced after cleaning.

Further mudholes are provided at the top and bottom of smokebox tube-plate and in the front-plate level with the firebox crown.

BOILER FITTINGS. A complete set of steam fittings of the most substantial and approved pattern is supplied as follows:—Two water gauges with stout brass guards: pressure gauge: whistle: blow-off cock: double safety valves: blast pipe and cock: special gland packed steam cocks for water lifter and injector (injectors are only fitted to special order at extra charge): special check valves or clack boxes for pump and injector (injectors are only fitted to special order at extra charge) having special cocks between clack box and boiler whereby the boiler may be completely disconnected when under steam: fusible plug: &c., &c.

FIREBOX. THE GARRETT CORRUGATED FIREBOX

of

UNEQUALLED STEAMING CAPACITY,

ECONOMY and

DURABILITY.

The special mudhole fitted in the external firebox front-plate over the firehole between the longitudinal stays gives easy access to the **Garrett Corrugated Crownplate**: and there are no rows of roof-stays as with flat-topped fireboxes to make difficult the task of cleaning the crownplate.

TESTS (BOILER AND ENGINE). The boilers of the Garrett Standard Single Cylinder General Purpose Type Traction Engines are tested by hydraulic pressure (cold water) to 320 lbs. per square inch for a regular working steam pressure of 160 lbs. per square inch.

The boilers of the Garrett Standard Compound General Purpose Type Traction Engines are tested by hydraulic pressure (cold water) to 360 lbs. per square inch for a regular working steam pressure of 180 lbs. per square inch.

RICHARD GARRETT & SONS, Ltd., Leiston Works, ENGLAND

Specification of the Garrett General Purpose Type Traction Engine.—*Continued.*

TESTS (BOILER AND ENGINE)—*Continued.*
Every Garrett General Purpose Type Traction Engine has to undergo a prolonged brake trial at its regular working steam pressure, carrying full load and lasting several hours, when indicator diagrams are taken: no Engine is allowed to leave Leiston Works without having passed through this trial satisfactorily.

In addition to the above tests every Garrett General Purpose Type Traction Engine is also tested with a full load behind it over a variety of roads.

TENDER. The tender is constructed of extra stout mild steel plates with capacious water tank underneath footplate and coal bunker on the top: all corners are flanged by special hydraulic machinery with large "rounding" curves instead of sharp corners, so as to assist cleaning and prevent the accumulation of mud and dirt, &c.

ASHPAN AND GEAR COVERS are of stout steel plates flanged by special hydraulic machinery with large "rounding" curves instead of sharp corners, to prevent the accumulation of dirt, &c., and to assist cleaning.

SPECIAL DRAWBAR ATTACHMENT so arranged that the draught from the drawbar is taken direct to the main axle **without passing through the tender**: the drawbar attachment is provided with a special wedge adjustment.

LAGGING. Boiler lagged with wood, neatly covered with sheet steel casing and secured with polished brass bands round boiler barrel.

PAINTING. The Engine is painted, lined out and varnished in best locomotive style.

OUTFIT. With every Garrett General Purpose Type Traction Engine the following outfit is provided:— Waterproof cover of best Willesdon or equal cloth: one pair of large head lamps and one tail lamp with sliding shutters, also one water-gauge lamp: tool box with all necessary spanners, also hammer, caulking tool and oil can: stoking tools: tube brush: complete sets of spuds or clips, also frost pegs for hind driving wheels: fusible plug: &c., &c.

EXTRAS. The following (when ordered specially) can be fitted to the Garrett General Purpose Type Traction Engines at extra charge (prices on application:—
High duty injector or independent steam pump.
Powerful locomotive type laminated steel springs to front and hind axles.
Specially large Colonial type firebox.
Oil burning apparatus.
Special "drop" or "rocking" grates.
Extra wide travelling wheels.
Special draught attachment and steering angles for front wheels, for direct ploughing.
Parts for converting into a steam road roller.
Awning (1) over tender (driver's stand) or (2) over full length of Engine.
Blow-off cock worked from footplate.
Double discharge water lifter for filling tank or water cart.
Injector specially arranged for watering ground, including necessary hose for same.
Spark arrestors of various types.
Jib or other types of cranes.
Dismantling and close packing for shipment.

APPENDIX 1 - Table of Dimensions of Traction Engines and Tractors c.1909

N.B. Engines on offer in 1909 are tabulated as listed at that date. Engines marked * are as listed 1920.

Type of Engine	Diameter of Crankshaft	Diameter of First Countershaft	Diameter of Second Countershaft	Diameter of Main Axle	Tank Capacity: Tender (gallons)	Tank Capacity: Belly (gallons)	Bunker Capacity: Cubic Feet	Bunker Capacity: Cwt.	Cylinder Diameter	Cylinder Stroke	Flywheel Diameter by Width	Hindwheels Diameter by Width	Fore Wheels Diameter by Width	Extreme Width of Engine	Extreme Length of Engine	Height to Top of Flywheel	Grate Area, square feet	Heating Surface, square feet
No. 3 tractor	2¼"	2¾"	—	3½"	53	60	4	1.6	5½"	9"	2' 6" × 4½"	4' 0" × 8"	3' 0" × 5"	4' 6"	12' 8⅝"	6' 1"	2.1	42.8
No. 4 S.C. tractor	2¾"	3¼"	—	4⅛"	65	85	9¼	3.8	6½"	10"	3' 3" × 5"	5' 0" × 1' 0"	3' 4" × 6"	5' 10¾"	14' 5"	7' 3"	3.0	68.8
No. 4 C.D. tractor	2¾"	3¼"	—	4⅛"	65	85	9¼	3.8	4½" & 6⅞"	10"	3' 3" × 5"	5' 0" × 1' 0"	3' 4" × 6"	5' 10¾"	14' 5"	7' 3"	3.0	68.8
*No. 4 C.D. tractor s/heater	2¾"	3¼"	—	4⅛"	65	75	9¼	3.8	4½" & 6⅞"	10"	3' 3" × 5"	5' 0" × 1' 0"	3' 7¾" × 6"	6' 0"	14' 10"	7' 3"	3.0	¶68.12
No. 4 C.D. Colonial tractor	2¾"	3¼"	—	4⅛"	65	75	9¼	3.8	4½" & 6⅞"	10"	3' 3" × 5"	5' 0" × 1' 0"	3' 7¾" × 6"	6' 0"	15' 9"	7' 3"	4.38	73.14
No. 4 S.C. traction	2¾"	3¼"	—	4⅛"	—	100	11	4.4	6½"	10"	3' 0" × 5½"	5' 4½" × 1' 2"	4' 0" × 6"	6' 7"	18' 0"	8' 0"	5.27	105.77
No. 5 S.C. English traction	2¾"	3¼"	—	4¼"	105	—	9	3.7	7"	10"	3' 3" × 7"	5' 4½" × 1' 4"	3' 8" × 8"	7' 3"	16' 6"	7' 10"	5.27	105.77
No. 5 S.C. Continental traction	3"	3¼"	—	4¼"	—	110	14	6.0	7"	10"	3' 0" × 7"	5' 6" × 1' 4"	4' 0" × 8"	7' 2"	18' 9"	8' 0"	6.5	139.0
*No. 5 S.C. Colonial traction	2¾"	3¼"	—	4¼"	—	100	13¾	5.8	7"	10"	3' 3" × 7"	5' 4½" × 2' 0"	3' 8" × 9"	7' 3"	18' 0"	7' 10"	6.1	109.27
*P.V.I. S.C. traction	3"	3¼"	—	4¼"	105	—	8¾	3.6	8"	10"	3' 3" × 7"	5' 4½" × 1' 4"	3' 8" × 8"	7' 3"	16' 7"	7' 9"	4.03	103.55
*50 b.h.p. C.D. ploughing–S. H. traction	3"	3½"	—	4⅜"	90	140	14	6.0	5" & 8½"	10"	3' 7" × 5½"	6' 0" × 2' 0"	4' 0" × 7"	9' 0"	19' 0"	8' 3"	7.18	129.8
No. 6 S.C. traction	3"	3¼"	3½"	4⅞"	128	—	9¼	4.0	8"	12"	4' 2" × 6"	6' 0" × 1' 4"	3' 9" × 9"	7' 0⅜"	17' 1"	8' 6"	4.75	119.5
No. 6 S.C. Colonial traction	3¼"	3½"	—	4⅞"	128	—	9¼	4.0	8"	12"	4' 2" × 7"	6' 0" × 1' 6"	3' 9" × 9"	7' 6⅜"	17' 5⅜"	8' 7⅜"	5.75	124.4
No. 6 C.D. traction	3¼"	3¼"	3½"	4⅞"	128	105	9	3.7	5½" & 9"	12"	4' 2" × 6"	6' 0" × 1' 4"	3' 9" × 9"	7' 2¼"	17' 0¾"	8' 7½"	4.75	124.0
*No. 6 C.D. Colonial traction	3¼"	4"	3½"	5¼"	145	—	10	4.0	6" & 10½"	12"	4' 2" × 6"	6' 0" × 1' 4"	4' 2" × 9"	7' 2"	19' 0"	8' 9"	5.90	127.0
No. 6 S.C. rigid N.Z. traction	3"	3¼"	3½"	5¼"	137	—	10¾	4.3	8½"	12"	4' 2" × 6"	6' 0" × 1' 6"	3' 9" × 9"	7' 3⅛"	17' 6"	8' 5"	5.70	122.0
No. 6 S.C. straw burner	3"	3¼"	—	4⅞"	106	105±	—	—	8"	12"	3' 10" × 10"	5' 9" × 1' 8"	4' 0" × 9"	7' 9¼"	§	8' 5"	8.00	173.50
No. 7 S.C. traction	3¼"	3¼"	3½"	4⅞"	128	—	9½	3.9	8½"	12"	4' 2" × 6½"	6' 0" × 1' 6"	3' 9" × 9"	7' 5⅜"	17' 4"	8' 6"	5.30	134.40
*No. 7 S.C. S.H. traction	3¼"	4"	3½"	5¼"	145	—	10	4.0	8"	12"	4' 6" × 6½"	6' 0" × 1' 4"	4' 3" × 9"	7' 2"	17' 4"	8' 10"	4.75	¶121.75
No. 7 C.D. traction	3½"	3¼"	3½"	4⅞"	128	—	9	3.4	6⅜" & 11"	12"	4' 2" × 6"	6' 0" × 1' 6"	3" 3" × 9"	7' 6¼"	17' 6¾"	8' 7"	5.30	134.40
*No. 7 S.C. rigid N.Z. traction	3¼"	4"	3½"	5¾"	145	—	10	4.0	8½"	12"	4' 6" × 6"	6' 0" × 1' 6"	4' 3" × 9"	7' 6"	18' 11"	9' 0"	6.58	138.40
No. 8 S.C. traction	3½"	3½"	4"	5¼"	185	120	13½	5.6	9"	12"	4' 6" × 6½"	6' 6" × 1' 6"	4' 3" × 9"	7' 10"	18' 11 13/16"	9' 5½"	6.09	160.00
No. 8 C.D. traction	3½"	3½"	4"	5¼"	185	—	13½	5.6	6" & 10½"	12"	4' 6" × 6½"	6' 6" × 1' 6"	4' 3" × 9"	7' 11"	18' 11 13/16"	9' 5½"	6.09	160.00
No. 8 S.C. Colonial traction	3½"	3½"	—	4⅞"	185	—	13½	5.6	9"	12"	4' 2" × 8"	6' 0" × 1' 8"	4' 3" × 10"	8' 2⅞"	18' 7 9/16"	9' 1½"	7.30	164.60
No. 8 S.C. rigid N.Z. traction	3½"	3½"	4½"	6¼"	193	—	15	6.2	9"	12"	4' 6" × 6½"	7' 0" × 1' 6"	4' 6" × 9"	8' 0"	19' 4½"	9' 7 9/16"	7.30	164.60
No. 10 S.C. straw-burner	3½"	4"	—	5¼"	127	—	—	—	9¾"	12"	3' 10" × 10"	6' 3½" × 2' 6"	4' 6" × 10"	9' 8¾"	21' 1⅞"	9' 8"	9.60	259.4
No 6 C.D. road locomotive	3½"	3⅜"	4"	5½"	185	135	13	5.4	6⅜" & 11"	12"	3' 7" × 6"	6' 6" × 1' 6"	4' 6½" × 9"	7' 7⅛"	18' 1⅛"	8' 9¾"	5.00	124.00
No 8 C.D. road locomotive	4"	3½"	4½"	6"	190	130	18	7.4	7" & 11½"	12"	4' 6" × 6"	7' 0" × 1' 6"	4' 3" × 9"	8' 1¼"	19' 5½"	9' 6"	6.80	187.80

§ not available ± optional ¶ superheat added 10 sq.ft. to No.4 tractor; 20 sq.ft. to 7NHP traction

APPENDIX 1 - Table of Dimensions of Traction Engines and Tractors c.1909 (continued)

N.B. Engines on offer in 1909 are tabulated as listed at that date. Engines marked * are as listed 1920.

Type of engine	Boiler Barrel Length by Diameter	Tubes		Working Pressure, lb. per sq. in.	Weight Empty (tons)	Weight in Working Order (tons)	Maximum b.h.p.	Coal per Hour per b.h.p. (lb.)	Wate per Hour per b.h.p. (lb.)	Engine Speed, r.p.m.	Gear Ratios		Speed in m.p.h.	
		Number	Diameter								Slow	Fast	Slow	Fast
No. 3 tractor	3′ 1⅛″ × 1′ 8½″	19	1¾″	160	3.75	4.25	18	5.00	39	250	1 : 14.8	1 : 7.66	2.41	4.65
No. 4 S.C. tractor	3′ 10 3/16″ × 1′ 10½″	28	1¾″	160	4.85	5.50	25	4.00	32	230	1 : 24.4	1 : 11.90	1.67	3.44
No. 4 C.D. tractor	3′ 10 3/16″ × 1′ 10½″	28	1¾″	180	4.95	5.60	25	3.25	26	230	1 : 24.4	1 : 11.90	1.67	3.44
*No. 4 C.D. tractor s/heater	3′ 10¾″ × 1′ 10½″	26	1¾″	180	5.15	5.80	25	3.00	26	230	1 : 24.4	1 : 11.90	1.67	3.44
No. 4 C.D. Colonial tractor	3′ 10 3/16″ × 1′ 10½″	26	1¾″	180	5,25	5.90	25	—	26	230	1 : 24.4	1 : 11.90	1.67	3.44
No. 4 S.C. traction	5′ 1 3/16″ × 1′ 10½″	28	2″	180	4.75	5.50	25	4.00	32	230	1 : 17.04	—	2.03	—
No. 5 S.C. English traction	5′ 1 3/16″ × 1′ 10½″	28	2″	180	8.05	8.50	30	4.00	32	230	1 : 37.02	1 : 12.73	1.16	3.38
No. 5 S.C. Continental traction	6′ 1¼″ × 2′ 4½″	28	2¼″	180	7.50	8.00	30	4.00	32	230	1 : 22.2	—	2.00	—
*No. 5 S.C. Colonial traction	5′ 1 3/16″ × 1′ 10½″	28	2″	180	8.15	8.60	30	—	32	230	1 : 37.02	1 : 12.73	1.16	3.38
*P.V.I. S.C. traction	5′ 1¾″ × 1′ 10½″	28	2″	160	8.10	8.55	30	§	§	230	1 : 37.02	1 : 12.73	1.16	3.38
*50 b.h.p. C.D. ploughing – S.H. traction	5′ 1¾″ × 1′ 10½″	28	2¼″	225	§	§	§	§	§	230	1 : 24.6	1 : 14.80	2.00	3.38
No. 6 S.C. traction	5′ 3¼″ × 2′ 5½″	32	2″	140	9.75	10.50	25	4.00	32	180	1 : 27.3	1 : 15.30	1.41	2.50
No. 6 S.C. Colonial traction	5′ 3⅛″ × 2′ 5½″	32	2″	140	9.00	9.75	25	—	25	180	1 : 18.73		2.05	—
No. 6 C.D. traction	5′ 0¼″ × 2′ 5½″	37	2″	180	10.25	11.00	25	3.10	25	180	1 : 29.69	1 : 15.30	1.30	2.56
*No. 6 C.D. Colonial traction	5′ 1 5/16″ × 2′ 5½″	32	2″	180	9.00	9.75	25	—	25	180	1 : 25.1	1 : 11.50	1.50	3.34
No. 6 S.C. rigid N.Z. traction	5′ 3 3/16″ × 2′ 5½″	32	2″	160	10.00	10.75	25	3.10	25	180	1 : 30.2	1 : 17.10	1.27	2.34
No. 6 S.C. straw-burner	5′ 3 3/16″ × 2′ 5½″	32	2″	140	8.50	9.50	38		25	195	§	§	2.00	—
No. 7 S.C. traction	5′ 3¼″ × 2′ 5½″	37	2″	160	10.25	11.00	30	3.10	25	180	1 : 27.3	1 : 15.30	1.41	2.50
*No. 7 S.C. S.H. traction	5′ 3 3/16″ × 2′ 5½″	32	2″	180	10.50	10.75	30	§	§	165	1 : 25.1	1 : 11.50	1.40	3.05
No. 7 C.D. traction	5′ 3¼″ × 2′ 5½″	37	2″	160	11.25	12.00	30	3.10	25	180	1 : 29.69	1 : 13.66	1.30	2.84
*No. 7 S.C. rigid N.Z. traction	5′ 3 3/16″ × 2′ 5½″	36	2″	180	11.50	12.25	30	—	25	165	1 : 28.10	1 : 15.20	1.26	2.32
No. 8 S.C. traction	5′ 9¼″ × 2′ 10⅜″	40	2″	180	11.75	12.75	35	3.00	24	165	1 : 28.99	1 : 16.90	1.31	2.26
No. 8 C.D. traction	5′ 6 1/16″ × 2′ 9½″	40	2″	180	12.25	13.25	35	3.00	24	165	1 : 28.99	1 : 16.90	1.20	2.84
No. 8 S.C. Colonial traction	5′ 9 1/16″ × 2′ 10¼″	40	2″	140	10.25	11.25	35	—	25	180	1 : 18.73	—	2.05	—
No. 8 S.C. rigid N.Z. traction	5′ 9 5/16″ × 2′ 10⅜″	40	2″	160	12.00	13.00	35	—	25	165	1 : 35.2	1 : 18.00	1.16	2.28
No. 10 S.C. straw-burner	6′ 9 11/16″ × 3′ 6″	41	2¾″	140	11.00	12.25	42	—	25	195	1 : 21.6	—	2.02	—
No. 6 C.D. road locomotive	5′ 0 1/16″ × 2′ 5⅛″	37	2″	180	12.00	13.50	35	3.10	25	180	1 : 25.6	1 : 12.00	1.63	3.47
No. 8 C.D. road locomotive	5′ 11⅜″ × 2′ 10⅜″	55	1¾″	180	14.00	15.50	48	3.10	24	180	1 : 30.0	1 : 12.00	2.38	6.00

No. 6 Tractions. Later versions of the No. 6 compound, No. 6 single and No. 6 S.C. Colonial all had the same **gear** ratios as those here given for the **No.** 6 compound Colonial. Likewise cylinder diameters increased to 10¼″ and 6″.

No. 7 Tractions. Later versions of the No. 7 single and the No. 7 compound had the same gear ratios as the No. 7 single superheater (i.e., the same as the late No. 6s).

No. 8 Compound road locomotive. Second speed $\frac{18}{24} \times \frac{14}{48} \times \frac{16}{56} = \frac{1}{16}$ giving a road speed of 4.8 m.p.h.

Coal capacities of bunkers. Note the slight divergencies in weights carried compared with cubic capacities. These were obviously calculated at different times using coal of various weights per cubic foot.

Tender tank capacities. Later No. 6 and No. 7 engines had 145 gallons capacity.

Fore wheels. No. 6 and No. 7 tractions had the front wheel diameters increased to 4′ 3″ in later engines.

Fuel consumption figures. Figures given are for coal about 14,000 B.T.U.s per lb. No figures are given for Colonial fireboxes intended for inferior coal. It is the author's opinion that, though the figures for coal and water consumption are taken from official tables, they are extremely optimistic and represent a much rosier picture than would occur in daily work.

§ not available

APPENDIX 2 - Garrett & Schmach Patent Differential Locking Arrangement.

The firm's description of the patent was as follows:
The compensating gear is locked by operating the lever 'A'. which works in conjunction with a notched quadrant, being held positively in either position. This lever turns about its pivot 'B', and moves laterally a clutch ring 'C', which is formed with projections 'D' The differential pinions 'E' are formed with a number of recesses 'F' adapted to be engaged by the projections 'D' on the clutch ring 'C'. Thus when the lever 'A' is operated, the differential pinions are prevented from rotating on their spindles, consequently the differential gear is rendered inoperative, and both road wheels rotate together.

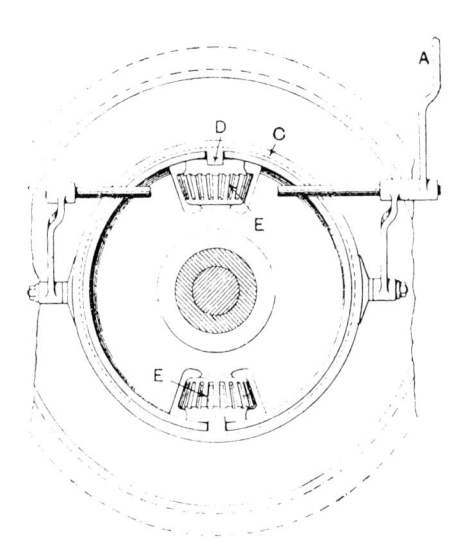

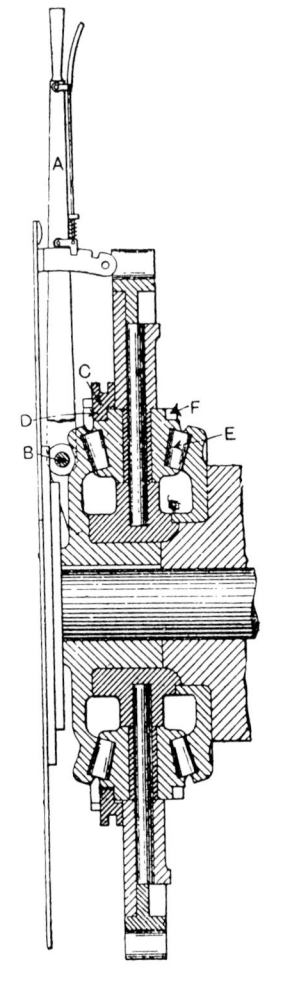

Fig.129

APPENDIX 3- Key to prefixes applied to drawing numbers and pattern numbers

N.B. The Garretts preferred to use the brake horse power rating as they believed the system of nominal horsepower ratings devised by the Royal Agricultural Society of England to be misleading since it took no account of, inter alia, working pressure or piston stroke. Customers, however, were habituated to the use of the RASE classification and as it was embedded also in the price fixing agreements of the Agricultural Engineers' Association Garretts had to continue to identify their engines in conformity with this despite their dislike of it. By way of slightly futile protest they referred to their engines as 'No.6' or 'No.8' instead of '6HP' or '8HP'. For better or for worse, however, 'NHP' has been used throughout this book.

TRACTIONS

TH	4 S/C Traction
AT	5 S/C Traction
ET	PV1 S/C Traction
T	6 S/C Traction
PT	6 S/C S/B Traction (Col.)
WT	6 S/C Traction (Col.)
TZ	6 S/C Traction N.Z.
BT	6 S/C S/H Traction
K	7 S/C Traction
U	8 S/C Traction
UZ	8 S/C Traction N.Z.
SU	10 S/C S/B Traction
XU	10 S/C Ploughing traction
TT	6 C/D Traction
UU	8 C/D Traction
CET	50 B.H.P Traction

ROAD LOCOS

HT	6 C/D Road loco
HU	8 C/D Road loco

APPENDIX 4 Garrett Tractions, Road Locomotives & Ploughing Engines

Works No.	Regn. No.	Date	Type	Purchaser	Notes
			Boydell	E.G.Clerk, Clerkness, N.S.W.	
			Boydell	Prokhoroff, Moscow.	
			Boydell		Not sold.
252		01/03/58	8 hp Chain	Jas. Barber, Snape, Suffolk.	Returned 8/58
5		12/07/58	12hp Loco		Chester Show
275		27/11/58	7 hp Chain	T.Sage, Colchester, Essex.	
3		29/08/63	10hp te	Mr. Hardy, Hartlepool.	Aveling No. 82
4		23/09/63	8 hp te	J.Edwards, Garboldisham, Norfolk.	Aveling No. 83
5		10/10/63	10hp te	Wrigglesworth	Aveling No. 89
6		--/10/63	8 hp te		Aveling No. 93
7		02/05/64	10hp te	Helmsing	Aveling No. 114
8		16/09/64	10hp te		Aveling No. 121
9		07/10/64	8 hp te	Possibly sold to Shaw, see below	Aveling No. 122
10		--/--/64	8 hp te	Ditto	Aveling No. 123 (Vienna Show)
		17/07/65	8 hp te	John Shaw, Wolverhampton.	Taken from Ledger No.7
		22/01/66	te	John Shaw, Wolverhampton.	Ditto
11	Export	27/10/66	10hp te	Th.Pilter, Paris, France	Aveling No. 246
12		09/09/67	8 hp te	J.Shaw & Sons, Wolverhampton.	Aveling No. 261 (Paris Show)
13	Export	31/03/68	8 hp te	W.S.Taylor, Toronto, Canada.	Aveling No. 247:1st. jacketted cylinder.
14	Export	02/12/67	10hp te	Th.Pilter, Paris, France	Aveling No. 262
2017		29/03/67	8 hp sm	C.Doubleday, Outwell, Norfolk.	
2040		24/12/67	8 hp sm	Wm.Jewell, Orpington, Kent.	Returned 9/69
2058		18/07/68	8 hp sm	Wiseman & Rix, Tittershall, Norfolk.	
2063		24/03/68	10hp sm	W&J Walker, Bosham, Sussex.	
2065		27/08/68	8 hp sm	Nathaniel Dring, Wisbech, Cambs.	
2142		20/10/68	10hp sm	W.W.Asplin, Foxton, Cambs.	
2167		20/10/68	8 hp sm	O.Kohan, Odessa, Russia.	
2199		28/08/69	8 hp sm	A.W.Wallace, Parsonstown, Ireland.	
2211		07/05/69	10hp sm	Wiseman & Rix, Tittershall, Norfolk.	
3309		04/08/69	8 hp sm	G.Warhurst, Knutsford, Cheshire.	
3350		25/08/69	10hp sm	Hambling & Son, E.Dereham, Norfolk.	
3358		24/11/69	8 hp sm	Wm.Street, Botesdale, Scole, Norfolk.	
3365		27/08/69	8 hp sm	Julien Arabin, Egham, Surrey.	
3386		15/12/69	10hp sm	G.Russell, Plumstead, Woolwich.	
3772		22/06/70	10hp sm	C.Farris, Shaftesbury, Dorset.	
3872		30/07/70	8 hp sm	A.Ashby, London Colney, Herts.	
4032		24/07/71	8hp sm	W.O'Neill, Athy, Ireland.	
4068		17/03/71	8 hp sm	General von Sederholm, S. Russia	Equipped with winding gear.
4160		10/04/71	8 hp sm	Obach	via E.Reuss & Co, London
4664		18/12/71	8 hp sm	Hetherington & Moore, Alton, Hants.	Islington Show 1871
4696		22/11/71	10hp te	T.C.Reed, Newington, Kent.	
4792		07/03/72	10hp sm	T.C.Collett, Ringleton, Kent	
7060		05/05/74	10hp sm	Wm.Eley, Cobham, Kent.	1st. with steerage on side of tender.
7428		26/08/74	10hp sm	Brassey	2nd. with steerage on side of tender.
7536		25/09/74	8 hp sm	Chas.Cass, Presdale, nr. Ware, Herts.	
7940		19/03/75	10hp sm	B.Garrett, Son & Co., Maidstone, Kent.	
8696		21/09/75	8 hp sm	W.Hunt, Culpho, Ipswich, Suffolk.	
8748		15/10/75	10hp sm	Binney, Ilford, Essex.	
8812		15/12/75	10hp sm	Robinson, Wilhamstead.	
8924		25/04/76	10hp sm	Wm.Turner & Son, Uckfield, Sussex.	At RG & S by Sept.89. Resold 1897 for £100.
9380		11/08/76	8 hp te	G.Goodyear, Markyate St., Beds.	1st. with gear instead of pitch chain.
9644		21/10/76	8 hp te	Hammond & Hussey, Croydon, Surrey.	
9648		19/10/76	8 hp te	H.Glover, Wrotham, Kent.	
9728		01/10/78	8 hp te	Page & Co.	
9740		22/12/76	8 hp te	B.H.Sturgeon, Norton, Suffolk.	
9800		20/01/77	8 hp te	E.K.Fisher, Market Harborough, Leics.	Not sold until 17/03/80
9804		03/07/78	8 hp te	Wm.Creasy, Bedfield, Suffolk.	
9884		21/06/77	8 hp te	Johns Bros., Swindon, Wilts.	
9916		14/04/77	8 hp te	Godwin	
10072		--/03/80	8 hp te	In stock 3/80	Suffolk Show June 1881
10512	Export	18/04/78	8 hp te	Th.Pilter, Paris, France	Returned
14040		13/01/82	8 hp te	W.Bennett, London Colney, Herts.	
17073		30/06/87	6 cd sm	T.Cooper, Gt. Ryburgh, Norfolk.	Newcastle Royal 1887
20485	Export	04/09/95	6 hp te	Henninger & Co. Darmstadt, Germany.	Shifting eccentric valve gear.
20548	NO3603	25/08/96	6 hp te	Saml Bull, Hitcham, Ipswich, Suffolk	
20800	AD8924	13/08/97	6 hp te	G.E.Coleberd, Romsey, Hants.	Smithfield Show '96.
21126	Export	/97	6 sc te	Henninger & Co. Darmstadt, Germany.	

Works No.	Regn. No.	Date	Type	Purchaser	Notes
21153	Export	08/07/97	6 sc te	Th.Pilter, Paris, France	
21315	CJ4173	18/12/97	6 sc te	Devon Trading Co. Ltd., Exeter.	Smithfield Show '97
21452	Export	26/03/98	6 sc pe	Rud. Sack, Leipzig, Germany	
21623		07/09/98	6 sc te	N.R.Etheridge, Wangford, Suffolk.	Converted to RR 11/01
22059	Export	21/03/99	6 sc pe	Rud. Sack, Leipzig, Germany	L.H. plougher.
22128	Export	18/05/99	6 sc te	Henninger & Co. Darmstadt, Germany.	German Royal Show
22223	Export	01/08/99	8 sc pe	Rud. Sack, Leipzig, Germany	R.H. plougher.
22224	Export	15/08/99	8 sc pe	Rud. Sack, Leipzig, Germany	L.H. plougher.
22442	AB8983	18/07/00	6 sc te	Cooper & Sherwood, Knodishall, Suffk.	Royal Show, York '00. P/ex. 11/10 for 28737
22867	Export	24/08/00	6 sc te	Henninger & Co. Darmstadt, Germany.	
23007	Export	22/11/00	8 sc pe	Rud. Sack, Leipzig, Germany	L.H. plougher.
23021		31/07/01	6 sc te	R.G.&S.	Smithfield Show '00. Works crane engine.
23036	Export	11/12/00	8 sc pe	Rud. Sack, Leipzig, Germany	R.H. plougher.
23098	Export	19/02/01	8 sc pe	Rud. Sack, Leipzig, Germany	R.H. plougher.
23126	Export	04/03/01	8 sc pe	Rud. Sack, Leipzig, Germany	L.H. plougher.
23375	Export	26/04/01	8 sc te	Bonnet & Quignon&Co. Boulogne, France	convertible to roller
23378	BJ6397	14/08/01	6 sc te	E.W.Brook, Hoo, Charsfield, Suffolk.	Royal Counties Show, June '01.
23403	NO3552	23/08/01	6 sc te	R.F.Oakley, Wethersfield, Suffolk.	Suffolk Show, June '01
23423	AH5670	21/12/01	8 sc te	C.G.Miles, Alburgh, Norfolk.	
23494	Export	03/10/02	6 sc te	Burn & Co., Burma.	Smithfield Show '01.
23510	Export	02/09/02	6 sc te	Clark & Fauset, Brisbane, Queensland.	
23641	BT3693	17/12/02	8 sc te	A.Kelly, Writtle, Essex.	Royal Counties Show, June '02.
23652	Export	16/05/02	8 sc te col	Th.Pilter, Paris, France	Strawburner for Algeria.
23674	Export	05/05/02	6 sc te	Henninger & Co. Darmstadt, Germany.	German Royal Show, Mannheim.
23730	Export	26/06/02	8 sc pe	Rud. Sack, Leipzig, Germany	L.H. plougher.
23734	Export	13/06/02	8 sc pe	Rud. Sack, Leipzig, Germany	R.H. plougher.
23785	HO5970	16/09/03	8 sc te	J.Drake, Winsor, Totton, Hants.	Built for show. Suffolk '02 & '03
23981		19/12/02	6 sc te	W.Rawlings, Collingbourne Ducis, Wilts.	Smithfield '02
23992	CF3472	13/11/02	6 sc te	W.Taylor, Bildeston, Suffolk.	
24001	Export	03/04/03	8 sc te sb	Eugen Behles, Bucarest.	1 speed
24062	Export	29/12/03	8 sc te col	T.M.Goodall & Co., Sydney, NSW.	
24068	Export	30/01/03	6 sc te	Henninger & Co. Darmstadt, Germany.	No. plate stamped 23981
24316	Export	29/05/03	8 sc te sb	Eugen Behles, Bucarest.	1 speed
24320	Export	08/09/03	6 sc te	Clark & Fauset, Brisbane, Queensland.	
24369	Export	07/07/03	8 cd rl	Mauritius Estates Co.Ltd.	
24398	AP9633	01/07/03	6 sc te	J.Drake, Totton, Hants.	Devon County Show, May '03. etc.
24420	Export	02/06/03	6 sc te	C.Haasemann&Sohne, Hanover, Germany	Hanover Show June '03
24424	Export	24/07/03	6 sc te	Dehle Bennison, Hobart, Tasmania.	
24429	Export	20/08/03	8 cd rl	Nees & Son, Wellington, NZ.	3 speed
24551	Export	22/12/03	8 cd rl	Tech. & Comm. Corpn. Johannesburg	3 speed
24552	Export	20/01/04	8 cd rl	Johannesburg Municipality, S.A.	3 speed
24594	FX6542	01/10/03	6 sc te	F.Payne, Redball, Somerset.	
24595	Export	20/01/04	8 cd rl	Johannesburg Municipality, S.A.	3 speed
24600	AH7485	15/08/04	7 sc te	J.Shilling, E.Dereham, Norfolk.	Smithfield '03
24601	MR8843	15/12/03	6 sc te	W.Rawlings, Collingbourne Ducis, Wilts.	Smithfield '03
24612	Export	07/03/04	8 sc pe	Rud. Sack, Leipzig, Germany	R.H. plougher.
24613	Export	11/03/04	8 sc pe	Rud. Sack, Leipzig, Germany	L.H. plougher.
24755	Export	25/04/04	7 sc te	Muscate, Danzig, Germany.	German Royal Show.
24835	Export	05/05/04	10 sc pe	Rud. Sack, Leipzig, Germany	R.H. plougher.
24836	Export	10/06/04	10 sc pe	Rud. Sack, Leipzig, Germany	L.H. plougher.
24845	Export	11/04/04	6 sc te col	Th.Pilter, Paris, France	
24864	Export	12/04/04	6 sc te col	Th.Pilter, Paris, France	
24869	Export	30/07/04	10 sc pe	Rud. Sack, Leipzig, Germany	R.H. plougher.
24870	Export	30/08/04	10 sc pe	Rud. Sack, Leipzig, Germany	L.H. plougher.
24889	CT4231	14/07/04	7 sc te	Abel Burton, Litcham, Norfolk.	
24890	DX3033	01/09/04	6 sc te	A.Moore, Winston, Debenham, Suffolk.	
24893		/04	8 cd rl	RG&S	Royal Show. Became 25363
24900	AF3361	31/10/04	6 cd te	H.Arden, Heavitree, Exeter, Devon.	Devon Show '04 "Sir Robert"
24938	Export	06/09/04	6 sc te	Dehle Bennison, Hobart, Tasmania.	
24996	EB3401	06/09/04	7 sc te	E.Farrow, Raveningham, Norfolk.	
25027		09/09/04	7 sc te	F.Heading, Downham Market, Norfolk.	"The Paragon"
25041	BJ5831	06/10/04	6 sc te	H.Davy, Laxfield, Suffolk.	
25060	Export	20/10/04	10 sc te sb	M.E.Mattos, Buenos Aires, Argentina.	2 speed
25066	NO3215	20/12/04	7 sc te	J.George, Wetherden, Suffolk.	Smithfield Show
25070	Export	27/12/04	6 cd te	Clark & Fauset, Brisbane, Queensland.	
25076	Export	15/12/04	10 sc pe	Rud. Sack, Leipzig, Germany	R.H. plougher.
25077	Export	30/12/04	10 sc pe	Rud. Sack, Leipzig, Germany	L.H. plougher.
25113	Export	25/08/05	8 sc te NZ	Jas.Macalister, Invercargill, N.Z.	Fitted as vertical drum plougher.
25114	Export	28/06/05	6 sc te NZ	Jas.Macalister, Invercargill, N.Z.	
25280	HR4291	16/01/05	7 sc te	A.M.Lucas, Granham, Wilts.	

Works No.	Regn. No.	Date	Type	Purchaser	Notes
25300	Export	28/03/05	10 sc pe	Rud. Sack, Leipzig, Germany	R.H. plougher.
25301	Export	03/04/05	10 sc pe	Rud. Sack, Leipzig, Germany	L.H. plougher.
25323	Export	13/03/05	8 sc te col	G.Chisnell & Son, Constantinople.	
25331	Export	14/10/05	8 cd te	Clark & Fauset, Brisbane, Queensland.	
25361	Export	18/04/05	6 sc te	Th.Pilter, Paris, France.	
25363		24/05/05	8 cd rl	J.Stanbury & Sons, Ashburton, Devon	Returned to RG&S and renumbered 25814
25365	AH6367	30/06/05	8 sc te	Wiseman & Silcock, Yarmouth, Norfolk.	
25366	AC9096	30/06/05	7 sc te	R.H.Draper, Shrewley, Warwick.	
25367	NO3289	30/06/05	7 sc te	E.W.Salmon, Elmstead, Essex.	
25368	MA5673	16/07/06	6 sc te	J.Bond, Rattlesden, Suffolk.	
25406	Export	08/09/05	10 sc te sb	M.E.Mattos, Buenos Aires, Argentina.	1 speed
25407	Export	25/09/05	10 sc te sb	M.E.Mattos, Buenos Aires, Argentina.	1 speed
25408	Export	25/09/05	10 sc te sb	M.E.Mattos, Buenos Aires, Argentina.	1 speed
25409	Export	02/10/05	10 sc te sb	M.E.Mattos, Buenos Aires, Argentina.	1 speed
25410	Export	02/10/05	10 sc te sb	M.E.Mattos, Buenos Aires, Argentina.	1 speed
25416	DL2628	06/07/05	6 sc te	G.Perkins, Newport, IOW.	Royal Show.
25428	FP1044	15/01/08	6 sc te col	H.Bennett, Stoke Ash, Suffolk.	
25429	BJ6404	31/07/05	7 sc te	A.H.Moore, Winston, Debenham, Suffolk.	
25448	E5236	30/08/05	7 sc te	W.Marriott, Bradfield St. George, Suffolk.	Returned to RG&S after a fire and re-sold.
25521	Export	31/08/05	6 sc te	Henninger & Co. Darmstadt, Germany.	
25523	BJ7851	14/09/05	6 sc te	R.Boulton, Holton, Suffolk.	
25563	AH6238	17/07/06	7 sc te	S.Hindes, Lingwood, Acle, Norfolk.	Royal Show
25575	Export	15/11/05	10 sc te sb	M.E.Mattos, Buenos Aires, Argentina.	1 speed
25576	Export	15/11/05	10 sc te sb	M.E.Mattos, Buenos Aires, Argentina.	1 speed
25577	Export	21/11/05	10 sc te sb	M.E.Mattos, Buenos Aires, Argentina.	1 speed
25578	Export	21/11/05	10 sc te sb	M.E.Mattos, Buenos Aires, Argentina.	1 speed
25579	Export	21/11/05	10 sc te sb	M.E.Mattos, Buenos Aires, Argentina.	1 speed
25608	Export	09/05/06	7 sc te	Muscate, Danzig, Germany.	German Royal Show
25698	Export	10/01/06	6 sc te	Th.Pilter, Paris, France	
25742	Export	07/04/06	10 sc te sb	O.Auschnitt, Galatz, Roumania.	1 speed
25814	KE3496	26/03/07	8 cd srl	H&S.Forrest, Forest Gate,	'Empress of Japan'. Renumbered from 25363
25816	NO369	27/07/06	6 cd te	Crawley Bros., Linton, Cambs.	3 speed.
25820	Export	30/05/06	6 cd gp te	Th.Pilter, Marseille, France	
25858	BP9562	19/07/06	8 sc te	G.F.Townsend, Exning, Suffolk.	
25890	NR34	23/07/06	7 sc gp te	Cooper & Sherwood, Knodishall, Suffolk.	
25904	Export	29/09/06	10 sc pe	Rud. Sack, Leipzig, Germany	R.H. plougher.
25905	Export	12/09/06	10 sc pe	Rud. Sack, Leipzig, Germany	L.H. plougher.
25920	CT4144	24/07/06	7 sc te	G.Bullimore, Deeping St. James, Lincs.	
25936	Export	16/06/06	10 sc te sb	M.E.Mattos, Buenos Aires, Argentina.	1 speed
25937	Export	03/09/06	10 sc te sb	M.E.Mattos, Buenos Aires, Argentina.	1 speed
25938	Export	22/09/06	10 sc te sb	M.E.Mattos, Buenos Aires, Argentina.	1 speed
25939	Export	22/09/06	10 sc te sb	M.E.Mattos, Buenos Aires, Argentina.	1 speed
26000	PU3158	24/07/06	7 sc te	A.Stevens, Aylsham, Norfolk.	
26009	BJ7919	11/08/06	6 sc te	H.Stammers, Beydon, Wangford, Suffolk	
26043		28/09/06	7 sc te	H.H.Baylis, Harford Manor, Berks.	
26045	EW2327	06/10/06	7 sc te	I.Sheldrake, Bunwell, Norfolk.	
26046	PU3157	06/10/06	7 sc te	I.Sheldrake, Bunwell, Norfolk.	
26061	HR3667	17/12/06	8 sc te	R.Lucas, Ramsbury, Wilts.	Smithfield Show.
26062	YA320	21/12/06	7 sc te	W.Rawlings, Collingbourne Ducis, Wilts.	
26084	CF3594	04/12/06	7 sc te	C.Debenham, Somersham, Suffolk.	
26085	NO985	09/08/07	6 sc te	J.Jefferys, Thaxted, Essex.	
26087	Export	04/03/07	10 sc pe	Rud. Sack, Leipzig, Germany	R.H. plougher.
26088	Export	23/02/07	10 sc pe	Rud. Sack, Leipzig, Germany	L.H. plougher.
26129	CE7956	02/02/07	7 sc te	G.F.Townsend, Exning, Suffolk.	
26145	Export	14/03/07	10 sc te sb	Furst Georg Alexander Sturdz, Niclauseni	1 speed; via Auschnitt
26354	SG5106	19/03/07	6 sc te	R.Pannell, Bryton, Cornwall.	
26411	Export	18/05/07	10 sc pe	Rud. Sack, Leipzig, Germany	R.H. plougher.
26412	Export	31/05/07	10 sc pe	Rud. Sack, Leipzig, Germany	L.H. plougher.
26446	Export	23/05/07	6 sc te	Henninger & Co. Darmstadt, Germany.	Dusseldorf Exhibn. Henninger patent superheater
26514	KE2282	27/07/07	7 sc te	J.George, Wetherden, Suffolk.	Royal Show.
26516	CF3964	21/06/07	7 sc te	Cornish & Lloyds Ltd., Bury St. Edmunds.	
26517	NN2114	18/09/07	6 cd te	F&J.Martin, Poundstock, Devon	
26521	CT3941	21/06/07	7 sc te	H.Hammond, Hethel, Norwich, Norfolk.	
26546	Export	19/04/07	8 sc te col	Ed.Zehder, Riga, Russia	
26569	TA660	26/07/07	7 sc te	W&J.H.Honey, Holsworthy, Devon.	
26618	AC9657	14/08/07	7 sc te	H.Upton, Clophill, Beds	
26632	CE8063	30/09/07	8 sc te	J.W.Desborough, Wiggenhall, Norfolk	
26685	EB2959	17/09/07	7 sc te	G.Hammond, Nayland, Suffolk.	
26694	AH6368	27/11/07	8 sc te	Wiseman & Silcock, Yarmouth, Norfolk.	
26695	NC2026	14/03/08	6 cd rl	Lalonde Bros.& Parham Ltd. Weston. Som	

Works No.	Regn. No.	Date	Type	Purchaser	Notes
26698	CT4145	12/10/07	7 sc te	G.Bullimore, Deeping St. James, Lincs.	
26699	CF3571	26/10/07	7 sc te	C.S.& H.L.Wilson, Beccles,Suffolk.	Eastern Counties Farmers Coop Assoc.
26710	CE7754	02/11/07	7 sc te	A.B.J.Chaplin, Fulbourn, Cambs.	Director of J.Taylor & Sons Ltd.
26711		02/10/07	7 sc te	F.B.Gibbons, Langtoft,	
26716	NK1006	19/10/07	7 sc te	S.C.Titmuss, Hatfield, Herts.	
26721	AW9230	14/01/08	7 sc te	W.Rawlings, Collingbourne Ducis, Wilts.	
26967	NK1937	25/07/08	7 sc gp te	B.Cannon, Buntingford,Herts.	
26968		25/08/08	6 cd srl	J.Purchase, Hounslow, Middx.	"Surprise"
26999	KE3497	27/05/08	6 cd srl	R.Body, Meopham, Kent.	
27015	AH6239	13/08/08	7 sc te	T.D.Nunn, Wix, Essex.	
27056	Export	11/06/08	8 sc gp te	Grimaldi, Milan, Italy	
27109	Export	06/06/08	8 cd gp te	Grimaldi, Milan, Italy	Angles to front wheels.
27111	Export	23/07/08	6 cd te col	Clark & Fauset, Brisbane, Queensland.	
27115	Export	22/08/08	8 cd te col	Clark & Fauset, Brisbane, Queensland.	
27118	Export	12/08/08	8 cd gp te	Grimaldi, Milan, Italy	
27160	AD1891	26/06/08	6 cd gp te	A.Dawson & Co., Rushmere, Ipswich.	
27162	AC9097	23/06/08	7 sc te	R.H.Draper, Shrewley, Warwicks.	
27165	NO297	23/06/08	7 sc te	E.Medcalf, Saffron Walden, Essex	
27176	Export	12/09/08	10 sc te sb	Ministerio Obras Publicas, B.A. Argentina	1 speed
27177	Export	28/08/08	10 sc te sb	Ministerio Obras Publicas, B.A. Argentina	1 speed
27179	Export	12/09/08	10 sc te sb	Ministerio Obras Publicas, B.A. Argentina	1 speed
27180	Export	26/09/08	10 sc te sb	Ministerio Obras Publicas, B.A. Argentina	1 speed
27181	Export	01/10/08	10 sc te sb	Ministerio Obras Publicas, B.A. Argentina	1 speed
27204	Export	18/11/08	8 cd te col	Clark & Fauset, Brisbane, Queensland.	3 speed.
27206	Export	08/08/08	8 sc te col	H.Jungclaussen, Ahrensbök, Germany.	Grooved flywheel.
27220		08/07/08	7 sc te	J.&T.McEwan, Cross House, Ayrshire.	A.Meikle, Glasgow owner & lessor.
27261	NO3631	02/10/08	7 sc te	W.J.Stride, Newport, Essex.	
27284	Export	23/07/08	6 sc te	Henninger & Co. Darmstadt, Germany.	
27286	Export	27/07/09	8 cd te col	H.Schnitz	Convertible to roller
27318	BJ6122	28/09/08	7 sc te	W.Turner, Hintlesham, Suffolk	
27332	NL1526	07/10/08	7 sc te	A.MckKay, Cornhill, Banff.	"Alexine"
27333		29/12/08	7 cd te gp	A.Kelly, Writtle, Essex.	Returned to RG&S 31/7/10 and rebuilt as srl
27341	BL8322	21/12/08	7 sc te	W.Rawlings, Collingbourne Ducis, Wilts.	
27343	WR6720	26/03/09	6 cd srl	J.Manders, Fulham, London.	"Frances"
27349	Export	27/02/09	10 sc pe	Rud. Sack, Leipzig, Germany	R.H. plougher.
27350	Export	25/03/09	10 sc pe	Rud. Sack, Leipzig, Germany	L.H. plougher.
27353	Export	26/10/08	10 sc te sb	M.E.Mattos, Buenos Aires, Argentina.	1 speed
27354	Export	13/11/08	10 sc te sb	M.E.Mattos, Buenos Aires, Argentina.	1 speed
27355	Export	13/11/08	10 sc te sb	M.E.Mattos, Buenos Aires, Argentina.	1 speed
27359	KE3498	18/03/09	7 cd te srl	R.H.Hayne & Co., London WC.	
27360	CK3407	29/03/09	7 cd te srl	R.H.Hayne & Co., London WC.	
27382	Export	19/08/10	6 cd te col	Clark & Fauset, Brisbane, Queensland.	
27556	TA2218	27/01/09	6 sc te	R.Parnell, Launceston, Cornwall.	
27565	Export	13/05/09	6 sc te	Henninger & Co. Darmstadt, Germany.	
27654		29/05/09	7 sc te	J.Chambers, Enniscorthy, Co. Wexford.	Dublin Show
27672		24/08/09	7 sc te	J.A.Gowing, Burgh St. Peter, Norfolk.	Renumbered 27901
27689	PB9630	31/07/09	7 sc te	G.Weller, Cranleigh, Surrey.	
27763	BT7469	02/11/09	6 cd rl	A.Dawson & Co., Rushmere, Ipswich.	Returned to RG&S.
27798		18/08/09	7 sc te	Murdoch & Sim, Inverkeithnie, Banff.	Highland Show.
27799	NY2393	06/07/09	7 sc te	Smith, Wilkinson, Llantwit Major, Glam.	
27803	TA1834	18/08/09	6 sc te	Bond & Tredinnick, Roborough, Devon.	
27804	AF4001	12/08/09	6 sc te	T.Crago, St.Mellion, Cornwall.	
27837	AH5510	20/08/09	7 sc te	F.Heading, Watlington, Norfolk.	
27838	Export	15/06/09	7 sc te	Th.Pilter, Algiers, N.Africa	
27841		20/08/09	6 sc te	J.J.Mcgee, Ardee, Co.Louth.	
27851	TA661	10/09/09	6 sc te	W&JH.Honey, Bridgerule, Devon.	
27854		19/10/09	6 cd rl	E.Hill, Swindon, Wilts.	
27855	Export	12/08/09	5 sc te col	Ed.Zehder, Riga, Russia	No 4 sc cylinder bore increased.
27856	Export	23/07/09	6 sc te col	H.Jungclaussen, Ahrensbök, Germany.	3 shaft; grooved flywheel.
27901	HO5605	15/09/09	7 sc te	R.F.Melsome, Christchurch, Hants.	Renumbered from 27672
27903	Export	16/04/10	10 sc pe	Rud. Sack, Leipzig, Germany	R.H. plougher.
27904	Export	02/04/10	10 sc pe	Rud. Sack, Leipzig, Germany	L.H. plougher.
27907	SE998	21/10/09	7 sc te	W.McKay,Abercheder, Banff.	
27908	SE3065	02/10/09	7 sc te	G.Morrison, Fisherie, Banff.	"Mabel"
27910		06/10/09	7 sc te	S.G.Addison, Keith, Banff.	"Ethel"
27913	Export		6 cd te gp col	Jas.Macalister, Invercargill, N.Z.	3 speed
27919	Export	06/09/09	6 sc te col	H.Jungclaussen, Ahrensbök, Germany.	3 shaft
27932	Export	06/10/09	8 cd te	Th.Pilter, Algiers, N.Africa	RH Steer
27946	OI6818	29/12/09	6 cd rl	J.Harkness & Co., Belfast.	"Vera"
27949	NO9002	13/12/09	7 sc te	J.Jeffery, Thaxted, Essex.	

Works No.	Regn. No.	Date	Type	Purchaser	Notes
27950		01/12/09	6 sc pv sh te		See 28272
27961	BJ5930	08/10/09	7 sc te	J.White, Raydon, Hadleigh, Suffolk.	
27977	CT3942	16/10/09	7 sc te	J.A.Leatherdale, Gt.Tey, Essex.	
28074	BJ5780	14/12/09	6 sc te	W.B.Barham, Bruisyard, Suffolk.	
28218	CF3556	20/12/09	7 sc te	H.Bennett, Stoke Ash, Suffolk.	
28249	FX8223	19/01/10	7 sc te	H.Caines, Corfe Castle, Dorset.	
28256		30/06/10	6 sc te	M.Farrell, Dungarvan, Co.Kilkenny.	
28257		20/08/10	5 sc te	P.Fenelon, Shangary, Myshall, Co.Carlow.	2 speed
28272	Export	07/05/10	6 sc pv sh te	Henninger & Co. Darmstadt, Germany.	Originally 27950
28284	Export	30/07/10	7 sc te	Henninger & Co. Darmstadt, Germany.	
28285	Export	14/05/10	6 sc te	Henninger & Co. Darmstadt, Germany.	
28288	Export	05/08/10	7 sc te	Henninger & Co. Darmstadt, Germany.	
28373	Export	16/08/10	6 sc te sb	Palmer Graham & Co., via Novorossisk.	1 speed
28375	SX901	28/07/10	6 sc te sh	Allan Meikle, Mt.Vernon, Glasgow.	"Bonny Jean" Dumfries Show. 3 Speed.
28376	Export	20/06/10	7 cd te gp	Grimaldi, Milan, Italy	
28377	Export	18/06/10	8 sc te col	Th.Pilter, Algiers, N.Africa	3 shaft colonial
28382	BJ8243	21/09/10	5 sc col te	E.Cheney, Kelsale, Suffolk.	
28385	AH6369	30/06/10	7 sc te	Wiseman & Silcock, Sutton, Norfolk.	
28387	Export	19/08/10	5 sc te gp col	Clark & Fauset, Brisbane, Queensland.	
28388	Export	19/08/10	5 sc te gp col	Clark & Fauset, Brisbane, Queensland.	
28389	Export	30/06/10	5 sc te col	Ed.Zehder, Riga, Russia	2 speed
28390	Export	29/07/10	5 sc te col	Ed.Zehder, Riga, Russia	1 speed
28392		26/07/10	6 sc te	D.Carroll, Ballyroebuck, Co.Wexford.	
28393	PR299	13/07/10	6 cd te	J.Davies, Redmarley, Worcs.	"Express"; Royal Show.
28394	Export	31/08/10	5 sc te col	Ed.Zehder, Riga, Russia	1 speed
28396	NK1387	16/07/10	7 sc te	B.Cannon, Rushden, Herts.	
28405	SA4139	27/03/11	6 sc te sh	A.Wilson, Bridgend, Forglen, Turriff.	
28406	MR12	30/08/10	7 sc te	J.Dalton, Abbotts Ann, Hants.	
28407	Export	15/09/10	5 sc te col	Ed.Zehder, Riga, Russia	1 speed
28410	NO1186	31/07/10	7 sc te	A.Kelly, Writtle, Essex.	
28412	HR3376	24/08/10	7 sc te gp	E.G.Warren, Salisbury, Wilts.	
28730	Export	22/11/10	5 sc te cont	Burn, Calcutta.	2 speed; Allahabad Exhibition. Oil burner.
28731	Export	13/06/10	5 sc te cont	C.Haasemann&Sohne, Hanover, Germany	2 speed
28732	NO2511	10/10/10	7 sc te	G.F.Townsend, Exning, Suffolk.	
28734	AB8829	04/10/10	6 sc te	E&J.Watson, Swineshead, Worcs.	
28737		29/11/10	6 sc te	Cooper & Sherwood, Knodishall, Suffolk.	
28738	SA4100	05/10/10	7 sc te	A.Gray, Huntly, Aberdeen.	"Royal George"
28740		10/09/10	6 cd te gp	Barndarrig Farmers Assn., Co.Wicklow.	"Saint Kevin"
28742		21/09/10	6 sc te	P.Cullen, Inch, Blackwater, Co.Wexford.	
28744	AB9054	14/12/10	7 sc te	W.Mortimer, Bourton, Berks.	
28747	NK1756	29/10/10	7 sc te	G.G.Cooper, Ashwell, Baldock, Herts	
28748	FS3607	29/03/11	7 sc te	W.Adamson, Hunterhall, Glencarse, Perth.	3 Speed "George V"
28751	Export	26/11/10	6 sc te gp NZ	Jas.Macalister, Invercargill, N.Z.	
28752	Export	26/11/10	7 sc te gp NZ	Jas.Macalister, Invercargill, N.Z.	
28753	Export	30/09/11	8 sc te col NZ	Jas.Macalister, Invercargill, N.Z.	
28754	Export	14/10/10	5 sc te cont	Ed.Zehder, Riga, Russia	1 speed
28755	Export	23/12/10	5 sc te Eng	Th.Pilter, Dieppe, France	2 speed
28756	BJ5940	01/12/10	5 sc te Eng	RG&S Works Engine.	2 speed
28757		21/07/11	6 sc te	T.Dalton, Gowram, Co.Kilkenny.	
28758	FX7239	31/12/10	7 sc te	The Earl of Eldon, Encombe, Dorset.	
28759	Export	23/12/10	5 sc te cont	Grimaldi, Milan, Italy	2 speed
28765	Export	10/02/11	5 sc te cont	Henninger & Co. Darmstadt, Germany.	1 speed
28766	Export		8 cd te gp	Fremantle; via J.W.Harker & Co. London	RH Steer; for direct ploughing.
28771	Export	03/05/11	8 cd te gp	Grimaldi, Milan, Italy	RH Steer
28772	Export	26/05/11	8 cd te gp	Grimaldi, Milan, Italy	RH Steer
28773	Export	11/07/11	8 cd te gp	Grimaldi, Milan, Italy	RH Steer
28987	Export	21/03/11	5 sc te cont	Th.Pilter, Bordeaux, France	2 speed
28989	Export	01/06/11	5 sc te cont	Ed.Zehder, Riga, Russia	1 speed
28990	Export	13/07/11	5 sc te cont	Ed.Zehder, Riga, Russia	1 speed
28991	Export	16/08/11	5 sc te cont	Ed.Zehder, Riga, Russia	1 speed
28992	Export	15/04/11	4 sc te cont	Ed.Zehder, Riga, Russia	1 speed
28993	Export	13/07/11	4 sc te cont	Ed.Zehder, Riga, Russia	1 speed
28994	Export	28/07/11	4 sc te cont	Ed.Zehder, Riga, Russia	1 speed
28995	Export	16/08/11	4 sc te cont	Ed.Zehder, Riga, Russia	1 speed
28996	Export	03/08/11	4 sc te cont	Ed.Zehder, Riga, Russia	1 speed
28997	Export	07/09/11	4 sc te cont	Ed.Zehder, Riga, Russia	1 speed
28998	Export	03/06/11	7 sc te	Henninger & Co. Darmstadt, Germany.	Cassel Show.
29001	Export	29/04/11	5 sc te cont	Grimaldi, Milan, Italy	2 speed; Turin Exhibition.
29003	SA4206	09/11/12	7 sc te	G.Morrison, Fisherie, Banff.	"Elsie Ann"
29009	AH6370	07/07/11	7 sc te	G.Nicholson, Stalham, Norfolk.	

Works No.	Regn. No.	Date	Type	Purchaser	Notes
29012	Export	24/06/11	5 sc te cont	Th.Pilter, Dieppe, France	1 speed
29020	Export	24/06/11	6 cd te	Th.Pilter, Tunis, N.Africa	
29024	Export	06/06/11	6 sc te sh pv	Henninger & Co. Darmstadt, Germany.	Cassel Show.
29025	BJ6478	07/07/11	7 sc te	M.Tubby jr., Gt.Yarmouth, Norfolk.	
29026	Export	11/07/11	6 sc te	Th.Pilter, Bordeaux, France	Dynamo stand
29027	HR3924	15/07/11	7 sc te	Exors of T.E.Mills, Elston Hill, Wilts.	
29029	PU86	22/07/11	6 sc te	W.Ives, Chrishall, Essex.	
29030	Export	14/07/11	5 sc te cont	Grimaldi, Milan, Italy	2 speed
29035	Export	02/08/11	8 cd te gp	Grimaldi, Milan, Italy	
29764	AC9326	10/08/11	6 sc te sh	R.J.Colcombe, Sellack, Ross.	"Olive"
29766	SA4096	31/07/11	7 sc te	J&J.Wilson, Macduff, Banff.	"Princess May"
29770	NK1853	04/09/11	7 sc te	W.W.Pack, Ashwell, Herts.	
29772		21/08/11	6 sc te	G.H.Bissell, Affpuddle, Dorchester.	
29773	Export	30/09/11	7 sc te col NZ	Jas.Macalister, Invercargill, N.Z.	
29774	Export	30/09/11	5 sc te Eng	Jas.Macalister, Invercargill, N.Z.	2 speed
29775	Export	30/03/12	5 sc te cont	Ed.Zehder, Riga, Russia	1 speed
29779	SP5541	13/07/12	7 sc te	W.Spence & Son, Kingsbarns, Fife.	
29780	Export	08/12/11	6 cd te gp col	M.E.Mattos, Buenos Aires, Argentina.	
29784	Export	08/02/12	6 sc te	Th.Pilter, Bordeaux, France	
29785	AH6570	02/10/12	7 sc te	W.G.Fulcher, Necton, Norfolk.	
29786	Export	22/09/11	5 sc te cont	H.Jungclaussen, Ahrensbök, Germany.	2 speed; grooved flywheel.
29787	Export	27/10/11	5 sc te	J.McIntosh, Hill Crest, Natal.	2 speed; wide gearing for direct ploughing
29788	Export	16/12/11	6 cd te col	Clark & Fauset, Brisbane, Queensland.	
29789	Export	30/03/12	4 sc te cont	Ed.Zehder, Riga, Russia	1 speed
29790	Export	02/12/12	6 sc te	Th. Pilter, Bordeaux, France	
30009		08/07/12	7 sc te	R.Robinson & Sons, Annan	
30096	Export	13/05/13	7 sc te gp	Th.Pilter, Bordeaux, France	
30111	Export	11/12/11	7 cd te gp	Soc.Italiana Ernesto Breda, Milan, Italy	
30112	Export		7 cd te gp	Soc.Italiana Ernesto Breda, Milan, Italy	
30288	Export	09/07/12	4 sc te cont	Ed.Zehder, Riga, Russia	1 speed
30289	Export	25/05/12	5 sc te cont	Ed.Zehder, Riga, Russia	1 speed
30310	Export	25/05/12	5 sc te cont	Ed.Zehder, Riga, Russia	1 speed
30369	Export	25/07/12	8 cd te col	Whitehead, Sumner, Harker & Co., Lisbon	New wide gearing throughout.
30410	Export	13/09/12	7 cd te	Grimaldi, Turin, Italy	Drawbar for direct ploughing.
30413	Export	05/06/12	8 sc te rigid	Th.Pilter, Bordeaux, France	
30802	Export	10/07/12	7 sc sh te	C. Randon, Rinxent, Pas de Calais, Franc	
30821	Export	29/06/12	5 sc te cont	Grimaldi, Turin, Italy	1 speed
30840	Export	14/08/12	5 sc te col	J.Chambers & Son Ltd., NZ	2 speed
30846	Export	30/04/12	5 sc te Eng	Henninger & Co. Darmstadt, Germany.	2 speed
30859	Export	11/09/12	6 sc te col	Th.Pilter, Oran, N.Africa	3 shaft colonial
30900	Export	06/08/19	5 sc te	Orenstein & Koppel, Durban, S.Africa.	Drawbar for direct ploughing.
30905	Export	01/08/12	5 sc te cont	Grimaldi, Turin, Italy	2 speed
30917	Export	24/08/12	6 cd te gp	Th.Pilter, Tunis, N.Africa	
30969	Export		5 sc te cont	C.Haasemann&Sohne, Hanover, Germany	2 speed
30991	Export	17/07/12	4 sc te cont	Ed.Zehder, Riga, Russia	1 speed
30995		24/09/12	6 cd te	Queens County C.C.	No. 1
31030	Export	22/08/12	5 sc te cont	Ed.Zehder, Riga, Russia	1 speed
31058	Export	13/08/12	4 sc te cont	Ed.Zehder, Riga, Russia	1 speed
31063	V7840	11/11/12	7 sc sh te	A.Meikle, Glasgow.	"Dreadnought"
31081	Export	29/08/12	4 sc te cont	Ed.Zehder, Riga, Russia	1 speed
31127	Export	24/01/13	7 sc te col NZ	Jas.Macalister, Invercargill, N.Z.	
31128	Export	19/11/12	5 sc te Eng	Jas.Macalister, Invercargill, N.Z.	2 speed
31129	Export	24/01/13	8 cd te col	W.C.Benbow, Temuka, NZ	3 speed, flywheel dished for 3rd speed.
31132	Export	07/05/13	8 cd te col	Harker, Sumner & Cia, Lisboa + Porto.	
31157	Export	26/11/12	5 sc te Eng	Jas.Macalister, Invercargill, N.Z.	2 speed
31371	Export	21/02/13	6 sc te gp	Th.Pilter, Bordeaux, France	
31378	Export	22/04/13	7 sc te pv	Henninger & Co. Darmstadt, Germany.	
31390	Export	13/02/13	5 sc te gp	Orenstein & Koppel, Durban, S.Africa.	Port Elizabeth Show.
31401	Export	15/05/13	5 sc te	Ed.Zehder, Riga, Russia	1 speed
31454	Export	16/04/13	6 cd te gp	Th.Pilter, Tunis, N.Africa	
31458	Export	15/04/13	5 sc te gp	Th.Pilter, Bordeaux, France	2 speed
31471		23/05/13	6 sc te	Scanlon Bros., Ballyhoe, Co.Cork.	
31508	Export	18/11/13	7 sc te gp	Th.Pilter, Paris, France	
31551	Export	13/10/13	5 sc te gp PV1	Henninger & Co. Darmstadt, Germany.	2 speed
31553	Export	04/06/13	4 sc te	Ed.Zehder, Riga, Russia	1 speed
31576	Export	12/06/13	4 sc te	Ed.Zehder, Riga, Russia	1 speed
31581	Export	03/06/13	7 sc te gp	Th.Pilter, Bordeaux, France	Dynamo on extended smokebox.
31611	CF3954	25/11/13	6 sc te	Cooper & Sherwood, Knodishall, Suffolk.	
31639	Export	25/07/13	4 sc te	Ed.Zehder, Riga, Russia	1 speed
31681	Export	10/07/13	4 sc te	Ed.Zehder, Riga, Russia	1 speed

Works No.	Regn. No.	Date	Type	Purchaser	Notes
31697	Export	25/07/13	4 sc te	Ed.Zehder, Riga, Russia	1 speed
31710	Export	31/07/13	5 sc te	Ed.Zehder, Riga, Russia	1 speed
31748	Export	14/08/13	5 sc te	Ed.Zehder, Riga, Russia	1 speed
31774	Export	04/09/13	5 sc te	Ed.Zehder, Riga, Russia	1 speed
31781	Export	31/07/13	5 sc te	Ed.Zehder, Riga, Russia	1 speed
31833		29/09/13	7 sc te	R.Robinson & Sons, Annan	
31836	ES3616	21/10/13	6 cd te gp	R.McLean, Aberfeldy, Perth.	"Pioneer"; convertible to roller.
31851	AB8193	27/11/13	7 sc te	T.Pegler, Clementsend Grn.Colliery Glos.	
31865	ES4454	19/12/13	7 sc te gp	P.White, Greenhead, Crieff.	
31952		17/12/13	7 sc te	F.O.Blaney, Lytchett Matravers, Dorset.	
32030	Export	07/03/14	5 sc te PV1	Henninger & Co. Darmstadt, Germany.	
32125	Export	27/03/14	6 cd gp col	Ed.Zehder, Riga, Russia	
32146	Export	12/02/14	7 sc te	Th.Pilter, Bordeaux, France.	From stock, no. changed.
32158	Export	03/04/14	6 sc te gp	Th.Pilter, Bordeaux, France	
32197		31/07/14	6 sc te	J.Dalton, Chancellors Mills, Kilkenny.	
32208	Export	29/05/14	50bhp pe	Dr.A.E.Parr, Aligarh, U.P. India.	Oil burner; spares 10/10/30
32273	Export	29/05/14	5 sc te PV1	Henninger & Co. Darmstadt, Germany.	2 speed
32300			50bhp pe	Wadhams Eng.Co. London, for Smyrna	Cancelled by War; renumbered 33781.
32316		31/07/14	6 sc te	P.Behan, Red Mills, Kildare.	
32317	Export	16/04/14	10 sc te sb	Eugen Behles, Bucarest.	1 speed
32323	NO1817	06/07/15	7 sc te gp	J.Jeffrey & Son, Thaxted, Essex.	
32343	Export	17/06/14	4 sc te cont	Ed.Zehder, Riga, Russia	1 speed
32344	Export	18/06/14	6 sc pv sh te	Th.Pilter, Marseille, France	
32346	Export	08/07/14	6 sc pv sh te	E.Lillamond, Bouches-de-Rhone, France.	
32444	Export	16/07/14	4 sc te cont	Ed.Zehder, Riga, Russia	1 speed
32474	Export	22/07/14	4 sc te cont	Ed.Zehder, Riga, Russia	1 speed
32505	Export	22/07/14	5 sc te cont	Ed.Zehder, Riga, Russia	1 speed
32508		07/10/14	6 sc te gp	Cork County Council.	
32510	W.O.	10/11/16	4 sc te cont	To Salonika	
32520		21/04/15	6 sc te	Cork County Council.	
32557	W.O.	10/11/16	4 sc te cont	Area Director of Works, BEF, Salonika.	1 speed
32560	W.O.	17/01/17	4 sc te cont	Area Director of Works, BEF, Salonika.	1 speed
32576	W.O.	17/01/17	5 sc te cont.	Area Director of Works, BEF, Salonika.	1 speed
32582	Export	07/11/14	6 cd te gp col	Shire of Benalla, Australia.	via Horrocks Roxburgh, Melbourne.
32702		09/07/15	6 sc te	J.P.Creen, Ballyculter, Co.Down.	
32890	M-o-M	30/12/16	6 sc te gp	Salonika	Returned to U.K. and regd. NK6184.
32936	NO6955	13/12/16	7sc te	C.Blewett, Yeldham, Essex.	
33066	HR3359	15/10/17	7 sc te gp	G.&H.Wilson, Ramsbury, Wilts.	
33068	AH5440	06/06/18	6 cd te gp	Norfolk Motor Transport Co.Ltd.	No.10
33120		25/10/17	7 sc te gp	Piltown Co-op. Socy. Ltd., Co.Kilkenny.	
33121		26/06/18	7 sc te gp	Piltown Co-op. Socy. Ltd., Co.Kilkenny.	
33129		14/11/17	7 sc te gp	Bagenalstown Thrshg Union, Co. Carlow.	
33130		15/12/17	6 sc te gp	W.&A.McMullan Ltd., Portaferry, Co.Down.	
33139		12/01/18	6 sc te	J.Campbell, Eyrecourt, Co.Galway.	
33202	AH6010	06/09/18	7 sc te gp	Eggleston Bros, Melton Constable, Norfolk	
33232	SP5461	31/12/18	8 sc te gp	Heggie & Robertson, Dunfermline.	
33251	MA6819	30/10/18	7 sc te	W.Fielding, Hyde, Cheshire.	
33331		07/06/19	7 sc te gp	R.Robinson & Sons, Annan.	
33390		11/07/19	7 sc te gp	Whithorn Steam Threshing Co., Wigtowns.	Highland Show.
33442	BL9009	13/08/19	7 sc te gp	H.Baylis, Faringdon, Oxon.	
33443	NO3548	02/05/19	6 sc te gp	Miss K.Courtauld, Colne Engaine, Essex.	
33493		25/07/19	6 sc te gp	W&A.McMullan Ltd., Portaferry, Co.Down.	
33560	HR3564	28/06/19	7 sc te	F.Swanton, Marlborough, Wilts.	
33561	AC9136	23/12/19	6 sc te gp	J.Cleave, Hatton, Warwick.	
33562		30/06/19	7 sc te gp	H&P.Nolan, Grangewath, Carlow.	Dublin Show.
33594	AP9579	27/08/20	7 sc te gp	J.Philipson, Salisbury, Wilts.	
33609	TA1913	30/06/19	6 sc te	H.H.M.Peeke, Slade Barton, Devon.	
33724	OS877	05/11/19	7 sc te gp	R.Crawley, Port William, Wigtownshire.	
33737	BJ8855	31/01/20	7 sc te	T.Cook, Bradwell, Gt.Yarmouth, Norfolk	
33781	BJ5911	01/11/20	50 bhp cd sh	W.E.Cooper & Sons, Parham, Suffolk.	Originally 32300
33827		17/06/20	6 sc te gp	MacArthur Bros., Cool Claudy, Co.Derry.	
33844		19/05/20	6 sc te gp	M.Egan, Johnstown, Co.Kilkenny.	
33845	MN9039	30/07/20	7 sc te gp	J.Hayes, Thurles, Co.Tipperary.	
33846	AH6011	02/07/20	7 sc te	K.Eggleton, Briston, Norfolk.	
34016	AP9659	09/08/21	6 sc te gp	J.Philipson, Alfriston, Sussex.	
34017	PW9017	27/09/26	7 sc te	J.W.Durrell & Bird, East Ruston, Norfolk.	
34039		06/09/22	5 sc te PV1	W.Logan, Coleraine.	2 speed
34045	BJ6628	11/09/22	5 sc te PV1	L.J.S.Cooper, Leiston, Suffolk.	2 speed; was yard engine.
34046	BJ7690	13/09/22	5 sc te PV1	H.Hawes, Stradbroke, Eye, Suffolk.	2 speed
34125		01/06/23	6 sc te gp	Roscommon C.C.	

Works No.	Regn. No.	Date	Type	Purchaser	Notes
34133	KK2427	18/08/22	7 sc te gp	H.E.Blunt & Son, Sholden, Deal, Kent.	
34176	Export	25/11/22	5 sc te	Ed.Zehder, Riga, Latvia	1 speed
34183	SP7321	29/09/22	7 sc te gp	W.Spence & Son, Kingsbarns, Fife.	
34186		03/07/24	7 sc te gp	F.B.McKee & Co.Ltd., Belfast.	
34187	AH9623	20/09/22	6 sc te	E.D.Lacon, Gt.Ormeby, Norfolk.	
34210	SM6605	02/08/27	7 sc te gp	R.Robinson & Sons, Annan.	Highland Show.
34292	Export	03/07/23	4 sc te cont	W.Schneider & Co., Reval, Estonia.	1 speed; via Zehder
34293	Export	13/08/23	4 sc te cont	W.Schneider & Co., Reval, Estonia.	1 speed; via Zehder
34304	Export	14/08/23	4 sc te cont	Ed.Zehder, Riga, Latvia	1 speed
34305	Export	15/05/23	5 sc te cont	Ed.Zehder, Riga, Latvia	1 speed
34306	Export	31/05/23	5 sc te cont	Ed.Zehder, Riga, Latvia	1 speed
34307	Export	31/05/23	5 sc te cont	Ed.Zehder, Riga, Latvia	1 speed
34353		06/05/27	6 sc te	W.McKane, Ballywatt, Dervock, Antrim.	
34417	Export	08/03/24	8 cd te gp col	W.A.Govt. Rlys, Dwellingup, W.Australia.	3 speed
34431	Export	03/03/24	4 sc te cont	R.Bitteniek, Nerata, Latvia.	1 speed; via Schneider
34432	Export	31/03/24	4 sc te cont	W.Schneider & Co., Reval, Estonia.	1 speed
34433	Export	12/04/24	4 sc te cont	H.Lessik, Estonia	1 speed; via Schneider
34479	Export	05/05/24	5 sc te cont	Ed.Zehder, Riga, Latvia	1 speed
34496	Export	05/05/24	5 sc te cont	Ed.Zehder, Riga, Latvia	1 speed
34518	Export	21/07/24	5 sc te cont	Ed.Zehder, Riga, Latvia	1 speed
34519	Export	16/09/24	5 sc te cont	Ed.Zehder, Riga, Latvia	1 speed
34520	Export	19/06/26	5 sc te cont	Ed.Zehder, Riga, Latvia	1 speed
34727		23/05/25	6 cd te gp	Dublin C.C.	No.2
34918	Export	09/06/26	7 sc te gp col	Sumner Harker, via Lisbon.	
34937	Export	29/09/26	80bhp cd sb te	W.H.Cullington, Buenos Aires.	1 speed
34964	Export	11/10/26	5 sc te cont	Ed.Zehder, Riga, Latvia	1 speed
35064	Export	26/08/27	5 sc te cont	Ed.Zehder, Riga, Latvia	1 speed
35067	Export	19/08/27	80bhp cd sb te	W.H.Cullington, Buenos Aires.	1 speed
35068	Export	31/08/27	80bhp cd sb te	W.H.Cullington, Buenos Aires.	1 speed
35069	Export	31/08/27	80bhp cd sb te	W.H.Cullington, Buenos Aires.	1 speed
35140	SM7869	07/09/29	7 sc te gp	R.Robinson & Sons, Annan.	
35461	OU9309	13/06/31	6 sc te gp	G.Ewen, Petersfield, Hants.	"Pride of Petersfield"

Notes & Abbreviations .
In addition to the engines listed in the foregoing pages of the appendix there were the four Savory type ploughing engines described in Chapter 5.

te = traction engine; sm = self-mover; sc. = single cylinder; cd = compound; sb = straw-burner; col = Colonial boiler;
pe = ploughing engine; rl = road loco; srl = showman's road loco; NZ = New Zealand type;
Eng = English type (as applied to 5NHP singles, to distinguish them from the light Continental type);
cont = Continental type; sh = superheated;
gp = general purpose - a term used by Garretts to denote an engine with features not covered by the
    A.E.A.agreement. These were charged as extras. Latterly, however, all tractions were called general purpose.
W.O. = War Office; M-o-M = Ministry of Munitions.

Registration numbers.   The numbers given are U.K. numbers only, and are the first known to have been carried.
Tractors used for road haulage were required to be registered from the inception of registration in 1905.
Registration for traction engines was introduced in 1921.
Before registration traction engines used for haulage were licensed county by county.
Certain engines were re-registered during their careers.
Nos.30009, 31833, and 33331, owned by R. Robinson & Son, were allocated the registration numbers
SM 2758, 2759 and 2760, but it is not known how these were carried in relation to Works numbers.